IS CONGRESS BROKEN?

IS CONGRESS BROKEN?

The Virtues and Defects of Partisanship and Gridlock

WILLIAM F. CONNELLY JR.
JOHN J. PITNEY JR.
GARY J. SCHMITT
EDITORS

BROOKINGS INSTITUTION PRESS
Washington, D.C.

1775 Massachusetts Avenue, N.W., Washington, D.C. 20036
www.brookings.edu

The Brookings Institution is a private nonprofit organization devoted to research, education, and publication on important issues of domestic and foreign policy. Its principal purpose is to bring the highest quality independent research and analysis to bear on current and emerging policy problems. Interpretations or conclusions in Brookings publications should be understood to be solely those of the authors.

Library of Congress Cataloging-in-Publication data are available.
ISBN 9-780-8157-3036-1 (pbk : alk. paper)
ISBN 9-780-8157-3037-8 (ebook)

9 8 7 6 5 4 3 2 1

Typeset in Adobe Caslon Pro

Composition by Westchester Publishing Services

Contents

IS CONGRESS BROKEN?

Introduction

WILLIAM F. CONNELLY JR.,
JOHN J. PITNEY JR.,
AND GARY J. SCHMITT

Much of the contemporary discourse about Congress among scholars, journalists, and politicians has its origins in the writings of Woodrow Wilson and early twentieth-century progressives. These thinkers saw Congress as a roadblock to needed change and ill-adapted to meet the requirements of modern government. Similarly, critics today complain that the constitutional system is not designed for dispatch and is particularly vulnerable to political forces that thwart progress. Congress, they conclude, lies at the center of this dysfunction.

We recognize that all is not well with Congress. But have these Wilsonian expectations intensified disappointment with congressional partisanship and legislative productivity?

No doubt Congress is not as effective as it should be. Problems obviously exist. This volume raises two questions: whether the reforms designed to make Congress more effective have, in fact, done so; and more fundamentally, if the standard by which we judge those reforms is the correct one to begin with. As a constructive alternative, we seek to revive a more traditional Madisonian perspective on Congress. This approach takes a more complex view of the institution, recognizing that there is room for both cooperation and conflict. Yes, the constitutional system is full of friction, as Justice Brandeis wrote, but friction creates light as well as heat.

Tough partisan conflict can promote needed oversight, give rise to serious deliberation, and prevent ill-considered legislative innovations. Since Congress is, first and foremost, a representative institution, partisan conflict reflects factional divisions within the polity.

James W. Ceaser gave the opening keynote address at the conference that was the genesis of this volume. Because Congress will never be loved by presidents, he said, it might as well be feared. This fear has been absent in recent years; thus Congress must regain its proper role in the policy process. Congress might, for example, revive the constitutional power of the purse as the best means to defend itself against the overgrown prerogatives of the executive branch. Perhaps Congress needs to revisit the 1974 Budget Impoundment and Control Act, as budgetary process scholar Peter Hanson recommends.[1] As James Madison noted in *Federalist* No. 58: "This power over the purse may, in fact, be regarded as the most complete and effectual weapon with which any constitution can arm the immediate representatives of the people, for obtaining a redress of every grievance and for carrying into effect every just and salutary measure."[2]

While many of the essays in this volume look back to the Founders for insight into what they saw as the proper functions of Congress, our focus is on the future of Congress. At present, Congress does not deliberate as thoughtfully, legislate as carefully, or oversee the executive branch as thoroughly as it should. Broadly, this collection is an attempt to promote analysis and develop ideas for returning Congress to its proper place in our constitutional system. For successive generations, congressional reforms have been supported as making the institution more "open," more "responsive," more "democratic." As several essays herein suggest, however, the cure for the ills of democratic governance might be, not more openness and more democracy but, rather, a greater respect for the complexity of the institutions and their intended place in producing responsive and sound government.[3] Today, Congress may be better at representing the factional parts of American society and, thereby, less adept at legislating in the interest of the whole. A Congress more Madisonian responsible than Wilsonian responsive may be more effective at fulfilling its other functions to deliberate, legislate, and oversee the executive.

Challenging the conventional wisdom begins with questioning whether Congress is, indeed, hopelessly dysfunctional and whether effective government requires a continued drift toward deference to presidents, courts, and executive bureaucracies. To restore public trust in Congress, we need the public to remember that Congress's task is both to represent and enlarge the public good. To accomplish the latter, we need to provide members with the institutional "space" to deliberate as the Constitution's architects intended republican institutions to do.[4]

Trusting politicians does not mean being naïve; it does require, however, not being endlessly cynical about our elected leaders. Madison, after all, was a realist who famously wished to unleash ambition to counteract ambition. He had confidence that politicians, acting within properly established institutions, could produce sound policies. In short, he expected elected representatives to be somewhere between the naiveté of Mr. Smith and the cynicism of Frank Underwood.

Madison's design was for a government limited in scope. Expecting a restricted structure to support a government whose ends now seem unlimited is to require that government to perform its role in a way that will inevitably lead the population to frustration, a sense that the system is broken, and distrust of the institutions themselves. A key theme of this volume is that reforms designed to transform the Constitution's architecture have only deepened this problem. Putting a saddle on an elephant does not make the elephant a racehorse. Hence, to regain public trust in government and its institutions, to manage expectations of what Congress was designed to do, we may need to think once again of what it means to have limited government. A fuller appreciation for our system of separated powers, federalism, and bicameralism is a critical, if not simply sufficient, starting point.

In his maiden floor speech first-term Senator Ben Sasse (R-Nebr.), who holds a Ph.D. in history, cited the Founders' Constitution and the "unique place in the architecture of Madisonian separation of powers" served by the Senate. Senator Sasse lamented "short-termism" and the "sound-bite culture" in today's Senate, calling for the "recovery of more honest Socratic debate." While he offered no magic bullet solutions, Senator Sasse focused on executive overreach and congressional abdication: "The growth of the administrative state, the fourth branch of government, is increasingly hollowing out the Article I branch, the legislature—and many in Congress have been complicit in this."[5] Senator Sasse appears concerned that a new president with an ever-expanding policy agenda may make even more aggressive use of executive power than his or her predecessors, making an institutionally stronger Congress more imperative than ever.

The authors in this volume agree there are no magical solutions to restoring Congress's place in our constitutional constellation, though they generally concur that, as important as changes in how Congress organizes itself may be, a return to a more nuanced and realistic perspective about Congress's role is a necessary first step.

Daniel Stid's chapter offers an ideal opening for our collection of essays, providing useful historical perspective. He argues that "we are not obliged to keep working against the grain of our longstanding constitutional arrangements." Instead, he calls for revitalizing the reform tradition embodied in the Legislative Reorganization Act of 1946, designed to uphold Madison's separation of powers, as an alternative to the Wilsonian perspective so popular among reformers for decades. Stid thinks we need to return to this alternative congressional reform tradition to restore Congress:

> An institution so restored would be much better positioned to serve as the first branch of government, to retain and actively exercise rather than continue to cede its power and authority to the President, administrative agencies, and the courts . . . For this restoration to occur, Congress needs to take back the power of the purse and oversee the executive branch much more systematically and effectively. The frayed and tattered "regular order" needs to be re-envisioned and reestablished. But the imperatives of representative democracy over the next 50 years will mean that any functional order will work much differently than it did 50 years ago.

Stid laments the "big lobotomy" of congressional staff cuts, blaming Wilson's preference for the unifying national executive versus the parochialism of Congress. Stid broaches the "careful what you wish for" quandary; to wit, Wilsonian reformers sought "responsible parties," yet now they lament red versus blue polarization. Responsible party government reforms may have begun with Democratic reformers but, ultimately, they proved bipartisan: "Gingrich's Republican majority represented the apex of responsible party government." Newt and Nancy are two peas in a pod.

Stid also suggests that elections may matter more than tinkering with institutional reforms. A critical election, not reform, may be better at resolving impasses, an argument echoed throughout this volume. Is reform a leading or lagging indicator? After all, large majority elections (1974, 1994) enabled significant institutional reforms. This raises another question: Is reform really a stalking horse for a particular policy agenda?

In his essay on congressional representation, chapter 3, Andrew Busch makes thoughtful use of the federalist/anti-federalist debate as a rubric for judging reform. Busch underscores the importance of thinking institutionally, faulting progressive reformers for following Woodrow Wilson's lead in slighting the importance of constitutional and institutional structure. He makes the case for revisiting the Seventeenth Amendment, refederalizing American politics, and curbing the growth of the administrative state. Busch also develops the constructive point that elections, not reforms, will provide the real solution to current purported dysfunction.

In chapter 4, Dan Palazzolo grounds his discussion of deliberation within congressional committees on the floors of the House and Senate in Madison's expectations of legislative politics and on the work of scholars such as Joseph Bessette and Randall Strahan. The Framers sought to design institutions that fostered deliberative lawmaking, but they realized that factional politics could overwhelm deliberation. In the contemporary Congress, institutional reforms, group activism, and heightened partisanship routinely trump (pun intended) deliberation in the legislative process. Yet Palazzolo challenges the simplistic notion that Congress is hopelessly gridlocked and incapable of deliberation. Notwithstanding partisan polarization, the degree of deliberation varies by issue, committee, chamber, and the strategic choices of parties and leaders. Palazzolo suggests that scholars should focus more attention on deliberation within parties. In addition, he recommends strengthening and closing committees, instituting a five-day work week, promoting a three weeks on–one week off schedule, and limiting the number of committees on which members serve, especially senators.

Donald Wolfensberger grounds chapter 5 on House rules in decades of personal experience on Capitol Hill, most notably as a longtime senior Rules Committee Republican staff member. He usefully draws on the work of scholar Greg Weiner, House Parliamentarian Charles Johnson, and others, and makes constructive use of his own long-term perspective on congressional history. Wolfensberger, too, makes apt use of the Madison versus Wilson debate. Like others, he criticizes the cutting of committee staff, along with the shift from committee to party leadership staff. But given his detailed knowledge of legislative rules and procedures, Wolfensberger outlines specific procedural prescriptions in the closing paragraphs of his chapter. First, he says:

> The current rule that allows recorded votes in committees to be postponed and clustered at the end of a bill markup session should be repealed so that members can reengage in the important deliberative stages of argumentation and persuasion. Leaders should desist in scheduling unreported bills on the floor except in emergency situations. Likewise, closed amendment rules on the floor should be reserved only for emergency bills, while opening up most other bills to modified open rules with time caps on the amendment process. And finally, leadership should refrain from substituting new bill language in the Rules Committee for that already agreed to by committees.

He finishes the chapter saying: "There are no procedural quick fixes that can instantly reverse the vice-like constrictions on members' individual rights and committees' deliberative roles. But the steps outlined above can begin an incremental process of reestablishing a balance between responsible party agenda-setting and responsive committee lawmaking in the nation's interest."

Placing such recommendations in context, Wolfensberger cites a speech that John Boehner gave just before he became Speaker about the need to return to regular order:

> the truth is, much of the work of committees has been co-opted by the leadership. . . . In too many instances, we no longer have legislators; we just have voters. In my view, if we want to make legislators legislate again, then we need to empower them at the committee level. If Members were more engaged in their committee work, they would be more invested in the final products that come to the floor.[6]

A return to regular order may be a worthy goal, yet implementing this change may be more difficult than some realize, placing the transition from Speaker Boehner to Speaker Ryan in context, as well.

In chapter 6, Melanie Marlowe argues that Congress has eviscerated itself, abdicating to the executive branch by delegating lawmaking to the administrative state. Entitlements are another example of the abdication of lawmaking responsibility. So, too, are the proliferating independent boards and commissions. Marlowe offers budget reforms to reverse this process. Further, Marlowe argues, Congress can promote public deliberation by using serious committee oversight hearings to educate members of Congress and the general public. As part of that reform, Congress should eliminate term limits on committee chairs and transfer staff resources from personal offices to professional committee staff. She concludes: "If Congress wants to be taken seriously, it must behave seriously" and "Congress must invest in itself."

Gary Schmitt and Rebecca Burgess, in chapter 7, bring a foreign policy and administrative state focus to this volume, explaining how, in conjunction with the rise of the president as party and popular leader, the presidency has become the dominant branch of government. That said, Congress remains the most powerful legislature in the world if only it would step up to its responsibility and functions. "Turf" lost to the executive may be less important than "ensuring that the authority" Congress "does wield is properly directed." This will require rolling back previous reforms that have weakened committees to promote more serious deliberation and oversight. Congress must "refine and enlarge the public view," as Madison argued, rather than simply reflect the "slice-in-time" partisan gamesmanship that dominates congressional–executive relations today. As such, Schmitt and Burgess argue, we need to change the terms of debate about Congress from our current simplistic populism to a more fully deliberative republican perspective. This might enable Congress to find both the incentive and capacity to act on its convictions.

In chapter 8, Kathryn Pearson offers a thoughtful perspective on contemporary congressional leadership in the context of separation of powers, including how institutional context affects the behavior of party leaders and members. She notes the deepest disagreements within congressional party caucuses are commonly over party strategy, not policy. The central leadership dilemma is managing party caucus divisions over "political strategy and institutional loyalty." Pearson's key conclusion is that we need to strengthen both committee and party leaders. Weak party and committee leaders leave "Congress with insufficient power and incentives to overcome institutional hurdles and fulfill its constitutional responsibilities." Stronger committee chairs can empower a Speaker to balance "the dual imperatives of the speakership—responsibility for the institution and for one's party." Therein lies the challenge for congressional leadership in Madison's constitutional context. Ironically, strengthening committee leaders may be the necessary predicate for strengthening party leadership. Newly minted Speaker Paul Ryan seemingly read Pearson's conference paper, since he adopted one of her recommendations, namely, reducing the Speaker's votes on the Steering Committee. Will he also end committee chair term limits?

In chapter 9, Peter Hanson offers insight into the budget piece of the reform puzzle in his short Brookings Institution essay, replicated here. This essay, however, may only whet the reader's appetite for his longer essay found on the George Mason University website, or for Hanson's recent book, *Too Weak to Govern: Majority Party Power and Appropriations in the U.S. Senate*. Here, Hanson argues that the annual appropriations process is on the verge of collapse given the decline of "regular order," by which he means the debating and passing of individual appropriations bills in the House and Senate. Instead, today's Congress often budgets by passing large omnibus packages at the end of the legislative session following a budget summit with the president, with little scrutiny or opportunity for amendment by rank and file members. Hanson blames primarily Senate rules and procedures for this breakdown. To restore regular order, Hanson recommends filibuster reform, concurrent House and Senate consideration of appropriations, restoring earmarks, and reducing transparency. A more deliberative and republican Congress might budget more effectively than the more open and democratic Congress does at present.

In his closing conference keynote address, Jonathan Rauch drew on his Brookings Institution "Political Realism" essay, which he abridges in chapter 10. Rauch argues that we cannot take the politics out of politics, because "governing is difficult and politics is transactional." Consequently, we need "political machines" in which we re-empower party and committee leaders with the carrots and sticks needed to lead. Congressional party and committee leaders require leverage and opportunities to deliberate behind closed doors. The Wilsonian push for transparency has failed. "The public sees more of the sausage making while getting less sausage." Rauch is willing to make the "case for corruption," complete with "honest graft." He wants a return to the smoke-filled rooms, though without the smoke. Rauch wants to "rescue compromise." Rauch's political realism reflects Madison's sober yet optimistic realism about human nature and Madison's confidence about republican self-government.

The concluding chapter, "A Return to Madisonian Republicanism: Strengthening the Nation's Most Representative Institution," by Bill Connelly and Jack Pitney, pulls together the various threads of the previous essays and reflects more broadly on what a Madisonian reform agenda would be to set Congress on a future path to retake its rightful place in the constitutional order.

A final note: The bulk of the essays in this volume were prepared for a working conference on "Congress, the Constitution, and Contemporary Politics" held at the American Enterprise Institute for Public Policy Research (AEI) in Washington, D.C., on October 15 and 16, 2015. We would like to express our deep thanks to the William and Flora Hewlett Foundation, whose generosity made this scholarship possible, and to AEI for hosting our workshop. Many thanks goes to the contributing authors, of course, but also to the following conference participants who imparted valuable feedback in their role as discussants: James Ceaser (University of Virginia), Gregory Weiner (Assumption College), Michael Malbin (Campaign Finance Institute), Frances Lee (University of Maryland), Charles Johnson (former Parliamentarian of the House of Representatives), Matthew Spalding (Hillsdale College), Yuval Levin (National Affairs), John Haskell (Congressional Research Service), and Mickey Edwards (former member of Congress and Aspen Institute). We would also like to thank the Brookings Institution for permission to reprint edited versions of the essays by Peter Hanson and Jonathan Rauch, and the editorial staff of Brookings for their professional assistance in preparing this volume. Finally, we want to note the invaluable assistance of Rebecca Burgess, program manager of AEI's Program on American Citizenship, for keeping both the conference and editorial process on track and running as smoothly and substantively as it did.

Notes

1. Peter Hanson, "New Ideas for Federal Budgeting: A Series of Working Papers for the National Budgeting Roundtable," Centers on the Public Service, George Mason University (http://psc.gmu.edu/wp-content/uploads/New-Ideas-for-Federal-Budget-Working-Paper-No.-1.pdf).

2. *Federalist* No. 58, Avalon Project at Yale Law School (http://avalon.law.yale.edu/18th_century/fed58.asp).

3. Martin Diamond, "The Separation of Powers and the Mixed Regime," *Publius* 8, no. 3 (1978), pp. 33–43.

4. Randall Strahan, "Personal Motives, Constitutional Forms, and the Public Good: Madison on Political Leadership," in *James Madison: The Theory and Practice*

of Republican Government, edited by Samuel Kernell (Stanford University Press, 2003).

5. Department of Defense Appropriations Act, HR 2685, 114th Cong., 1st sess., *Congressional Record* 161 (November 3, 2015) (www.congress.gov/congressional-record/2015/11/3/senate-section/article/s7697-1).

6. Representative John A. Boehner, "Congressional Reform and 'The People's House,'" remarks delivered at the American Enterprise Institute, September 30, 2010 (www.aei.org/publication/congressional-reform-and-the-people-house/print).

2

Two Pathways for Congressional Reform

DANIEL STID

In the 1940s, two different committees of political scientists worked under the auspices of the American Political Science Association (APSA) to grapple with pressing issues then facing democracy in the United States. The crises of the Great Depression and World War II, and the ways in which American political institutions struggled to respond to them, had raised important questions about the viability of our system of government. In a nutshell—to borrow the title of an influential book published in 1945—informed observers were asking, "Can representative government do the job?"[1]

We are now, once again, asking ourselves this question. The role of Congress—ostensibly the first branch of government—has greatly diminished relative to the other branches. The institution is riven by polarized parties. Opinion polls routinely find that only one in ten Americans approves of Congress.

As contemporary reformers consider how we might respond to these challenges, we would do well to revisit the legacies of the two APSA committees. One must admit that this is not a straightforward case to make. Both committees acknowledged that they had not marshaled the analytical rigor and empirical research that have come to be the hallmarks of modern political science. Their respective reports, like most documents written by committees, glossed over some conflicts and inconsistencies; hence, our tendency to regard them as the youthful indiscretions of a discipline that has since matured.

If we actually take the time to read and understand the final reports of these two committees, we can appreciate that they present clear and compelling alternatives—one focused on congressional capacity, the other on responsible partisanship—for how to improve representative democracy in the United States. Moreover, both committees reshaped Congress in ways still observable today. We need to understand how they did so.

We begin with the work of the APSA Committee on Congress, then turn to its further development in the Legislative Reorganization Act of 1946. Next, we take up the work of the APSA Committee on Political Parties and how liberal reformers in Congress used it as a bearing point in their long march toward more responsible partisanship from 1950 to 1975. We continue tracing the arcs of these two reform impulses in recent decades, marked as they have been by increased polarization and decreased institutional capacity in Congress. We conclude by considering how, in the face of these outcomes, those of us concerned about the health of representative democracy in the United States might proceed.

The APSA Committee on Congress

The Committee on Congress originated in discussions among political scientists working in universities, nonprofits, and government agencies in Washington, D.C., during the late New Deal era. They wanted to assess the health and functioning of the legislature in a period of expanding executive and administrative powers. In January 1941, APSA president Frederic A. Ogg appointed George Galloway, an industrial planner who had previously worked for the National Recovery Administration, to lead the five-member committee.[2]

In the preface to its final report, issued in 1945, the committee noted: "We have proceeded on two assumptions: first, that the present tripartite pattern of the federal government will continue; and second, that Congress should be equipped effectively to discharge its constitutional functions as one of the three coordinate grand divisions of our national government."[3]

The committee's two assumptions reaffirmed our Constitution's separation of powers, but with a twist. In *Federalist* No. 48, James Madison had warned that, because of its proximity to the people, the wellspring of popular government, "the legislative department is everywhere extending the sphere of its activity, and drawing all power into its impetuous vortex." However, as Representative Madison came to realize in the 1790s, when the executive branch was led by an energetic executive and determined administrators, it, too, could be a vortex. This was even more the case after the transformation of presidential power and influence brought about by Franklin Roosevelt and the expansion of the administrative state.

The committee concluded that "Congress must modernize its machinery and methods to fit modern conditions if it is to keep pace with a greatly enlarged and active Executive branch." The goal was not that of "reducing and hamstringing the Executive"; far from it. Rather, "a strong and more representative legislature, in closer touch with and better informed about the Administration, is the antidote to bureaucracy."[4]

In helping develop this antidote, the committee acknowledged that it sought to serve as a "catalytic agency"—today we might call it an advocacy group—"seeking to stimulate congressional interest in self-improvement and public interest in legislative reform."[5] The committee's work led to a flurry of meetings, speeches, panels, reports, and newspaper stories on congressional reforms. The committee joined forces and met frequently with a bipartisan, bicameral group of "procedural entrepreneurs," legislators who were likewise concerned about the institutional health and independent role of the legislative branch vis-à-vis the executive. Galloway and his colleagues also spent plenty of time on Capitol Hill engaging with these legislators.[6]

"The Reorganization of Congress," the committee's final report, offered multiple recommendations. Beyond discrete calls to eliminate private bills and local legislation, register lobbyists, and increase salaries and retirement benefits for legislators, the core recommendations fell into three categories: 1) increasing the expertise and staff capacity of Congress; 2) rationalizing and revitalizing the committee system; and 3) better positioning Congress to oversee and set the agenda for its "external relations" with the executive branch.[7]

The committee's call for Congress to augment its staff reflected a frustration among legislators that their institution was more and more reliant on executive branch officials for its information and was, thereby, losing its initiative. The recommendations for more staff resources took three forms: first, that "the committees of Congress be adequately equipped with independent, qualified experts to aid them in making laws," second, that "the

Legislative Reference Service and the Office of Legislative Counsel be substantially increased," and third, that "each member's annual allowance for clerical hire be substantially increased."[8]

The report also proposed that elected officials and citizens recognize committees as "the center of legislative activity where criticism of administration and decision upon proposed legislation is largely made." Rather than lament the central importance of committees for deliberation, as Woodrow Wilson had famously done in his *Congressional Government*, "The Reorganization of Congress" celebrated this reality. Indeed, it advocated that "most of the days and most of each day of a congressional session should be legally and specifically devoted to committee hearings" and that these hearings were the way for "constituents and sightseers to see Congress at work."[9]

But the members of the Committee on Congress also recognized that the committee system would have to be modernized. A core thrust of this was rationalizing and streamlining the number of committees, which had grown "like Topsy since the early days of the Republic," to the point where there were forty-eight standing committees in the House and thirty-three in the Senate. The plethora of committees left too many members with more committee assignments than they could master, hence the report's recommendations for "(a) eliminating the inactive committees; (b) consolidating those with overlapping jurisdictions; (c) creating twin committees organized functionally in both houses; and (d) correlating them with major areas of public policy and administration."[10]

The Committee on Congress also considered whether to take on an emerging problem arising from the norm of selecting committee chairs on the basis of seniority. The report acknowledged that the norm "settles harmoniously the problem of priority without dispute or controversy." But it noted that the seniority system meant some committees were chaired by legislative deadwood or by those who treated their committees as fiefdoms. On balance, the Committee on Congress felt that the seniority norm needed to change, though it recognized the political challenge of doing so and the corresponding need for a "compromise solution." One option was putting an age limit of sixty-five or seventy on chairs. Another was imposing term limits of six years in the chair. Both had "the great merit of the automatic feature." A third option that clearly did not have this "automatic feature" was to have chairs selected by leaders of the majority party in each house.[11]

However committee chairs were to be selected, the final report also recommended that they be obliged to hold committee meetings when a majority of members called for one, report bills passed in committee to the floor in a timely way, and keep a public record of all nonexecutive committee sessions. These disciplines would also serve to counteract problems arising from the seniority system.[12]

The third thrust of the report was to enable Congress to interact more effectively with the president and the burgeoning executive branch. Franklin Roosevelt and then Harry Truman had been inviting the "Big Four"—the vice president, Senate Majority Leader, Speaker of the House, and House Majority Leader—to a weekly White House meeting to plan the administration's and the Democratic Party's legislative agenda. The Committee on Congress proposed to build on this model, but bring the initiative back to Capitol Hill, by establishing a new "Legislative Council" consisting of the Big Four plus the chairmen of the standing committees in both houses. The remit of the new council would be to "plan and coordinate the legislative program of Congress and to promote more effective liaison and cooperation with the Executive."[13]

The central element of the interbranch recommendations of the Committee on Congress was for a concerted response to "the growing concern in and out of Congress for more adequate supervision and control of an expanding bureaucracy." This was, in many respects, the key issue the committee was addressing in the report, and it arose from undeniable historical circumstances: "Recurring wars and depressions have caused a great expansion of the public services, with more and more intervention by the State in the control of industry and the protection of individual welfare. There is no reason to expect a reversal of this long-run trend after the war, regardless of fluctuations in party control."[14]

In response to the expanded scope of the administrative state, the Committee on Congress recommended centralizing the oversight function within the subcommittees of the House Committee on Appropriations to capitalize on their expertise and primary responsibility for government expenditures. Other members of Congress could submit inquiries to the relevant appropriators to pursue, and records of their proceedings would be made available to the public.[15]

Looking back over the main thrusts of the Committee on Congress's final report, we can see they all reflected the perspective that Congress was an autonomous branch of government that needed to preserve and enhance its primary constitutional function of deliberation, especially relative to the growing energy in the executive branch. Hence the imperative tone of "The Reorganization of Congress." With a few exceptions (discussed later), the recommendations of this report would assume concrete and implementable form in legislation that Congress passed the following year.

The Legislative Reorganization Act of 1946

In early 1945, as the APSA Committee on Congress was finishing its report, it passed the reform baton to a bipartisan, ten-person Joint Committee on the Organization of Congress. Its cochairs, Senator Robert La Follette Jr. of Wisconsin and Representative Mike Monroney of Oklahoma, had been active informants of the APSA Committee on Congress. They hired George Galloway, leader of the APSA Committee, to be the staff director of their Joint Committee. The men clearly sought to build on the assessment and plans they had already developed together.[16]

The House and Senate instructed the members of the Joint Committee to study the "organization and operation" of Congress to "recommend improvements in such organization and operation with a view toward strengthening the Congress, simplifying its operations, improving its relationships with other branches of the United States Government and enabling it better to meet its responsibilities under the Constitution." The Joint Committee spent most of 1945 holding hearings and receiving testimony from witnesses in Congress (forty-five members spoke with the Joint Committee, and thirty-seven submitted written statements) as well as citizens at large.[17]

On March 4, 1946, the Joint Committee submitted its report. It echoed the recommendations of its APSA predecessor, albeit with a few noteworthy modifications. The Joint Committee did not touch the institutionally delicate seniority issue, relying instead on meeting and reporting requirements for committees as the way to bring the chairs in line.[18] And rather than concentrating oversight in the House Appropriations subcommittees, the Joint Committee recommended that all the standing committees of both houses "be directed and empowered to carry on continuing review and oversight" of policies and agencies in their jurisdiction and that they be given the subpoena power to help do so.[19]

One important new recommendation was the establishment of a legislative budget process that would operate independently of the executive branch and enable Congress to set overall revenue and spending targets for itself via a concurrent resolution, with mechanisms for reconciliation should the spending plans outstrip expected revenues. Another was to establish and provide staff for majority and minority policy committees in both houses that would set their respective caucuses' agendas.[20] Both ideas reflected a desire to integrate and organize the work being done across committees in ways that would enable the institution to speak with a more coherent voice.

The Joint Committee submitted its report in March 1946. It was promptly converted into legislation, though the proposed package of reforms did not pass through Congress unscathed. The bids to formalize a legislative–executive council as well as majority and minority policy committees were knocked out by Sam Rayburn, who preferred informal arrangements to these integrative functions. But the rest of the package passed before the summer recess with large bipartisan majorities.[21]

The effect was immediately apparent. When the 80th Congress convened in January 1947, the number of standing committees was reduced from thirty-three to fifteen in the Senate and from forty-eight to nineteen in the House. Congress had also, for the first time, delineated the jurisdictions of these committees. The standing committees began hiring the four professional staff members that each was now allotted. Congress increased the number of specialists providing support in the Legislative Reference Service and doubled the size of the Legislative Counsel staff. Individual members had more resources to pay for administrative and clerical support. The standing committees of both houses began a new phase of systematic oversight of the executive branch, equipped with more professional staff, the subpoena power, and the expectations written into law that they all "exercise continuous watchfulness of the execution by the administrative agencies" under their jurisdictions.[22]

For all of the immediate changes wrought by the Legislative Reform Act, some observers of Congress have downplayed its impact. The legislative budget process fell by the wayside; the appropriators, in particular, did not want to be limited by it. And by dramatically streamlining the number of committees, the act consolidated the power of the committee chairs, many of whom were out of step with liberal reformers. While the number of standing committees stabilized at the lower levels provided by the

LRA, over time there was an increase in the number of subcommittees and assignments to them, which undermined the goal of focusing members' attention on fewer policy domains.[23]

Nevertheless, the main provisions of the act proved resistant to shifting tides. Passed in the 79th Congress that had Democratic majorities in both houses, the act would weather the transitions to and from Republican majorities in the 80th and then again in the 83rd Congress.

Consider also the echoes of the Legislative Reorganization Act of 1946 in several of the institutional reforms during the "resurgence" of Congress during the 1970s. These changes included a major expansion of professional staff and expertise working support of Congress, not only in committees, subcommittees, individual member offices, and the existing legislative support organizations, but also in new bodies, like the Office of Technology Assessment and the Congressional Budget Office (CBO). With the Budget Impoundment and Control Act of 1974 that established the CBO, Congress also provided for a legislative budget process of the sort it had taken a false start on in 1946. This one would have much more staying power. The 1970s also witnessed a new era of congressional oversight that brought a rogue presidency and intelligence agency to heel and spurred an especially creative period of legislation. Finally, the Senate further streamlined its committee system and refined the jurisdictions that it had first delineated in 1946 (the House tried but largely failed to do likewise).[24]

These developments in the 1970s, like those that had been embodied in the Legislative Reform Act of 1946, all reflect a perspective that sees Congress as an autonomous and deliberative policy-making body. Congress had made progress in realizing these qualities in the three decades following the Legislative Reform Act of 1946. However, it ran into mounting headwinds from a countervailing set of reforms that sought to subordinate these internal features and attributes of the legislative body to achieve more responsible partisanship within it. We turn to them now.

The APSA Committee on Political Parties

In 1946, just after the Committee on Congress had wrapped up its work, another set of political scientists was drawing inspiration from its example and approached the APSA to propose a similar committee on political parties. In early 1947, Association President Arthur MacMahon appointed a twelve-member Committee on Political Parties and named Elmer Eric (E. E.) Schattschneider of Wesleyan University as its chair.

Schattschneider was a well-known and outspoken advocate of responsible party government. He and many of his colleagues were inspired by recent events in the parliaments of Europe—in Britain in particular, where the Labor Party had swept to power in July 1945 and was then proceeding to carry out its promise to nationalize the "commanding heights" of the economy. Schattschneider and his colleagues on the Committee on Parties believed the more disciplined and principled—that is, more "responsible"—political parties in the European mold could unite what the separation of powers and federalism had put asunder in the United States.[25]

Like its predecessor, the Committee on Political Parties did not undertake an "extensive fresh study of the subject" but, rather, worked with each other and select informants in academia, civil society, party politics, and government. It released its report, "Toward a More Responsible Two-Party System," in the fall of 1950.

In the forward to this report, the Committee on Political Parties flagged what it regarded as the key problem the country was facing, namely, that "either major party, when in power, is ill-equipped to organize its members in the legislative and the executive branches into a government held together and guided by the party program. Party responsibility at the polls thus tends to vanish." For much of American history these challenges may have been tolerable, but in a period in which the country was striving to provide full employment at home and successfully prosecute the Cold War abroad, this situation presented a grave danger. The report underscored two imperatives: "first, that the parties are able to bring forth programs to which they commit themselves and, second, that the parties possess sufficient internal cohesion to carry out these programs."[26]

If James Madison served as the intellectual forebear for the Committee on Congress, then Woodrow Wilson did so for the Committee on Political Parties. In *Congressional Government*, Wilson had called the Founders' separation of powers a "radical defect" in the original constitutional design as, in his view, it led to irresponsible behavior among officeholders and their parties; everyone could always point the finger at someone else, and this left voters in the dark. Admiring the clarifying concentration of legislative and executive power in Westminster cabinets, Wilson argued that "*Power and strict accountability for its use* are the essential constituents of good government."[27]

Like Wilson, the Committee on Political Parties saw Congress, in particular, as the nut that had to be cracked open to get at responsible party government. It was in Congress that the "radical defect" was so problematically manifest, preventing the fusion of legislative and executive power, and the subordination of the former to the latter, that characterized the Westminster parliamentary model these reformers admired. The committee devoted an entire chapter to the reform of Congress, the only branch of government it singled out for such treatment.[28]

The committee's assessment began by noting that, so long as it was left to its own devices, Congress would remain incorrigible: "a higher degree of party responsibility in Congress cannot be provided merely by actions taken within Congress." There would need to be a forcing function brought to bear through national party programs presented to the electorate for their approval or rejection, for "above all, the basis of party operations in Congress is laid in the election process."[29]

But the committee proposed that, while the country waited on clearing electoral winds, "Action within Congress can be of decisive significance . . . the materials for responsible party operations in Congress are already on hand. The key to progress lies in making full scale use of them."[30] A central thrust here was to strengthen the legislative parties by establishing party leadership committees in each house that would guide the caucus and periodically be accountable to it through "a vote of confidence"; by having party caucuses meet more frequently and make more use of a "binding caucus decision . . . to carry out the party's principles and programs"; and by punishing any caucus members who did not hold the party line with unfavorable committee assignments, less patronage to distribute to constituents, and public excoriation. In keeping with its push for more majoritarian government, the report also called for majority cloture in the Senate.[31]

The Committee on Political Parties criticized what it saw as the pathologies of the committee-based system of congressional organization. Speaking of the seniority norm that served as the lynchpin of this system, the report argued: "It is not playing the game fairly for party members who oppose the commitments in their party's platform to rely on seniority to carry them into committee chairmanships. Party leaders have compelling reason to prevent such a member from becoming chairman—and they are entirely free so to exercise their influence."

The report did not specify how exactly party leaders should go about exercising this influence, and it acknowledged that "the task of party leaders when confronted with revolt on the part of committee chairmen . . . is not easy."[32] Still, there was no mistaking that the task had to be done.

The report also called for subordinating the committee system to the party system in a number of other ways: having slates of all committee assignments drawn up by the party leaders and presented to the party caucus for its approval; having the party caucus revisit and reaffirm those assignments on a regular basis; manipulating committee ratios so that the majority would enjoy a "comfortable margin of control"; and taking the reporting, scheduling, and rule-setting for floor consideration of legislation out of the hands of the committee chairs, including the House Rules Committee, and placing it under the control of the majority party leadership in each house.[33]

The Committee on Political Parties acknowledged that this vision faced an uphill climb in the face of constitutional arrangements designed to preclude party government, such as the separation of powers. Yet they did not call for any formal amendments. Schattschneider and his colleagues asserted that "the weakness of the American two-party system can be overcome as soon as a substantial part of the electorate wants it overcome."[34]

The committee downplayed another potentially complicating factor—whether the more responsible party system they were advocating would worsen the "mischief of faction." America's ideologically diverse and pragmatic political parties, focused more on winning offices than on using them to advance coherent programs, reflected and reinforced constitutional arrangements meant to encourage negotiation and compromise. The committee argued that the parties could sharpen the political debate and clearly array themselves on either side of it but, nevertheless, keep that debate within moderate bounds. "There is no real ideological division in the American electorate," the report claimed, "and hence programs of action presented by responsible parties for the voter's support could hardly be expected to reflect or strive toward such division."[35] We turn now to see how this gambit played out.

Toward a More Responsible Two-Party System: 1950–75

"Toward a More Responsible Two-Party System" received plenty of attention, garnering a front-page story in the *New York Times* and an endorsement by the *Washington Post*. White House officials shared the document with President Truman, who liked, in particular, the push to strengthen the party organizations.[36]

The committee's call for more principled and programmatic parties resonated with a nascent coalition seeking to move the Democratic Party in a more consistently liberal direction on civil rights and economic policy. In Congress, the coalition was led by Midwestern members elected in the wake of World War II, including Senators Hubert Humphrey of Minnesota and Paul Douglas of Illinois and Representatives Richard Bolling of Missouri and Eugene McCarthy of Minnesota. These legislators worked closely with liberal activist groups to develop and advocate for their common political agenda, including the newly formed Americans for Democratic Action and Eleanor Roosevelt's National Committee for an Effective Congress as well as established organizations like the NAACP, the ACLU, and the AFL-CIO.[37]

Shortly after the report's publication, Humphrey invited Schattschneider to Washington, D.C., to meet with the leaders of this coalition to discuss the report's recommendations. Now that Schattschneider was free to speak on his own, he could give more direct voice to his liberal political views. And liberals like Humphrey, who had recently put "the Senate on trial" in an article he had written, were eager to talk about how to apply responsible partisanship in Congress, which they saw as a precondition for realizing their policy agenda.[38]

Paul Butler, Chair of the Democratic National Committee, 1954–60, also mainlined "Toward a More Responsible Two-Party System" directly into the American body politic. Butler spoke on behalf of the party's liberal faction, the "amateur democrats" in James Q. Wilson's phrase, who saw principles and ideas, not patronage and pork, as the proper currency of politics. Butler had read "Toward a More Responsible Two-Party System" just before taking the position of chair and regularly invoked its vision of responsible partisanship in his speeches. Butler also established an institutional innovation called for in the report, the Democratic Advisory Council (DAC), whose main job was to issue policy statements, much like an opposition party's shadow government in a Westminster-style parliament. The DAC became a platform used by the liberal faction to push their policy agenda. This development caused much consternation on the part of Sam Rayburn and Lyndon Johnson. But rather than deferring to the leaders of his party's divided congressional majorities, Butler pressed on. His innovative DAC experiment "achieved an outsized impact precisely by sharpening rather than papering over the party's institutional and ideological tensions."[39]

Butler's innovation was paralleled by similar developments within the party in government. In 1957, a group of eighty Democrats in the House, known loosely as "McCarthy's Mavericks," signed a "liberal manifesto" outlining their policy agenda. In 1959, the members of this legislative party faction formally organized the Democratic Study Group (DSG) to advance their policy agenda and the institutional reforms they saw as preconditions for achieving it. Their primary initial target was overcoming the House Rules Committee, where Chairman Judge Howard Smith of Virginia had bottled up floor consideration of liberal and civil rights legislation. Due in no small part to the DSG's pressure, in 1961 Rayburn finally expanded the Rules Committee to enable more liberal legislation to flow through it.[40]

DSG members continued to advocate procedural reforms throughout the 1960s. Richard Bolling, who had been instrumental in the expansion of the Rules Committee, was outspoken and prolific on the need for more responsible parties, most of all his own. Bolling wrote two books arguing that the constraints imposed on majority party rule by the committee system and the modes of policymaking it perpetuated were undemocratic and unacceptable.[41]

Democratic presidencies and growing Democratic majorities on Capitol Hill released some of the pressure behind these reform efforts. Indeed, the extraordinary achievements of Lyndon Johnson and the 89th Congress in passing the Great Society, including long awaited civil rights measures, demonstrated that the U.S. political system in general and Congress in particular could still respond to ripe moments and pressing demands for policymaking, the constraints of the separation of powers, the traditional committee system, and the filibuster notwithstanding.

Then, beginning with the election of Richard Nixon in 1968, Democratic congressional majorities once again began setting the direction for the party in government. Over the next seven years they would systematically implement a slate of party reforms that represented the core provisions of the APSA Committee on Political Parties' congressional reform agenda. This was not an accident. A new generation of liberal reformers had come into the vanguard of the DSG, including Philip Burton of California and Donald Fraser of Minnesota, a protégé of Hubert Humphrey. They regularly invoked "Toward a More Responsible Two-Party System" as a blueprint for their efforts. Fraser, who in these years led, with Senator George McGovern, the Democratic Party's Commission on Party Structure and Delegate Selection, was especially influential in the liberals' fight for party reform.[42]

In this period the liberal reformers in Congress gained some additional allies in the new citizen activist groups led by Ralph Nader and John Gardner, the founder of Common Cause. These groups were influential in the passage of the Legislative Reorganization Act of 1970, the key measures of which focused on greater transparency, including pushing committees in both houses to open up more hearings and meetings to the public, recording votes in House and Senate committees, recording roll call votes in the House Committee of the Whole, introducing electronic voting in the House (which would ease and, thus, increase the number of recorded roll call votes), and allowing television and radio coverage of hearings in the House. While not directly called for by the Committee on Political Parties, these procedural changes advanced the goal of increasing members' accountability to public opinion.[43]

Congressional reformers were just getting started. Over the next five years the DSG and its reform coalition allies implemented the core planks of their sweeping reform agenda for the House. These included meeting regularly as a caucus; voting in the caucus to approve nominations for committee chair positions as well as committee assignments for the rank and file; establishing a Steering and Policy Committee that worked in service of the party leadership; and effectively making the House Rules Committee an arm of the party leadership.

The effort culminated in the subordination of the seniority system to the House Democratic Caucus. The DSG had carefully set the stage for this battle through a series of procedural reforms in the first part of the decade. The arrival of seventy-five new Democratic members of the Class of 1974, elected in the aftermath of Watergate, put them over the top. At the start of the 94th Congress, the caucus unhorsed three chairs—Eddie Hebert of Louisiana (Armed Services), Wright Patman of Texas (Banking and Currency), and William Pogue of Texas (Agriculture)—and thereby put the rest on notice.[44]

Democrats in the Senate took a less dramatic path to reform but still empowered the Democratic Policy Committee to make recommendations to the conference with a two-thirds vote and reaffirmed the power of the Democratic Conference relative to the committee chairs and the seniority system. In 1975, Senate Democrats began voting on the committee chairs nominated by their steering committee on a secret ballot. That same year they also tackled filibuster reform, lowering the threshold of votes needed for invoking cloture from two-thirds of senators voting to three-fifths of all senators.[45]

The sweeping changes in congressional structures, rules, and procedures that paved the way for more responsible partisanship in Congress in the 1970s were inextricably connected with and served to reinforce changes in the broader party system. The transformation in electoral alignments and regional party footprints set in motion by the civil rights legislation of the mid-1960s was making the Democratic Party more uniformly liberal and the Republican Party more conservative. The national party organizations had come into their own and were gaining strength relative to state and local parties, especially in the areas of policy development and coalition formation. The decline of the patronage system and the advent of the primary system of nominations led to the triumph of the issue-oriented amateur activists over the local machines and political professionals in the party organizations.

On each of these dimensions, the vision of the Committee on Political Parties was being realized. But it was not clear this was leading to effective party government of the sort that Schattschneider and his colleagues had wanted. Indeed, in 1961, reflecting on what the advent of national, issue-based parties driven by amateur activists would entail, James Q. Wilson imagined that "the need to employ issues as incentives and to distinguish one's party from the opposition along policy lines will be intensified, social cleavages will be exaggerated, party leaders will tend to be men skilled in the rhetorical arts, and the party's ability to produce agreement by trading issue-free resources will be reduced."[46] We will see that Wilson was all too prophetic.

Polarization and Its Discontents, 1975–2015

During the 1980s, propelled by these multifaceted changes in the party system, House Democrats came to be more and more unified around a liberal policy agenda. In keeping with the theory of conditional party government, the rank and file members in this more aligned majority delegated more power to its leadership.[47] Jim Wright's ascension to the speakership in 1987 pushed the doctrine of responsible party government into the territory of second order, and unintended, consequences. As Nelson Polsby observed:

> Unlike his predecessors in the Speakership, Wright pursued a strategy of leadership that explicitly mobilized the Democratic caucus to pursue a broad-gauged Democratic program. In the single-minded pursuit of this goal, Wright accentuated tendencies already present to do without the participation of Republicans in the conduct of legislative business. An important byproduct was to further weaken the credibility of go-along, get-along Republicans among their Republican colleagues. By drawing sharp partisan lines, Wright gave Republican moderates—moderates in style, not necessarily in policy preferences—no place to go but into the camp of the Republican Militants.[48]

The militants, of course, were led by Newt Gingrich of Georgia. Throughout the 1980s, as the APSA Committee on Political Parties would have recommended, he was actively working as an "opposition party leader" to perturb the party system into a more sharply defined conflict.[49] Were Gingrich to succeed in this quest, it would help him rise to a leadership position in the GOP and, he believed, help the GOP win a majority in the House. It is fair to say that, when he began these dual campaigns, he was perhaps the only one who saw both outcomes as possible. The two efforts began to reinforce each other; the more his actions provoked a heavy-handed response from the Democratic leadership, the more the GOP rank and file, growing weary of being in the minority under the "go-along, get-along" style of Minority Leader Bob Michel of Illinois, rallied to Newt's banner. This support, in turn, gave him that much more backing for his next attack on the Democratic Party and, ultimately, the institution of Congress itself.[50]

Gingrich understood that, given the decades of Democratic dominance, by attacking the legitimacy of Congress as well as the vestiges of committee-based, bipartisan policymaking within it, he would shift the electoral odds in favor of his insurgent minority. It was no accident that the preamble to the 1994 Contract with America was a broadside aimed squarely at the institution that the GOP wanted to conquer:

On the first day of the 104th Congress, the new Republican majority will immediately pass the following major reforms, aimed at restoring the faith and trust of the American people in their government:

FIRST, require all laws that apply to the rest of the country also apply equally to the Congress;

SECOND, select a major, independent auditing firm to conduct a comprehensive audit of Congress for waste, fraud or abuse;

THIRD, cut the number of House committees, and cut committee staff by one-third;

FOURTH, limit the terms of all committee chairs;

FIFTH, ban the casting of proxy votes in committee;

SIXTH, require committee meetings to be open to the public.[51]

In earlier decades, it had been liberal reformers like Hubert Humphrey and Richard Bolling that had put Congress—and the longstanding internal arrangements it had established to foster deliberation, negotiation, and compromise—on trial. Now the House Republicans were doing so.

In asking for a national electoral mandate on the concrete policy agenda contained in the contract, then passing all but one of its planks through the House of Representatives during the first 100 days of the new Congress, Gingrich's Republican majority represented the apex of responsible party government in the United States. Most accounts of this period tend to emphasize the political strife it produced, but as Randall Strahan has documented, by 1998, sixteen bills generated by the Contract or reflecting its recommendations had become law, including major legislation reforming welfare, reducing taxes, and supporting ballistic missile defense. After the budget brinksmanship and government shutdowns of 1995–96, President Clinton concurred in a State of the Union address that "the era of big government is over," and Congress and the White House agreed on the Balanced Budget Act. "Whatever political problems followed from Gingrich's Contract strategy," Strahan observed, "the evidence is clear that the Contract was consequential in leading to some major changes in public policy."[52]

As Gingrich and his majority worked toward these legislative accomplishments, they discovered that their goal to establish what the Speaker had first described on the floor of the House in 1980 as "accountable party government" would be stymied by enduring features of the American constitutional order. In his 1998 book, *Lessons Learned the Hard Way*, Gingrich admitted upon reflection that "We had not only failed to take into account the ability of the Senate to delay us and obstruct us, but we had much too cavalierly underrated the power of the President. . . . A legislator and an executive are two very different things, and for a time we had allowed ourselves to confuse the two."[53]

While these constitutional arrangements forced Gingrich and his majority to compromise with the Senate and president, they were free to structure the operations of the House as they saw fit, and inside that body they did not hold back from the full sweep of changes advocated by the party government reformers. In doing so, Gingrich and his majority cut down institutional developments with roots that could be traced back to the Legislative Reorganization Act of 1946 and its echoes in the augmentation of expert staffing and congressional oversight in the 1970s. The committee system was already primed to be undermined by the GOP majority through the contract provisions already noted, including the imposition of term limits for chairs. It was even more profoundly altered when, in the wake of the election, Gingrich decided to bypass the seniority system altogether. He went down the seniority lists to identify activists whose loyalty he could count on and put them into the chairs of key committees. Gingrich also created a new steering committee dominated by his leadership team and allies to control the committee assignment process for rank and file members. The incoming majority, many members of which had been groomed and inspired by Gingrich over the years, including the GOP's seventy-three freshmen representatives, endorsed these rule changes in December 1994. These changes moved in the same direction but went beyond what liberal reformers bolstered by the "Watergate Babies" had done in the Democratic caucus two decades earlier.[54]

Congressional staffing and oversight were also changed during the 104th Congress. Following through on the Contract's pledge to reduce House committee staff by one-third, the GOP also eliminated the Office of Technology Assessment, with its specialized expertise meant to give Congress an independent perspective vis-à-vis the executive branch's technocrats, and lowered the budgets and staffing of the General Accounting Office and the Congressional Research Service. These changes were connected to the GOP's push for party government, as they reduced the capacity of Congress to operate autonomously and to deliberate on policy in ways that were not simply driven by public opinion brought to bear from outside of the institution. Taken together, however, these changes greatly reduced the staff expertise available to support policymaking and oversight by legislators. Critics of this shift have likened it, harshly but not unfairly, to a self-administered "big lobotomy" from which Congress has yet to recover. Alongside these shifts, the House GOP also centralized control of the oversight agenda in the leadership offices to sharpen and coordinate its political confrontation with the Clinton administration. This more intentionally political approach to oversight of the executive branch led to fewer hearings, with greater interbranch conflict arising from those that were held.[55]

It might be tempting to see the penchant for ideological combat between the parties that characterized Gingrich and his majorities as a Republican approach to partisanship in the modern House. But as Bill Connelly has shown, a mirror image played out among House Democrats in their own fight back from minority to majority status. Nancy Pelosi argued, as Gingrich had, for unstinting confrontation and delineation between the parties. In the run up to the 2006 election, as she led her party's push to win control of the House, Pelosi developed the parliamentary-style "Six for '06" policy agenda, including a set of reforms that the Democratic majority enacted as promised in the first 100 hours of the new Congress.[56]

More ideological and uncompromising partisanship, and the confrontation that it engendered, also came to characterize the U.S. Senate in this period. Beginning in the mid-1970s, when the Senate lowered the cloture threshold to sixty votes, the use of the filibuster by the minority party began to increase. It grew more or less steadily over the next three decades, regardless of which party was in the minority. Meanwhile, the party confrontation in the Senate continued to sharpen given the narrower majorities and persistent electoral contest for control of the institution, which changed hands nine times between 1980 and 2015.[57]

The GOP took the use of filibusters, or the threat of them, to new heights after they lost control of the Senate in 2006. On the Democratic side, Majority Leader Harry Reid escalated use of "filling the tree" to prevent consideration of GOP amendments. Then in late 2013 the Democratic majority unilaterally resorted to a series of arcane parliamentary maneuvers, the so-called "nuclear option," to establish majority cloture for consideration of presidential nominations for most executive branch positions and lower court appointments. How long the remaining uses of the filibuster will be preserved remains to be seen. What is clear is that, as in the House, more responsible partisanship in the Senate has undermined the prospects for bipartisan deliberation, negotiation, and compromise in that body.

Where Do We Go from Here?

Despite the well-intentioned and influential recommendations of the APSA committees, we have come full circle. Trust in and appreciation for Congress is at an all-time low. Presidents of both parties have been taking increasingly assertive unilateral actions and, given the gridlock in Congress, have been free to do so without being checked and balanced. Once again we are asking fundamental questions about the future of representative democracy in the United States.

Without a sense of the irony that would seem warranted given how the responsible party government reform tradition has helped bring us to where we are today, a new generation of commentators is once again hailing the superiority of the parliamentary model. They view the separation of powers as an outdated device that prevents the resolution of political impasses and that will, sooner or later, bring democracy in America to ruin. Like an earlier generation of advocates for parliamentary-style reforms, these observers regard conservatives in Congress as the primary source of our current political difficulties. Unlike their predecessors, the new parliamentarians are pessimistic and do not believe that anything can effectively be done by way of formal or informal reform, hence their general conclusion, aptly summed up by Matt Yglesias, that "American government is doomed!"[58]

Long-time Congress watchers Tom Mann and Norm Ornstein share the deep frustration and pessimism of these commentators, and they are even more outspoken in their conviction that, well, "Let's just say it: The Republicans are the problem." Their approach to institutional reform is to pursue "changes consistent with our current constitutional framework" that would, nonetheless, "improve the fit between our current parliamentary-style parties and the policy-making process." The first of two institutional reforms they advocate would be making the Senate more majoritarian by "eliminating or reducing the scope of Senate actions subject to filibuster-related obstruction." The second would be to "shift decision-making power between Congress and the executive branch" through the use of more unilateral executive actions and greater reliance on independent, nonpartisan, expert bodies like the Federal Reserve or the Affordable Care Act's Independent Payment Advisory Board.[59]

The preceding analysis of efforts to make American politics in general and Congress in particular operate in a more parliamentary fashion, and to try to work around rather than through the separation of powers in making policy, would suggest that these latest reform proposals would likely continue to be confounded by our constitutional checks and balances. They would serve to accelerate rather than moderate the forces of polarization, as well as the whipsawing of policy as parties with very different agendas gain and lose majorities in Congress.

But we are not obliged to keep working against the grain of our longstanding constitutional arrangements. There is another reform tradition we could seek to revitalize. This alternative tradition, embodied in the Legislative Reform Act of 1946, and echoed in several of the 1970s reforms, would have us working with the grain of our system of government by developing the capacity for deliberation, negotiation, and compromise in Congress. An institution so restored would be much better positioned to serve as the first branch of government, to retain and actively exercise rather than continue to cede its power and authority to the president, administrative agencies, and the courts.

For this restoration to occur, Congress needs to take back the power of the purse and oversee the executive branch much more systematically. The frayed and tattered regular order needs to be reenvisioned and reestablished. The imperatives of representative democracy over the next fifty years will mean that any functional order will work much differently than it did fifty years ago, but some corrective for the current ad hoc and dysfunctional disorder is necessary. Finally, rather than starving itself of the support and expertise it needs to represent the American people, Congress needs to amply provide for them.

It would be tempting at this stage in the argument to begin listing specific reform proposals. But this would be premature. Instead, we need to start by completing some essential spade work in three areas and beginning it in a fourth. First, we need to revitalize the reform tradition that recognizes and seeks to enable Congress to play its rightful part in our constitutional system; flags the self-imposed obstacles that keep it from doing so; and affirms that negotiation and compromise are not shortcomings but, rather, core constitutional values. Some clarion calls have been sounded along these lines from across the political spectrum.[60] They need to build into a sustained chorus.

Second, to avoid the sort of problematic unintended consequences that reformers working toward more responsible partisanship fell into, we need to ground all calls for reform in the best scholarship about the problems of polarization, the dynamics of negotiations and policymaking in Congress, and the prospects and pitfalls facing different types of reform efforts. In this regard, a group of leading scholars participating in a 2013 APSA task force have shed important new light on the challenge of negotiating agreement in politics generally and in Congress in particular.[61] In addition, a group of scholars is now scrutinizing reform shibboleths about transparency, campaign finance, and direct democracy, and finding them wanting.[62]

Third, we need to cultivate an outside coalition of civil society organizations who share the goal of a healthier and more robust congressional role. Some advocacy groups have developed indices and scorecards to measure how well the institution is functioning, with an emphasis on deliberation, negotiation, and compromise. Others are working to improve specific congressional processes like oversight and budgeting. Still others are seeking to foster relationships and dialog across the aisle.[63] As we saw in both of the reform efforts just described, the support and advocacy of outside groups helped reformers within the institution develop and carry out their agendas. A great deal of philanthropy and nonprofit activity is now invested in pulling Congress to the left or the right in both politics and policy, thereby contributing to the problem of polarization. More effort is needed to help the institution bear up and improve its ability to deal with this cross-pressuring.

Finally and perhaps most important, to start moving down the path to productive reforms, those interested in strengthening the institution's capacity have to begin engaging with and supporting "procedural entrepreneurs" in Congress who are thinking along similar lines. If the Legislative Reorganization Act of 1946 is any indication, a successful reform effort will require a bipartisan, bicameral group of such legislators working over multiple congresses toward this end. There have been some promising initial developments along these lines. At the end of the 114th Congress, a concurrent resolution to establish just such a Joint Committee on the Organization of Congress was introduced and co-sponsored by a bipartisan group of 39 representatives.[64] To be sure, the ongoing sharp conflict between the parties for control of Congress, already unusually long in duration and showing no sign of letting up, means that any reforms that stand a chance of getting enacted and being sustained will need to work for both parties. The odds of this occurring may seem especially daunting at present. That is all the more reason to get started right away.

Notes

The author would like to thank Jean Bordewich, Kelly Born, William Connelly, Lee Drutman, Paul Glastris, Larry Kramer, Frances Lee, Jack Pitney, Jonathan Rauch, Eric Schickler, Greg Weiner, and Don Wolfensberger for their comments on earlier drafts of this paper.

1. Thomas K. Finletter, *Can Representative Government Do the Job?* (New York: Reynal and Hitchcock, 1945).

2. Donald R. Matthews, "American Political Science and Congressional Reform," *Social Science History*, 5, no. 1 (Winter 1981), pp. 92–94.

3. *The Reorganization of Congress: A Report of the Committee on Congress of the American Political Science Association* (Washington, D.C.: Public Affairs Press, 1945), pp. 3–4.

4. Ibid., pp. 80–81.

5. Ibid., p. 4.

6. Ibid., pp. 86–87; Roger H. Davidson, "The Advent of the Modern Congress," *Legislative Studies Quarterly* 15, no. 3 (August 1990), pp. 60–63; Matthews, "American Political Science and Congressional Reform," pp. 95–98.

7. *Reorganization of Congress*, pp. 79–80.

8. Ibid., pp. 27–29, 79–80.

9. Ibid., p. 70; Woodrow Wilson, *Congressional Government* (New York: Houghton Mifflin, 1885), pp. 60–79.

10. "Reorganization of Congress," pp. 29–31, 79.

11. Ibid., pp. 33–37, 80.

12. Ibid., p. 80.

13. Ibid., p. 79.

14. Ibid., pp. 56–57.

15. Ibid., p. 80.

16. U.S. Congress, "Organization of Congress: Report of the Joint Committee on the Organization of Congress," 79th Congress, 2nd Session, March 4, 1946, prefatory sheets.

17. Ibid., p. 1.

18. George Galloway, *Congress at the Crossroads* (New York: Thomas Y. Cromwell Company, 1946), p. 343.

19. U.S. Congress, "Organization of Congress," p. 5.

20. Ibid., pp. 12–14.

21. Eric Schickler, *Disjointed Pluralism: Institutional Innovation and the Development of the U.S. Congress* (Princeton University Press, 2001), pp. 142, 145–46; Davidson, "Advent of the Modern Congress," p. 364.

22. U.S. Congress, Legislative Reorganization Act of 1946, 79th Congress, Public Law 601, p. 24; Eric Schickler, "Entrepreneurial Defense of Congressional Power," in *Formative Acts: American Politics in the Making*, edited by Stephen Skowronek and Matthew Glassman (University of Pennsylvania Press, 2007), pp. 310–12.

23. Davidson, "Advent of the Modern Congress," pp. 357, 365–72.

24. James L. Sundquist, *The Decline and Resurgence of Congress* (Brookings Institution Press, 1981), pp. 199–237, 315–43, 402–14, 430–31. For the aborted committee reform effort in the House, see Roger H. Davidson and Walter J. Oleszek, *Congress Against Itself* (Indiana University Press, 1977).

25. American Political Science Association, Committee on Political Parties, "Toward a More Responsible Two-Party System," *American Political Science Review* 44, 3 (September 1950), pp. vii–ix; Paul T. David, "The APSA Committee on Political Parties: Some Reconsiderations of Its Work and Significance," *Perspectives on Politics* 20, no. 2 (1992), pp. 70–79.

26. "Toward a More Responsible Two-Party System," pp. v, 1.

27. Wilson, *Congressional Government*, p. 284, Wilson's emphasis.

28. "Toward a More Responsible Two-Party System," p. 56.

29. Ibid.

30. Ibid., p. 57.

31. Ibid., pp. 59–61, 65.

32. Ibid., pp. 61–62.

33. Ibid., pp. 62–65.

34. Ibid., pp. v, 35–36.

35. Ibid., pp. 20–21.

36. Sam Hoffman Rosenfeld, "A Choice, Not an Echo: Polarization and the Transformation of the American Party System," Doctoral Dissertation, Harvard University, 2014, p. 51. More broadly, Rosenfeld's important new assessment traces the myriad ways in which the ideas presented in the report of APSA Committee on Parties filtered directly into the Democratic Party and congressional reform efforts in the ensuing decades.

37. Julian Zelizer, *On Capitol Hill: The Struggle to Reform Congress and Its Consequences, 1948–1950* (Cambridge University Press, 2004), pp. 33–62.

38. Hubert Humphrey, "Notes and Memoranda: The Senate on Trial," *American Political Science Review* 44, no. 3 (September 1950), pp. 650–60; Rosenfeld, "A Choice, Not an Echo," p. 51.

39. Ibid., pp. 53–103, quotation from p. 53; James Q. Wilson, *The Amateur Democrat: Club Politics in Three Cities* (University of Chicago Press, 1962).

40. Nelson Polsby, *How Congress Evolves: Social Bases of Institutional Change* (Oxford University Press, 2004), pp. 21–35, 184.

41. Richard Bolling, *House Out of Order* (New York: Dutton & Company, 1964), and *Power in the House* (New York: Dutton & Company, 1968).

42. Rosenfeld, "A Choice Not an Echo," pp. 175–225.

43. Zelizer, *On Capitol Hill*, pp. 99–105, 126–28; Walter Kravitz, "The Advent of the Modern Congress," *Legislative Studies Quarterly* 15, no. 3 (September 1990), p. 378.

44. Polsby, *How Congress Evolves*, pp. 59–74; Zelizer, *On Capitol Hill*, pp. 129–38, 156–71.

45. Ibid., pp. 131, 172–75.

46. Wilson, *Amateur Democrats*, p. 358.

47. David W. Rohde, *Parties and Leaders in the Postreform House* (University of Chicago Press, 1991).

48. Polsby, *How Congress Evolves*, p. 133.

49. Steven Roberts, "One Conservative Faults Two Parties," *New York Times*, August 11, 1983.

50. For more on factional dynamics in the House GOP in this period, see William F. Connelly Jr. and John J. Pitney Jr., *Congress' Permanent Minority? Republicans in the U.S. House* (Lanham, Md.: Rowman and Littlefield, 1994).

51. Representative Dick Armey, "Speech introducing the Contract with America," September 27, 1994 (www.udel.edu/htr/American/Texts/contract.html). There were two additional Day 1 actions specified in this plank: "SEVENTH, require a three-fifths majority vote to pass a tax increase; EIGHTH, guarantee an honest accounting of our Federal Budget by implementing zero baseline budgeting."

52. Randall Strahan, *Leading Representatives: The Agency of Leaders in the Politics of the U.S. House* (The Johns Hopkins University Press, 2007), pp. 165–67.

53. Newt Gingrich, *Lessons Learned the Hard Way* (New York: Harper Collins, 1998), p. 10.

54. Strahan, *Leading Representatives*, pp. 148–52.

55. Paul Glastris and Haley Sweetland Edwards, "The Big Lobotomy: How Republicans Made Congress Stupid," *Washington Monthly*, Summer 2014.

56. William F. Connelly Jr., *James Madison Rules America: The Constitutional Origins of Congressional Partisanship* (Lanham, Md.: Rowman and Littlefield, 2010), pp. 49–84, 225.

57. See Frances Lee, *Beyond Ideology: Politics, Principles, and Partisanship in the U.S. Senate* (University of Chicago Press, 2009).

58. Vox.com, March 2, 2015. See also Dylan Matthews, "This Is How the American System of Government Will Die," *vox.com*, March 3, 2015; Johnathan Chait, "Obama, Republicans, and the Crisis of Legitimacy," *New York Magazine*, September 17, 2013.

59. Mann and Ornstein, "Let's Just Say It: Republicans Are the Problem," *Washington Post*, April 22, 2012; Tom Mann and Norm Ornstein, *It's Even Worse than It Looks: How the American Constitutional System Collided with the New Politics of Extremism* (New York: Basic Books, 2012), p. 163–66.

60. See, for example, Gregory Weiner, "Congress and Deliberation in the Age of Woodrow Wilson: An Elegy," *Liberty Law Blog*, May 1, 2013 (http://www.libertylawsite.org/liberty-forum/congress-and-deliberation-in-the-age-of-wilson-an-elegy); Jonathan Rauch, "Rescuing Compromise," *National Affairs*, Fall 2013; Glastris and Edwards, "The Big Lobotomy"; Chris DeMuth, "A Constitutional Congress?" *The Weekly Standard*, October 27, 2014; Steven Teles and Lee Drutman, "A New Agenda for Political Reform," *Washington Monthly*, Spring 2015; Kevin Kosar, "How to Strengthen Congress," *National Affairs*, Fall 2015.

61. Sarah A. Binder and Frances E. Lee, "Making Deals in Congress," in *Political Negotiation: A Handbook,* edited by Jane Mansbridge and Cathie Jo Martin (The Brookings Institution Press, 2016).

62. Bruce Cain, *Democracy More or Less: America's Political Reform Quandary* (Cambridge University Press, 2015); Rick Pildes, "Romanticizing Democracy, Political Fragmentation, and the Decline of American Government," *Yale Law Journal*, 2014, pp. 804–52.

63. See, for example, the work of the Bipartisan Policy Center, the Lugar Center, the National Budgeting Roundtable, the Project on Government Oversight, and the Millennial Action Project.

64. Establishing a Joint Committee on the Organization of Congress, H.R. 169, 114th Congress (2016) (https://www.congress.gov/114/bills/hconres169/BILLS-114hconres169ih.pdf).

3

Congressional Representation and Contemporary Critiques

ANDREW E. BUSCH

One of the most fundamental questions surrounding Congress and the Constitution is representation. It is also one of the broadest, encompassing issues as diverse as the size of the House, term length and limits, campaign finance, redistricting, and even the roles of federalism and of the presidency in relation to Congress. And Congress's role as a representative body is under increasing stress and scrutiny. Public opinion surveys in recent years show that only about one in five Americans feel that the federal government now operates on the basis of consent of the governed,[1] a view that must be considered at least partially an indictment of Congress. When considering these issues, it makes sense to begin at the beginning, with the original debate over the Constitution, and go from there. Contemporary critiques of congressional representation are actually traceable to federalist, antifederalist, or progressive strands of thought applied to modern issues, sometimes unknowingly.

The U.S. Constitution has provided a compact framework for thinking about representation and congressional elections. Members of the House of Representatives are to be elected every two years, and are to be apportioned to states on the basis of population to be adjusted after a census every ten years. Few qualifications are placed on representatives. To be eligible for election, they must be twenty-five years old, residents of the state from which they were elected, and United States citizens for at least seven years prior to their election. There is no religious test for this or any other office under the United States, nor are there property qualifications. House elections, seen by James Madison as a "national" feature of the "compound republic,"[2] nevertheless, respect federalism in several ways. Every state is guaranteed at least one representative, regardless of population; the "times, places, and manners" of election are to be set by state legislatures, though Congress is allowed to alter such regulations by law. The federal Constitution in its original form did not establish any uniform voting rules, specifying only that the electorate for the U.S. House in each state would be the same as the electorate for the most numerous branch of the state legislature. The Constitution of 1787 was silent about many of the issues related to elections and representation that fill debates today. There was no explicit requirement that congressmen be elected by single-member districts, let alone that those districts be equal in population. The Constitution was also silent on the subject of campaign finance, except implicitly, to the extent that the First Amendment guaranteed freedom of speech and press.[3]

With relatively long terms of six years staggered so that only one-third of the Senate would be elected every two years, the Senate was designed to introduce greater stability into the legislature. Indicative of the greater executive and international responsibilities held by the Senate, senators had to be thirty years of age, citizens of the United States for at least nine years, and residents of the state from which they were elected. The Senate was the component of Congress more openly advancing the "federal" principle, with two senators per state, elected not by the people directly but by the state legislatures. Just as there was a limit to the "national" character of election to the House, the "federal" feature was not undiluted in the Senate. Senators had fixed terms and were not subject to recall by their states, and each state had two votes as well as two senators.[4] In contrast, under the Articles of Confederation, states had to cast a single unified vote and legislatures could recall their representatives at will.[5]

The Original Debate

Though they were a disparate lot, anti-federalists generally complained that the supporters of the Constitution were aiming toward "consolidation," or destruction of the autonomy of the states in favor of a unified and centralized government. For evidence, they could point to the expanded powers of Congress, but they could also point to the structure and mode of election of Congress, and to the structure of the federal government as a whole. Bicameralism was not necessary in a confederation of limited jurisdiction, nor was any electoral scheme based on anything but state equality or selection by the state government. The new Congress would be structured and elected much like the legislative body of a sovereign government, not the assembly of a compact among sovereign governments. It would, of course, be joined by fully formed executive and judicial branches; the Constitution proposed to form a complete government.[6]

The anti-federalists also had a number of more specific concerns about Congress and representation in the proposed Constitution. Indeed, issues of representation were one of the most salient issues dividing the sides.[7] To anti-federalists, two-year terms for the House of Representatives and six-year terms for the Senate were too long to assure adequate accountability; anti-federalists remembered the colonial mantra that "where annual election ends, tyranny begins." More crucially, too few representatives would be elected and, correspondingly, there would be too many constituents per representative. Consequently, members of the House would be too removed, too insulated, and too different from their constituents to know them, understand their lives, and adequately represent them. In contrast, anti-federalists hoped for a representative body that would be an "exact miniature of the people." Anti-federalists also feared that large electoral districts would place a premium on organizing the vote rather than allowing majorities to naturally form. Altogether, the Constitution would lead to a government of "the wealthy and well-born" at the expense of the "middling sort."[8]

Not least, the anti-federalists strenuously objected to the right of Congress to set times, places, and manners of congressional election, and called for term limits for senators and president, a religious test for officeholders, and the right of states to recall their legislators. Fearing that election was insufficient to assure fidelity in officeholders, they also sought to strengthen institutional constraints on the legislative powers of those who were elected to Congress.[9]

The federalist response provides considerable insight into their very different conception of representation. Overall, supporters of the Constitution vigorously denied that the House would be disconnected from the people.[10] Defenders of the Constitution conceded the general principle of the anti-federalists in regard to congressional terms—that they should be short enough to compel accountability—but denied that the Constitution violated that principle. They ultimately suggested that the two-year term, which some of their opponents saw as a grievous flaw, was, instead, beneficial. Madison agreed that the House should have "an immediate dependence on, and an intimate sympathy with, the people," and frequent elections were "unquestionably the only policy by which this dependence and sympathy can be secured."[11] Officeholders must be made to anticipate the moment when they will be stripped of their power unless they faithfully discharge their duties.[12] (Indeed, the federalists seemed to put more faith in election as an instrument of representation than did anti-federalists.)[13] But just how frequent must elections be to achieve this objective?

As Publius showed, there was no commonly agreed upon understanding of this question at the state level, as states varied considerably in the length of their legislative terms. The British House of Commons, seen by many Americans as the seminal model of a popular legislature, did not have to stand for election more than once every seven years. To Publius, the safety of the two-year term was also attested by the relatively limited power to be held by the U.S. Congress. Parliament possessed a plenary power to act in all areas. State legislatures, likewise, possessed a general police power, now to be constrained only by certain prohibitions written into the federal Constitution. In contrast, the *Federalist* claims repeatedly, the federal Congress would possess only limited, enumerated powers defined by the Constitution, making it safe to give the U.S. House a longer term than state houses.[14]

There was also a positive argument for the longer terms found in the Constitution. Members of the U.S. House must acquaint themselves with the affairs of a larger number of constituents than members of state legislatures, and must pass judgment on issues that involve the United States as a whole. In short, they simply need to learn more than their state-legislative counterparts. Moreover, Publius observed that reelection to Congress in the Articles of Confederation was almost a matter of course, but contended that the new Congress would be different. Although "a few members with superior talents will become members of long standing," this outcome was not to be expected.[15] Hence, the duration of a single term must be bolstered to guarantee a sufficient opportunity to gain the necessary expertise.

The *Federalist*'s defense of the size of the House—or, to put it another way, the ratio of constituents to representatives—again conceded the general principle proclaimed by the anti-federalists, that there must be a sufficient number of representatives to understand and represent the people. Again, however, the provisions of the Constitution were judged by federalists to be both as safe as and more efficient than the preferences of their opponents. Madison agreed that it was important for the representative to be acquainted with "the interests and circumstances of his constituents."[16] However, he argued that not many representatives were needed in a state to be able to achieve that. On the other side of the ledger, "fit representatives" were more likely to be found in large than in small constituencies, and they were more likely to behave moderately.[17] The anti-federalists perceived a danger that "fit" would come to mean wealthy and elite, but Madison saw the answer to that danger in the broad electorate, the broad eligibility for office, and the frequency of election. Merit would prevail, and the winners would be characterized by gratitude to the people and attachment to the form of government that allowed them to attain power. Large constituencies were actually necessary for a beneficial "refinement" of the popular will, allowing for reconciling the potentially contrary goals of justice and consent.[18]

Defenders of the Constitution also noted that the size of the House could, and almost certainly would, be augmented every ten years, at least for the foreseeable future, though federalists saw danger as well in too many representatives. As Madison famously noted, "In all legislative assemblies, the greater the number composing them may be, the fewer will be the men who will in fact direct its proceedings."[19] Anti-federalists were cognizant of this danger, but saw it as another decisive argument against a consolidated republic. Once there are enough representatives to satisfy the needs of safety, local information, and diffusive sympathy with the whole society, no more should be added. Here, as elsewhere, the analysis of Publius merged concern with representation understood in a manner not entirely unlike the understanding of anti-federalists—asking how accountable the representatives are, and how capable of understanding and conveying the interests and views of their constituents—with a concern with the quality of representation, or institutional capacity of the representatives to do their jobs effectively.

Finally, although the Constitution did not require it, Publius seemed to assume that the House would be comprised of members elected by districts, probably single-member districts.[20] And in fact even in the earliest Congresses, single-member districts were the predominant mode of election. In general, the Framers endorsed a geographical conception of representation in which representatives were tied to local constituencies. Of course, anti-federalists were even more committed to the connection between local constituencies and their representatives.

Although the Senate was not to be popularly elected, the arguments surrounding the Senate can also illuminate the constitutional understanding of congressional representation. Federalists conceded that the Senate found in the new Constitution was the result of compromise, but the equality of state representation in the Senate was also touted as consistent with the concept of a compound republic and a guard against "consolidation." The Senate's role, Publius argued, was to correct the tendency of popular assemblies to yield to passions and to produce too much mutability in the laws, a particularly dangerous result of short terms that led to loss of respect abroad, was inimical to the rule of law at home, and provided unfair advantages to the "sagacious and moneyed few."[21]

According to Publius, longer terms would allow the Senate to form long-term plans and be held accountable for the results, and to reflect the "cool, deliberate sense of the people."[22] Because the Senate, through its influence on treaties, would have a scope of responsibility that was not merely national but international, members would have to be even more knowledgeable than members of the House, also justifying their longer terms. Just as the limited size of the House would promote the elevation of fit characters, the even smaller Senate would mean that senators would likely be "the most able and the most willing to promote the interests of their constituents."[23]

On balance, the federalists placed greater emphasis on merit and expertise, the anti-federalists on similarity to the people; the federalists on stability, the anti-federalists on immediate popular accountability. The federalists leaned toward representation that was built on a "trustee" model that valued independent deliberation, anti-federalists toward a "delegate" model that relied on "interest group representation" or descriptive representation rather than simple election.[24] Yet both valued consent of the governed, ultimate accountability, and similar conceptions of equality and natural rights, and some versions of the anti-federalist thinking were a hybrid, calling for the elevation of the best men from each interest.[25]

A Federalist Critique?

Given this outline, it is possible to argue against contemporary congressional representation on federalist grounds. For example, there are two developments relevant to Publius's defense of the two-year term for House members that have contradicted the expectations of the federalists themselves. History has not confirmed the expectation that House elections would be different from the tendency under the Articles of Confederation to return incumbents as a matter of course. Although rotation in office was quite normal and incumbent reelection rates much lower through much of the nineteenth century, by the 1890s careerism had taken hold in the House.[26] Only twice between 1976 and 2014 has the incumbent reelection rate in the U.S. House fallen below 90 percent.[27] Similarly, history has belied the claim of Publius that the two-year House term was safe because Congress, unlike state legislatures, did not possess general or plenary police power but was to be limited to its enumerated powers. Eight decades after commencement of the New Deal, it is difficult to argue that the U.S. Congress conforms to those limits. To the contrary, federal authority has spread into every corner of American life on the basis of generous readings of the General Welfare Clause, the Necessary and Proper Clause, and the Commerce Clause.

However, hardly anyone actually argues against the two-year House term on those grounds today. Indeed, public opinion surveys show that only 18 percent of Americans would support reducing House terms to one year.[28] Given the federalists' appreciation of stability in the legislature, and their opposition to term limits in other contexts,[29] it is not at all clear that they would have found the disparity between prediction and reality troubling. Moreover, perhaps counterbalancing these failed assumptions, the extent of contemporary federal authority—commanding a $3.6 trillion government with more than four million civilian and military employees—may actually enhance the power of the federalist argument that a longer term is necessary for members to gain the knowledge and expertise they need to perform their service.

Another concern based on contemporary deviation from federalist expectations has to do with the Seventeenth Amendment, which altered the method of electing the Senate from election by state legislatures to direct popular election by voters of each state. The effects of this change are a matter of debate among scholars. One school argues that the Seventeenth Amendment led to substantial weakening of the federal system.[30] The other points out that voters in many states had long made their state legislative selections on the basis of their preferred U.S. Senate candidate, mirroring the evolution of the Electoral College from a representative to a more democratic mode of indirect election.[31] In defense of federalism and a limited federal government, repeal of the Seventeenth Amendment has gained some support within the Tea Party movement and among some other conservatives, and has become prominent enough to draw attention (and criticism) from National Public Radio, the *Huffington Post*, and *Slate*. However, it remains far from the top of the political agenda.[32]

An Anti-Federalist Critique

More common are contemporary representational concerns that are expressed in terms familiar to the anti-federalists. These could be summarized in the following way: Congress is too disconnected from the people. It consists of the elite of society, with more attorneys than any other profession, not the "middling sort" that has intimate knowledge of and sympathy with most people. It is insulated by long terms, incumbency advantage leading to routine reelection, and geographical distance and, hence, has lost the capacity to act consistent with consent of the governed. Ultimately, there are simply too few Representatives, as the House has not grown past 435 for a century despite the nation roughly tripling in population.

This critique returned in force to the public square in the 1980s and 1990s, when incumbency advantage and insulation of representatives became a renewed topic of national conversation. At the heart of much of this critique was a desire for congressional representatives to act more as delegates. The passage of the Affordable Care Act in 2010, despite large rallies and public opinion polls showing consistent public opposition to the measure, crystallized these concerns more recently, corresponding with a series of surveys showing that only about one in five Americans believe that the United States was still operating on the basis of consent of the governed.[33]

One anti-federalist solution proposed by many over the past quarter-century has been congressional term limits, the drive for which peaked in the mid-1990s. Term-limit proponents failed at the federal level but were much more successful at the state level, ironically hobbling legislators at the level of government preferred by the anti-federalists. There was also a justification for term limits grounded in an extrapolation of federalist logic that was occasionally heard: by releasing representatives from the need for reelection, term limits would free them to act on their conception of the public good rather than on short-term calculations of public opinion.[34]

The anti-federalist critique has also led to proposals, which have never advanced far beyond the academic or journalistic realm, to increase the size of the House of Representatives for the first time in a century. Most such proposals suggest increasing the size of the House to roughly the size of the British House of Commons, or around 600 to 650 members, a number that would provide a modest and temporary reduction in the ratio of constituents to congressmen.[35] Even after such a reduction, however, the average congressional district would retain a population several times larger than that of 1788, which the anti-federalists already saw as too large. Consequently, while proposals for augmentation of the House are a nod to the anti-federalist spirit, it is impractical to imagine that they could actually meet anti-federalist specifications.

Another "anti-federalist" approach to the issue of an "unrepresentative" Congress is the ongoing structural call to strengthen the role of the states and, hence, of state legislatures, in the federal system.[36] This approach suggests that if Congress by its nature cannot be made significantly more representative, perhaps it can be made less important in the overall governance of the country, with some power transferred to those legislative bodies that are more closely connected to the people.

However, states vary widely in the degree to which they conform to the anti-federalist model of representation. At one end, farthest from that model, are states with professional legislatures using long sessions and highly populous districts. Perhaps the best example is California, with a small, highly paid, year-round legislature; the California state senate, with only forty members, has more residents per district than U.S. House members. According to the National Conference of State Legislatures, only three states fit this model fully, with another seven close behind. At the other extreme is New Hampshire, with a part-time House of Representatives boasting 400 members, or about one for every 3,300 inhabitants. As the NCSL categorizes them, fifteen state legislatures are near this end of the spectrum. The rest (half of all state legislatures) are in-between. Many are part-time and/or term limited, and most have significantly smaller districts than those represented by U.S. Congress members, though not as small as New Hampshire's.[37] Since the 1980s, there have been repeated attempts to move in the direction of enhancing the power of state legislatures, with a key victory coming when the federal welfare system was decentralized in 1996. However, the decentralizing position has, on balance, lost more ground than it has gained, in areas ranging from criminal justice to health care to family law to education.

The Progressive Critique

The third strand of contemporary criticism of congressional elections and congressional representation is represented by the progressive movement of the early twentieth century and its descendants. This critique sometimes overlaps with one of the original constitutional arguments—scholar Elvin T. Lim has argued for considerable confluence between progressives and anti-federalists, for example[38]—but it generally emphasizes different concerns and often operates well outside the assumptions of both federalists and anti-federalists.

The progressive doctrine as a whole is grounded in several key assertions. One is that notions of natural rights, adhered to by both federalists and anti-federalists, are illusory. As progressive theorist Charles Merriam argued, while it cannot be said that there are no limits to the state, "The question is now one of expediency rather than of principle."[39] Consequently, there is little value to limited government as a principle, and little value to structures like separation of powers or federalism meant to bolster limited government. There is, on the other hand, great value to government action to address developing problems and to institutional reforms that lubricate such action. In particular, the great task of modern government is to serve as an active counterbalance to the power of private economic forces. In the progressive view the Constitution should be seen as malleable, not fixed. In general progressives were not favorably disposed to the principle of representation, which they chipped away at—from one end through direct democracy and from the other end through the decisive place given to administrative "experts" who act outside the constraints of messy democratic politics. This overarching progressive critique has a number of important implications for congressional elections and representation.

First, a key progressive impulse has been the desire to significantly limit the flow of private money into election campaigns, starting with passage of the Tillman Act of 1907 prohibiting federal campaign contributions by corporations and interstate banks. After the revelations of Watergate, the Federal Election Campaign Act Amendments of 1974 placed limits on individual, party, and interest group contributions to federal campaigns and established spending limits on campaigns for election to U.S. Congress. (It also created a system of public financing for presidential elections.)

In 1976, the Supreme Court in *Buckley v. Valeo* ruled the spending limits unconstitutional on grounds that preventing candidates from spending their own money on their own campaigns was an impermissible restriction on freedom of speech. On similar grounds, the Court also ruled out limits on independent expenditures (expenditures made by outside individuals or groups to support or oppose a candidate without the coordination of the candidate who benefits).

Since 1976 the Supreme Court has repeatedly ruled that campaign contributions or independent spending have a large degree of constitutional protection as a form of speech or as instrumental to speech. In one of the most notable of these decisions, the Supreme Court in 2010 ruled in *Citizens United v. Federal Election Commission* that corporations and labor unions must be free to engage in independent expenditures, though the Court did not upset the ban on direct corporate or labor donations to candidates.

Though not alone in their concerns, those in the progressive tradition have found this line of decisions most distressing. President Obama publicly rebuked the Court in his 2010 State of the Union Address, and some critics of *Citizens United* have called for a constitutional amendment to reverse the decision and elaborate on the right of Congress to restrict campaign contributions. The so-called Udall Amendment, named after its chief sponsor, Senator Tom Udall (D-N. Mex.), would establish the power of Congress "to regulate the raising and spending of money and in-kind equivalents with respect to Federal elections." To some extent, these concerns simply reflect understandable concerns voiced to one degree or another by wide swaths of the American public about the influence of big money in politics, and majorities of the Supreme Court have never abandoned the view formulated in the 1970s that avoiding the appearance of improper influence was sufficient justification for limits on direct contributions. On the surface, these complaints intersect with anti-federalist concerns about Congress falling into the hands of the "wealthy and well-born." However, this drive diverges from the anti-federalists in important ways.

It is ultimately grounded in the progressive conception that the key purpose of modern government is to counterbalance private economic power. Here, progressives apply a distinctive approach to the problem of how to manage private interests in a republic. For one thing, the approach of contemporary progressive campaign finance reformers shows none of the solicitude toward rights that one might have expected from the anti-federalists. Indeed, anti-federalists would likely have been quite suspicious about the uses to which government might put the power to control the landscape of elections (recall their deep hostility to even secondary federal regulation of the times, places, and manners of election). That approach is consistent, however, with the progressives' dismissal of natural rights, such as (in this case) rights of freedom of speech and press codified in the First Amendment and insisted upon by anti-federalists. Progressives, seeing rights as highly contingent creations of the state, are willing to subordinate freedom of speech to an alternative governmental purpose. That they are actually engaged in the subordination of rights is understood by both conservatives and the American Civil Liberties Union, which has harshly criticized the Udall Amendment as a threat to fundamental rights.[40]

More broadly, the federalists addressed the question in Madison's famed *Federalist* No. 10, in which the author proposed to mitigate the dangers associated with private interests by expanding the scope of the republic and, hence, expanding the number and diversity of interests. By doing so, Madison hoped interests would balance each other, leaving none strong enough to dominate. To abolish liberty so as to eliminate faction, Madison held, was like abolishing air to fight fire—a cure worse than the disease.[41] For their part, the anti-federalists hoped to manage the danger by limiting the scope of the polity, reducing the number of interests with which each polity had to contend, then making sure that each was adequately represented. Here, too, liberty was a primary goal, but could only be safeguarded on a smaller scale in a more homogeneous polity. In both cases, the demands of interests would be filtered through a representative electoral system at the federal and/or state level. Both historical and contemporary progressives eschew such structural thinking and, instead, rely on the force of law to simply suppress the involvement of private interests in congressional or other elections.

The other common contemporary critique grounded in progressivism is that the constitutional arrangement of presidential, House, and Senate elections does not produce a result that is representative of the popular desire for governmental action. Rather, because there are multiple institutions, each with its own constituency, and staggered timeframes for election, it is difficult to construct—and even more difficult to maintain for long—demonstrated public support that can be plausibly presented as a policy "mandate." (Of course, political scientists have long questioned whether elections can ever be said to truly confer a policy mandate, but that is a separate question.) In short, the current design of American elections is likely to produce a disjointed result inimical to transformative action.

The problem here, highlighted by progressive writers for over a century, is separation of powers, undergirded by separated elections and exacerbated by decentralized, localized political parties. Woodrow Wilson complained that the American system was based on an outmoded Newtonian view of systems in balance. Instead, he urged, government should be seen as an organic whole, with the president in the lead.[42] Along progressive lines, a committee of the American Political Science Association called in a 1950 report for "responsible"—that is, centralized and ideologically homogeneous—parties.[43] More recently, progressives have complained bitterly about "gridlock" in Congress, suggesting that the American system was broken when Congress defied the president.

Like the progressives' approach to the electoral control of private economic power, their critique of separation of powers contrasts sharply with views of federalists and anti-federalists alike. To Madison, the accumulation of all powers in one set of hands "may justly be pronounced the very definition of tyranny,"[44] and the federal convention, ultimately, took pains to separate the selection of the officers of each branch (for example, rejecting proposals that the president be selected by Congress and that the upper house be selected by the lower house). The anti-federalists complained that the Constitution did not provide for enough separation between branches, and often suggested what would have amounted to a fourth branch, an independent advisory council for the president.

Progressives have, over the years, suggested two remedies for separation of powers. The formal solution, requiring a constitutional amendment, would seek to limit the effects of separation of powers by coordinating presidential and congressional terms and elections as far as possible. In 1980, despairing of Jimmy Carter's difficulties dealing with Congress (controlled by his fellow Democrats), presidential advisor Lloyd N. Cutler endorsed giving the president, vice president, senators, and congress members simultaneous six-year terms, perhaps requiring voters to vote on party nominees for all offices as a team, and allowing the president to dissolve Congress and call for new elections.[45] Cutler hoped such a system would not only make government divided between the parties much less likely but would bind the president's co-partisans in Congress more closely to him. The goal would be to deliberately arrange the electoral system to emphasize representation of national or presidential majorities and to deemphasize the representation of sometimes-conflicting local majorities. This proposal, however, fell by the wayside in the wake of Ronald Reagan's election and successful presidency and has not been revived.

The other progressive answer to a congressional election system that inhibits activist government has been to informally supersede congressional elections by strengthening the president and executive branch bureaucracy at the expense of Congress. Just as anti-federalists might seek to bypass an unrepresentative Congress by placing more power in the states, progressives seek to do so by shifting power to the institutions they prefer for their ability to exert unified activist leadership or to define expert administrative opinion. This approach has manifested itself in a systematic strengthening of the policymaking capacities of the executive branch (starting with FDR's establishment of the Executive Office of the President), increasingly aggressive uses of executive actions to bypass Congress, and use of independent regulatory commissions and other regulatory agencies to fill in the details of vague congressional statutes. All this has been undergirded by Theodore Roosevelt's and Woodrow Wilson's goal of making the president the preeminent lawmaker and policymaker in Washington.

Of course, arguments for a strong president go back to Alexander Hamilton, who contended: "Energy in the executive is a leading character in the definition of good government."[46] Again, however, the progressives only briefly intersect with an original constitutional argument, in this case that of the federalists. Hamilton may have supported an energetic executive, but his view that the president was allowed to do anything not prohibited by the Constitution (expressed in his Pacificus letters) was limited to the realm of foreign affairs, where "secrecy, energy, and dispatch" were at a premium and normal lawmaking faced its greatest challenges. Theodore Roosevelt's "stewardship" theory of the presidency greatly advanced the argument that the president was a superior representative of the nation because he was the only official elected by the whole people and that the right of the president to do anything not prohibited extended to domestic as well as foreign affairs and to everyday policymaking as well as crisis.[47] Anti-federalists feared the president might become an overwhelming presence in the polity, and federalists denied that he would. Only the progressives welcomed it, although elevation of the presidency has become so universally embraced—and Congress itself so complicit—that it is easy to forget its ideological origins.

The Complicated Case of Gerrymandering

Although the three schools—federalist, anti-federalist, and progressive—are often simply at odds, there are also important representational issues regarding which their relationship is much more complicated. Gerrymandering, or the practice of deliberately drawing congressional boundaries for the purpose of advancing a particular electoral outcome, is such a case. Gerrymandering has been an issue in congressional representation since the first congressional districts were formed (though the term itself originated in Massachusetts after the 1800 census). The potential for redistricting mischief has grown since the Supreme Court ruled in the 1960s that congressional districts must be as equal in population as possible, thus subordinating traditional criteria such as geographic features, compactness, and respect for communities and political subdivisions that placed some limits around the manipulation of district boundaries.

Political gerrymandering (that is, gerrymandering for reasons of partisan advantage or incumbent protection) has been criticized from every possible direction. Federalists, anti-federalists, and progressives all shared some degree of aversion to a partisan system, as well as to artificial entrenchment of officeholders. In recent years, the progressive approach of replacing politics with neutral expertise has been at the heart of an assault on political gerrymandering in the form of citizen redistricting commissions adopted by seven states for congressional redistricting. However, while the federalists might well have applauded the objective, they may have been skeptical of the mechanism of a redistricting commission superseding the state legislature and would likely have rejected outright the direct democracy ballot initiative (introduced by progressives) that has typically been used to adopt it. Similarly, while anti-federalists might have condemned political gerrymandering in principle, it often leads to more homogeneous congressional districts that are easier to represent as a delegate.

Moreover, contemporary critics who "point to the need for greater attention to group interests, be they economic, sexual, racial, or ethnic," are speaking the anti-federalists' language.[48] One manifestation is the drive since the 1980s for "racial gerrymandering," or congressional redistricting criteria that maximize the potential for "majority–minority districts." Based on an interpretation of the Voting Rights Act Amendments of 1982, the U.S. Justice Department and federal courts have pushed states to pack their racial minorities into a small number of districts so they have greater capacity to elect a minority officeholder. Though observers have rarely noted the link to anti-federalist thinking, this drive is a selective attempt to alter the system of congressional election to make more likely the election of representatives who are "like their constituents" in some descriptive sense.

Conclusion

The Constitution sets out a few basic rules around the issue of congressional elections and representation. These provisions are grounded in a broader theory of representation favored by the federalists, one that emphasized expertise, merit, stability, deliberation, and moderation. Anti-federalists contested this model of representation, prioritizing accountability and descriptive similarity of the representatives to the people. Roughly speaking, the former leaned in the direction of trustee representatives, the latter in the direction of delegates. At the same time, federalists and anti-federalists shared basic principles, and their disagreements were often a matter of different emphases or different expectations about the result of particular institutional arrangements rather than of fundamental values.

Debates today sometimes feature echoes of that contest. It is possible to contend that contemporary congressional elections and representation are flawed because they do not adequately hew to the federalists' original design. Others perceive Congress as having ultimately proved the anti-federalists right, standing today as an institution that is too elitist and too far removed from the people. As a remedy, a variety of voices have promoted term limits, augmentation of the House, decentralization of power, and reform of congressional districting to assure better matching of the race or ethnicity of representatives with their minority constituents.

Added to this debate is the progressive critique, which is sometimes alien to the constitutional arguments of both federalists and anti-federalists. Included are arguments challenging the value of intrinsic rights to political expression, asserting that those rights in the context of election campaigns should be subordinated to governmental balancing of private economic interests, and arguments proposing that separation of powers should be overcome with a new centralized system revolving formally or informally around the president, in essence superseding the local geographic bias of congressional representation. To this extent, many contemporary complaints about Congress might well baffle founders in both of the camps of 1787–88, if not be perceived by them as harbingers of tyranny. Nevertheless, in the broadest sense, debates about representation—the size of the House, the character of House districts, congressional terms, the intersection of private interests and political life, and the structure and structural role of Congress—remain active, and in most cases each school of thought contributes something to the debate.

It is also clear that the question of representation is so central to Congress's place in the Constitution that it cannot be considered or critiqued seriously without touching a wide range of significant constitutional provisions that might seem to the casual observer to be peripheral, such as federalism and executive power. Implicit in this fact is that it may be even more difficult than many imagine to restore a sense among Americans that Congress represents them well. No matter which historical strand of thinking one looks to as a guide, Congress is but one part of a large and interconnected system, and there is no silver bullet.

Notes

1. "19% Think Federal Government Has Consent of the Governed," *Rasmussen Reports*, April 11, 2014 (www.rasmussenreports.com/public_content/politics/general_politics/april_2014/19_think_federal_government_has_consent_of_the_governed).

2. *Federalist* No. 39, in *The Federalist Papers*, edited by Clinton Rossiter (New York: Mentor, 1961).

3. United States Constitution, Article I, Sections 2 and 4.

4. Ibid., Article I, Section 3.

5. Articles of Confederation, Article V.

6. Herbert Storing, *What the Anti-Federalists Were For* (University of Chicago Press, 1981).

7. Walter Berns, "Does the Constitution 'Secure These Rights'?," in *How Democratic Is the Constitution?*, edited by Robert A. Goldwin and William A. Schambra (Washington, D.C.: American Enterprise Institute, 1987), p. 68.

8. "Report of the Pennsylvania Minority," December 18, 1787, pp. 247–49; *The Federal Farmer*, October 9, 1987, pp. 264–69; *Brutus I*, October 18, 1787, pp. 277–80. *The Anti-Federalist Papers and the Constitutional Convention Debates*, edited by Ralph Ketcham (New York: Mentor, 1986). See, also, Cecilia M. Kenyon, "Men of Little Faith: The Anti-Federalists on the Nature of Representative Government," *The William and Mary Quarterly* 12, no. 1 (January 1955), pp. 3–43.

9. See Kenyon, "Men of Little Faith," especially pp. 15, 17, 21–29.

10. *Federalist* No. 39, p. 244.

11. *Federalist* No. 52, p. 327.

12. *Federalist* No. 57, p. 352.

13. Jean Yarbrough, "Thoughts on the *Federalist*'s View of Representation, *Polity* 12, no. 1 (Autumn 1979), pp. 65–82.

14. *Federalist* No. 52, pp. 329–30. See, also, *Federalist* No. 53, pp. 330–32.

15. *Federalist* No. 53, pp. 335.

16. *Federalist* No. 56, p. 346.

17. *Federalist* No. 57, p. 354. See, also, *Federalist* No. 10, pp. 82–83.

18. Yarbrough, "Thoughts on the *Federalist*'s View," pp. 68–70.

19. *Federalist* No. 58, p. 360.

20. *Federalist* No. 57, p. 355.

21. *Federalist* No. 62, p. 381.

22. *Federalist* No. 63, p. 384.

23. *Federalist* No. 64, p. 395.

24. Joseph M. Bessette, "Deliberative Democracy: The Majority Principle in Republican Government," in *How Democratic Is the Constitution?*, edited by Robert A. Goldwin and William A. Schambra (Washington, D.C.: AEI, 1980), pp. 102–16; Yarbrough, "Thoughts on the *Federalist*'s View."

25. Berns, "Does the Constitution 'Secure These Rights?'," pp. 62–63; Joel A. Johnson, "Disposed to Seek Their True Interests: Representation and Responsibility in Anti-Federalist Thought," *The Review of Politics* 66, no. 4 (Autumn 2004), pp. 649–73.

26. Nelson Polsby, "The Institutionalization of the U.S. House of Representatives," *American Political Science Review*, 62, no. 1 (March 1968), pp. 144–68.

27. "Reelection Rates Over the Years" (www.opensecrets.org/bigpicture/reelect.php).

28. Larry J. Sabato, *A More Perfect Constitution: 23 Proposals to Revitalize Our Constitution and Make America a Fairer Country* (New York: Walker & Company, 2007), p. 192.

29. In *Federalist* No. 72, for example, Hamilton offers numerous arguments against presidential term limits.

30. See Ralph A. Rossum, *Federalism, the Supreme Court, and the Seventeenth Amendment: The Irony of Constitutional Democracy* (Lanham, Md.: Lexington Books, 2001).

31. William H. Riker, "The Senate and American Federalism," *American Political Science Review* 49, no. 2, pp. 452–69.

32. For support of repeal, see The Campaign to Restore Federalism (www.restorefederalism.org). See, also. Alan Greenblat, "Rethinking The 17th Amendment: An Old Idea Gets Fresh Opposition," NPR, February 5, 2014 (www.npr.org/sections/itsallpolitics/2014/02/05/271937304/rethinking-the-17th-amendment-an-old-idea-gets-fresh-opposition); David Schleicher, "States' Wrongs," *Slate*, February 24, 2014 (www.slate.com/articles/news_and_politics/jurisprudence/2014/02/conservatives_17th_amendment_repeal_effort_why_their_plan_will_backfire.html); Search results for "Seventeenth Amendment Repeal" on *Huffington Post* (www.huffingtonpost.com/news/17th-amendment-repeal).

33. "19% Think Federal Government Has Consent of the Governed," *Rasmussen Reports*, April 11, 2014 (www.rasmussenreports.com/public_content/politics

/general_politics/april_2014/19_think_federal_government_has_consent_of _the_governed).

34. For example, George F. Will, "A New Case for Congressional Term Limits," *Washington Post*, October 1, 2014 (www.washingtonpost.com/opinions/george-will-a-new-case-for-congressional-term-limits/2014/10/01/f924bf5a-48bc-11e4-891d-713f052086a0_story.html).

35. See Phil Duncan, "Enlarging the Congress: Boon for Democracy," *CQ Weekly*, October 28, 1989, p. 2914; James Glassman, "Let's Build a Bigger House: Why Shouldn't the Number of Congressmen Grow with the Population?," *Washington Post*, June 17, 1990, p. D2; Wilma Rule, "Expanded Congress Would Help Women," *New York Times*, February 24, 1991, p. E16; Charles A. Kromkowski and John A. Kromkowski, "Why 435? A Question of Political Arithmetic," *Polity*, 24, no. 1 (Autumn 1991), pp. 129–45; Christopher St. John Yates, "A House of Our Own or a House We've Outgrown? An Argument for Increasing the Size of the House of Representatives," *Columbia Journal of Law and Social Problems* 25 (1992), pp. 157–96; Michael Mevill and Sean Wilentz, "The Big House: An Alternative to Term Limits," *The New Republic*, November 16, 1992, pp. 16–18; DeWayne L. Lucas and Michael D. McDonald, "Is It Time to Increase the Size of the House of Representatives?," *American Review of Politics* 21 (2000), pp. 367–81; Jeff Jacoby, "A Bigger, More Democratic Congress," *Boston Globe*, January 13, 2005; Jeffrey W. Ladewig and Matthew P. Jasinski, "On the Causes and Consequences of and Remedies for Interstate Malapportionment of the U.S. House of Representatives," *Perspectives on Politics*, March 2008, pp. 89–107.

36. For example, Michael S. Greve, *Real Federalism: Why It Matters, How It Could Happen* (Washington, D.C.: AEI Press, 1999).

37. "Full and Part-Time Legislatures," National Conference of State Legislatures (www.ncsl.org/research/about-state-legislatures/full-and-part-time-legislatures.aspx).

38. Elvin T. Lim, "The Anti-Federalist Strand in Progressive Politics and Political Thought," *Political Research Quarterly* 66, no. 1 (March 2013), pp. 32–45.

39. Charles Merriam, "Recent Tendencies," chapter VIII in *A History of American Political Theories* (New York: Macmillan, 1903).

40. See ACLU Statement for Senate Hearing on Udall Amendment (www.aclu.org/sites/default/files/assets/6-3-14_—_udall_amendment_letter_final.pdf). See, also, Luke Wachob, "Udall's Futile Fight Against Free Speech," *National Review*, September 8, 2014 (www.nationalreview.com/article/387387/udalls-futile-fight-against-free-speech-luke-wachob).

41. *Federalist* No. 10, p. 78.

42. Woodrow Wilson, *Constitutional Government in the United States* (Columbia University Press, 1908).

43. American Political Science Association, "A Report of the Committee on Political Parties: Toward a More Responsible Party System," *American Political Science Review* 44, no. 3 (part 2) (September 1950).

44. *Federalist* No. 47, p. 301.

45. Lloyd N. Cutler, "Time for Constitutional Change?," *Foreign Affairs* 59, 1980–81.

46. *Federalist* No. 70, p. 423.

47. Sidney Milkis and Michael Nelson, *The American Presidency: Origins and Development* 7th ed. (Washington, D.C.: CQ Press, 2016), chapter 8.

48. Jean Yarbrough, "Representation and Republicanism: Two Views," *Publius* 9, no. 2 (Spring 1979), p. 88.

Return to Deliberation?

Politics and Lawmaking in Committee and on the Floor

DANIEL J. PALAZZOLO

The Framers of the U.S. Constitution designed institutions that made deliberation an essential and variable aspect of lawmaking. Ideally, Congress would be a chosen body of virtuous citizens who possessed the knowledge, experience, and time to make reasonable decisions that reflected the public interest.[1] But a large republic would also encourage a diverse range of factions—parties and like-minded groups—to protect and advance their policy and political interests.[2] The Framers also expected representatives to vary in terms of wisdom, patriotism, virtue, and motives; some would be motivated by public service, others by personal fame or political power.[3] Political goals and self-serving interests will always be present in the policy process,[4] but some degree of deliberation is necessary for Congress to legitimize its policy decisions, educate the public, and make intelligent choices.[5] Deliberation is what transforms Congress "from a collective of representatives to a community of legislators."[6]

This chapter assesses the essential and variable aspects of deliberation in committees and on the floors of the House of Representatives and the Senate. Beginning with the Framers, deliberation has always competed with factional politics in the lawmaking process. Over time, increases in the number and diversity of interests, an expansion of the federal government, the rise of the modern president, and a communication system that demands instantaneous and persistent responses to current events and issues have transformed American government and the context within which factions operate. Deliberative lawmaking has become increasingly more difficult. Today, advocacy groups, party polarization, and institutional reforms have accentuated politics and weakened Congress's capacity for deliberation.[7] Advocacy groups push members of Congress to take unbending positions and focus on narrow policy goals; polarized, competitive parties limit policy choices, obstruct legislative business, accentuate differences, and pursue tactics to seek and hold power[8]; and institutional reforms have strengthened party leaders and weakened committee chairs. Policymakers tend to use facts, information, and arguments to validate preconceived positions rather than to consider alternative ways to solve problems.

Even with those tendencies and constraints, though, the extent and quality of deliberation vary across issues, between the Senate and the House, and by institution (committee, floor, and party) within each chamber. The committee is a better institutional setting for deliberation than the floor, though some committees are better organized for deliberation than others, and the Senate is more conducive to debate than the House floor. Deliberation may be facilitated by the necessity of passing laws,[9] individual member goals (particularly gaining influence and making policy to solve problems), unsettled policy preferences, and the majority party's interest in building a successful record of governance.[10] The size of majority parties in Congress and presidential leadership may also affect the balance of politics and deliberation.[11]

Of course, the temptation of politics is always present and capable of preventing, derailing, or disrupting deliberative efforts to seek compromise and address public problems.[12] Thus, scholars and organizations have proposed reforms aimed to enhance the deliberative capacity of Congress.[13] From among a broad range of proposals, committee reforms offer the best prospects for improving deliberation. Ultimately, though, deliberation will depend on the capacity of leaders to manage factions within a system of separated powers, bicameralism, and mixed representation.

Constitutional Considerations: Deliberative Democracy and Factionalism

The Framers designed Congress to serve as the forum for deliberative democracy, a body of representatives capable of making "informed and wise judgments about public policy" that are "firmly grounded in the interests and desires of the American citizenry."[14] As James Madison put it, Congress should "refine and enlarge the public views" so that "the public voice, pronounced by the representatives of the people, will be more consonant to the public good, than if pronounced by the people themselves, convened for the purpose."[15]

Deliberation would be facilitated by institutions: a large republic, a bicameral legislature consisting of relatively small bodies of representatives and senators, longer terms for representatives than many of the state legislatures at the time (especially for senators), and a separation of legislative and executive powers. By enabling factions to flourish, a large republic would prevent unjust majorities from violating the rights of individuals and minorities. Madison famously argued in *Federalist* No.10: "Extend the sphere and you will take in a greater variety of parties and interests; you make it less probable that a majority of the whole will have a common motive to invade the rights of others citizens. . . ." The "greater variety of parties" provides security "against the event of any one party being able to outnumber and oppress the rest," and creates "greater obstacles" to the formation of an "unjust and interested majority." A large republic would also increase the probability of electing "fit characters," or "enlightened statesman," and make it harder for "unworthy candidates" to win office.[16]

Bicameralism would delay the legislative process by requiring laws to be passed by two different chambers of representatives elected by different constituents for different lengths of time—the House by the people every two years and the Senate by state legislatures every six years. The public trust is less likely to be betrayed when "the concurrence of separate and dissimilar bodies is required in every public act."[17] In addition, senators would lend greater stability, experience, and knowledge to the lawmaking process; deter Congress from the temptation to yield "to the impulse of sudden and violent passions, and to be seduced by factious leaders into intemperate and pernicious resolutions";[18] and improve the chances that laws will reflect the "cool and deliberate sense of the community."[19] The small size of the two bodies and the relatively long term lengths were designed to facilitate deliberation among representatives and discourage impulsive responses to ill-informed public opinion.[20]

The separation of powers was the last line of defense against poorly designed laws. One purpose of the president's authority to veto, according to Alexander Hamilton, is to "furnish additional security against the enactment of improper laws." The presidential veto would "increase the chances in favor of the community against the passing of bad laws, through haste, inadvertence, or design."[21]

Yet, in describing the effects of a large republic, bicameralism, and separation of powers, Madison and Hamilton spoke in terms of probabilities. Those institutions would improve the likelihood of deliberation but not guarantee it. In addition to promoting deliberation, the system of separated and overlapping powers was designed to limit the concentration of power, particularly in the legislative branch.[22] Although a large republic increased the chances of electing representatives "whose wisdom may best discern the true interest of their country and whose patriotism and love of justice will be least likely to sacrifice it to temporary or particular considerations," Madison warned, "Enlightened statesmen will not always be at the helm. . . ."[23] He claimed that representatives have three possible motivations: 1) ambition, 2) personal interest, and 3) the public good. "Unhappily," said Madison, "the two first are proved by experiences to be the most prevalent."[24] Madison's political theory suggests that even a large republic will yield its share of "factious leaders," ambitious power seekers and self-serving demagogues pursuing personal glory or short-term gain, together with "fit characters," "enlightened statesman," and virtuous individuals with "generous principles" or "extended views."[25]

Madison's belief that institutions could be designed to foster deliberation in service to the public interest was mixed with the underlying assumption that the legislative process is ridden with factions and parties that pursue their self-interests. Thus, Madison contends: "The regulation of these various and interfering interests forms the principle task of modern legislation and involves the spirit of party and faction in the necessary and ordinary operations of government."[26] Legislators themselves may be attached to such interests or parties, and the legislature may be overtaken by political parties whose members are guided by "passion, not reason."[27] Factions and parties may be motivated by influencing public policy or gaining power.[28]

In sum, the struggle between deliberation and politics is as old as the Constitution. The institutions were designed to promote good government and effective national policy, yet depending on the power of interests and parties, they could also produce gridlock or stalemate.[29] The question is: How do current conditions affect deliberation among representatives with competing ideological views and policy preferences, allegiances to parties and groups, and aspirations to win public office and gain political power?

Politics and Deliberation in the Contemporary Congress

Scholars have defined "deliberation" in different ways.[30] Joseph Bessette calls deliberation "reasoning on the merits of public policy," a process that involves information, argument, and persuasion, ultimately to address the national interest.[31] Bessette distinguishes deliberation from bargaining, which may require logrolling, splitting differences, or side payments.[32] Gary Mucciaroni and Paul Quirk define deliberation as "the weighing of substantive information and considerations in making public policy decisions."[33] Unlike Bessette, Mucciaroni and Quirk do not assume that deliberation requires members of Congress to serve a specific goal, like the public interest; they are interested in the "intelligence" of deliberation, or "the ability . . . to reach decisions that are informed, instrumentally rational, and consistent with decision makers' goals or values."[34] Steven Smith emphasizes "careful consideration of alternatives," broad participation, reasoning together rather than argumentation, and equal ability of members to exchange views.[35]

Conceptual distinctions are important, if only because they affect normative claims about the quality of deliberation in Congress. Rather than evaluate the conceptual merits of different definitions, I identify the essential, if not the least objectionable, aspects of deliberation: 1) reliable information about problems, issues, and programs;[36] 2) time and opportunity for analysis, debate, and careful consideration of alternative policy choices;[37] 3) institutional settings that are large enough to facilitate a range of differing viewpoints among a broad range of participants[38] but small enough to allow serious discussion;[39] and 4) the capacity for members of Congress to be persuaded by information learned[40] or claims made about the effects of policy choices.[41] Although political realities prevent either chamber from achieving the "ideal form of debate or deliberation," as Smith points out, "deliberation and debate occur frequently and everywhere. A great deal of debate and deliberation transpires before most major policy decisions are made. . . ."[42] Thus, the analysis considers how different aspects of deliberation in committee and on the floor withstand the political or nondeliberative factors in the lawmaking process.

Three general factors affect the capacity for deliberation in the contemporary Congress: interest group activism, party polarization, and institutional changes, both within Congress and between Congress and the president. Those factors tend to promote political tactics and weaken deliberation. Although Congress is awash in information about problems and policy choices, members may ignore the most valid or reliable information; House party leaders limit floor time and amendments; both the Senate Majority Leader and the minority party block legislation from floor consideration; committee deliberations are often subordinated to partisan priorities; and, on many issues, members are not open to being persuaded.[43] Nevertheless, there are important exceptions to the general effects of groups, parties, and institutional constraints on deliberation. Moreover, because members, leaders, and groups are motivated by governing as well as politics, deliberation varies by institutional setting, issue type, and choice.

Proliferation of Advocacy Groups

Madison contended that a minority faction is relatively harmless because "relief is supplied by the republican principle, which enables the majority to defeat its sinister views, by regular vote. It may clog the administration, it may convulse the society; but it will be unable to execute and mask its violence under the forms of the constitution."[44] Yet, a proliferation of interest groups[45] and ideological think tanks[46] from the 1960s to the 1990s pose greater challenges to deliberation than Madison may have imagined.[47] Too many groups, "hyperpluralism," can cause paralysis or gridlock, especially when it comes to reducing or eliminating benefit programs guarded by rent-seeking and entrenched interests.[48] In addition, some think tanks furnish members of Congress with arguments based on studies that reinforce ideological viewpoints and reduce the credibility of public policy research.[49]

Advocacy organizations representing specialized causes push individual members to pledge support for or against policy preferences in advance of legislative debate.[50] As Morris Fiorina points out: "representatives devoted increased attention to the narrow agendas of such groups, detracting attention from the more general concerns of the larger public and distorting the priorities of American politics." The competition between such groups encourages "the uncivil, exaggerated, 'politics of total war' style of contemporary American politics."[51] The adverse effects of advocacy groups on deliberation are compounded when they align with political parties.

Party Polarization

Heightened partisanship stemming from increased party polarization beginning in the 1980s has also adversely affected deliberation in Congress. A combination of alignment between ideology and party identification in the mass public, particularly among engaged citizens,[52] activist groups,[53] and procedural and confrontational tactics[54] have increased party polarization in Congress. On highly salient issues, the parties stake out positions opposite one another and use committees and especially the floor to send messages to voters rather than engage in constructive debate.[55] Even when the two parties are not strongly divided over policy they compete for power using tactics that may ignore or undermine deliberation.[56]

Partisan polarization has strengthened the power of legislative leaders, who have informational advantages over rank-and-file members. Thus the decision-making process often requires members to defer to legislative leaders, increasing party strength, but weakening deliberation.[57] Polarization has also strengthened party leaders at the expense of committees. Party leaders deploy various tactics—for example, post-committee adjustments and committee bypass—that displace or override the deliberative functions of committees.[58] William Bendix shows that the percentage of bills that bypass committee markups, a key indicator of deliberation, has increased significantly in the House and even more so in the Senate since the 105th Congress. Committees with the most polarized memberships held fewer markups, as did committees with a higher portion of moderates and moderate chairs.[59]

In the House, restrictive rules on floor amendments limit the ability of members to present alternatives to committee bills.[60] In the Senate, heightened partisanship combined with individualism has increased the frequency of filibusters, leaving the majority party with few options but to let the majority leader negotiate "structured consent" agreements with the minority leader. Such agreements weaken deliberation by precluding broad involvement of senators in the decision-making process.[61] Bills influenced by partisan tactics are less likely to pass either chamber and be enacted into law.[62]

Institutional Reforms and Executive Power

In the House, institutional reforms enacted in the 1970s gave the Speaker of the House the power to refer bills to multiple committees and strengthened the role of party leaders in making committee assignments. Party leaders have used committee assignments to reward party loyalty rather than policy expertise,[63] and the Speaker's power to nominate members to the Rules Committee has enabled the party leadership to impose restrictive rules that limit floor amendments and debate. The Speaker's power of multiple referral has weakened committee autonomy, invited the party leadership to resolve jurisdictional conflicts and policy differences between committees, and given the Speaker direct influence over committee decisions.[64] Term limits on committee chairs may also weaken the capacity of committees by short-circuiting the careers of experienced leaders.[65]

The rise of the modern president in the twentieth century has weakened deliberation in Congress. The president's ability to formulate policy and issue executive orders undermines the lawmaking capacity of Congress. In addition, to the extent that the public looks to the president to address the nation's problems[66] and the president's priorities take precedent in Congress,[67] presidential leadership can fuel partisanship and weaken deliberation.

Institutional Dysfunction?

In the view of some scholars the combination of advocacy groups, polarized parties, and institutional reforms has made Congress the "broken branch."[68] The Republican House majority failed to check the excesses of executive power exercised by President George W. Bush, and under divided party control President Barack Obama has circumvented Congress with executive orders. A breakdown in regular order has undermined Congress's capacity to gather good information and deliberate over policy options, and it has allowed interest groups to exploit the policymaking process. Accordingly, reformers argue that a dysfunctional legislative process produces either poorly designed public policy or gridlock. Meanwhile, partisan wrangling has poisoned public discourse and further eroded public confidence.

Yet, while interest group activism, partisanship, and institutional changes have generally weakened deliberation in Congress, several caveats about the generalized effects of current conditions on deliberation are worth noting. To begin with, not all interest groups are rent-seeking factions, and their influence over individual members of Congress and policy outcomes is often overstated.[69] Moreover, interest group involvement and competition can improve the quality of debate and legislation,[70] and lobbyists can provide information that may contribute to deliberation.[71]

With respect to partisanship, although party polarization measured by roll call voting in Congress is high by historical standards, members from opposite parties continue to cosponsor legislation.[72] Moreover, although polarization mixed with divided government adversely affects legislative output,[73] bipartisan and cross-partisan coalitions continue to be built on a range of issues.[74] Political goals do not always favor partisanship; party leaders must gauge the costs and benefits of highlighting partisan differences as opposed to passing legislation and establishing a record of governance.[75] Based on their extensive analysis of legislative proposals, Scott Adler and John Wilkerson argue that the effects of party polarization are exaggerated: "it is one thing to draw attention to the increasing role of partisanship in congressional deliberations, and another to conclude that partisanship is the driving force of legislative operations. Partisan politics does not infuse every legislative issue—far from it."[76]

It is worth pointing out that partisanship is nothing new in American politics.[77] Party leaders have forever had to deal with the clamor and conflicts associated with interest group demands and internal party factions. The resignation of Speaker of the House John Boehner (R-Ohio) amid protests by the Republican Freedom Caucus over both policy differences and procedural actions during the 114th Congress is a recent example. Among other things, the Freedom Caucus expressed concerns about the lack of representation on committees, lack of time to review bills, and rules restricting floor amendments.[78] Upon assuming the duties of the speakership, Paul Ryan (R-Wis.), Boehner's successor, pronounced: "We are not solving problems; we are adding to them. . . . We are wiping the slate clean. Neither the members nor the people are satisfied with how things are going. We need to make some changes, starting with how the House does business."[79] The Freedom Caucus revolt reminds us that strong party leadership has its limits in the House, and party leaders must always be conscious of the need to balance the critical functions of representation, lawmaking, and deliberation.[80]

The institutional effects of congressional reforms and presidential power on deliberation are also mixed. Although some institutional reforms of the 1970s empowered the Speaker, weakened committee chairs, and loosened constraints on member pursuit of self-serving political goals,[81] committee reorganization has had some positive effects on committee deliberation. Based on their analysis of bill referral data, Adler and Wilkerson find that committee reforms of issue jurisdictions can be explained as much by efforts to improve policy coordination as to protect legislative turf or advance constituent interests. Committee reforms "clarified committee issue responsibilities in ways that served to promote information sharing and reduce policy duplication."[82] As for the effects of presidential power, although the president's legislative leadership exceeds anything envisioned by the Framers, Congress remains a formidable lawmaking body.[83]

In sum, conditions that define contemporary politics generally weaken incentives and institutional capacity for deliberation, but they do not undermine deliberation in lawmaking. Deliberation continues to vary by committee, issue, chamber, and the strategic choices of leaders.

Deliberation in Committee

In his seminal work on congressional committees, Richard Fenno developed the theme that "committees matter" and "committees differ."[84] Committees are essential for deliberation. Hearings provide information and arguments for debating legislation, markup sessions create opportunities to amend and refine bills, and committee reports contain arguments for and against committee actions. Fenno argues that decision-making processes and decisions made by committees vary by three factors: multiple member goals, strategic premises, and environmental constraints. At least two of the three member goals identified by Fenno—gaining influence and making good public policy—are conducive to deliberation, particularly the value of policy expertise, reliable information, and efforts to persuade others. Committees with clear decision rules that define influence by success on the floor implement processes that feature participation and specialization. In terms of environmental constraints, committees are affected in varying degrees by the parent chamber, clientele groups, the executive branch, and political parties. Fenno noted two major differences between House and Senate committees: "senators do not specialize as intensely or as exclusively in their committee work," and "Senate committee chairmen have less potential for influence inside their committees."[85]

Committee Organization

Since Fenno's study, increased partisanship and polarization have compromised committee autonomy and power over legislation,[86] yet the organizing principle of variation across committees remains valid.[87] Three theories to explain committee organization and decision-making—distributive, informational, and partisan—reflect varying incentives for deliberation. Distributive committees[88] designed to support reelection goals are less inclined to deliberation than informational committees, which provide the parent chamber with policy expertise and, assuming the committee is representative of the chamber, a reliable way to make good public policy.[89] Under party cartel theory, committees are beholden to party leaders,[90] whereas under conditional party government the degree of committee autonomy from party leaders depends on policy agreement within parties and disagreement between them.[91] Partisanship has had a growing influence on three prestigious House committees—Appropriations, Rules, and Ways and Means.[92] Still, John H. Aldrich and David W. Rohde point out, "much of Congress' business does not involve party conflict" and "the agenda that Congress deals with is multifaceted and diverse, and only a portion of it deals with the types of issues that provoke interparty disagreement."[93]

Problem Solving and Issue Contexts

Looking beyond organizational and preference structure to the problem solving capability of committees, Adler and Wilkerson show that the informational advantage of committees depends on issue type. Committee expertise is more evident on compulsory bills (those Congress must deal with) compared with discretionary bills. Moreover, bills sponsored by members of a committee are less likely to be rolled on the floor: "the chamber values the domain expertise of the committee of jurisdiction, particularly when the issues involved originate in committee."[94]

Deliberation is also more likely with issues that are less familiar to committee members or that require technical knowledge of outside experts, particularly when policy experts reach a broad consensus on the need for reform and the process is not overpowered by interest groups.[95] Examples include deregulation of the trucking and airline industries,[96] welfare reform,[97] telecommunications,[98] and election administration.[99]

Issues that do not clearly divide the parties are also more susceptible to deliberative decision-making.[100] Congress passed several bills in the 114th Congress with bipartisan or cross-partisan coalitions: Sustainable Growth Rate (SGR) Repeal and Medicare Provider Payment Modernization Act, Keystone XL Pipeline Act, Bipartisan Trade Priorities and Accountability Act, the Justice for Victims of Trafficking Act, and the USA Freedom Act. Some bills (like the SGR repeal) required years of committee consideration; others (like the trafficking bill) had short legislative histories. Coincidentally perhaps, after the 113th Congress, which some called the "worst Congress ever,"[101] the Bipartisan Policy Center (BPC) reported that Congress performed relatively well on several indicators during the First Session of the 114th Congress.[102] The BPC's Healthy Congress Index revealed increased numbers of working days, bills reported from committees, and Senate amendments compared to recent Congresses. If nothing else, the data show that deliberative aspects of Congress vary from Congress to Congress.

Of course, bills that pass with bipartisan majorities are not, by definition, acts of pure deliberation. The processes leading to passage of bills in the 114th Congress involved varying degrees of lobbying, tactical maneuvers, and deliberation over the merits of public policy. Yet, bipartisan or cross-partisan coalitions suggest that members of Congress do not begin every policy debate with a clear partisan preference; rather, they weigh a variety of factors and the information and preferences of various sources (leaders, groups and lobbyists, policy experts, and constituents). On many issues, the committee is a vital source of preference formation.[103]

Moreover, even though party polarization hampers deliberation between parties, issues that separate the two major parties are not, by definition, void of deliberation. The parties may be polarized yet still internally divided over policy choices. During the 111th Congress, Democrats debated numerous approaches to increasing health care coverage before settling on the Affordable Care Act (ACA), which seeks to achieve the goal through a combination of private insurance purchased through health care exchanges and Medicaid expansion. That debate resumed during the 2016 presidential nomination contest, with Hillary Clinton arguing to maintain and improve the ACA and Bernie Sanders advocating for a single-payer, Medicare-for-all, program. Meanwhile, Republican elected representatives and candidates engage in spirited debates over the proper way to handle immigration, international trade, defense spending, entitlements, tax policy, intelligence surveillance, and foreign policy. Although this chapter focuses on deliberation in committee and on the floor, scholars should devote more attention to deliberation within parties, particularly given the rise in party polarization.[104]

Thus deliberation continues to compete with political forces in the era of heightened partisanship. As Bessette argues, "The point is not that non-deliberative factors are unimportant, but rather that policymaking within Congress is best understood as a complex mix of politics *and* deliberation, of the 'play of power' and the reasoned effort to promote good policy."[105]

Strategic Choices of Committee Leaders

Deliberation also depends on the choices and actions of party leaders and committee chairs. Party polarization and advocacy group politics increase the likelihood of "strategic disagreement,"[106] and the decline of seniority as a norm for advancement and term limits on committee chairs may weaken incentives for members to gain policy expertise. Yet, Congress still has "serious lawmakers" who develop the expertise required for deliberative lawmaking.[107] Lawmaking depends on legislative entrepreneurs who devote the time needed to acquire information, draft legislation, build coalitions, and push legislation.[108]

Two former committee chairs (one a conservative Republican and the other a liberal Democrat) illustrate the importance of policy expertise and factual analysis to probe issues and frame policy debates. Speaker of the House Paul Ryan (R-Wis.), formerly chair of both the House Budget Committee and the Committee on Ways and Means, recounts a story of a conversation he had with Representative Barney Frank (D-Mass.) during his orientation to the House in 1999. Ryan asked Frank: "What do you know now that you wish you knew when you started?"[109] Frank, an ideological rival of Ryan and, at that time, a nine-term member of the House, advised Ryan, "If you want to be effective . . . *do not be a generalist.* Don't spread yourself too thin. Specialize in two or three things, study up, and know those issues better than anyone else. Get yourself on the relevant committees, know everything there is to know about your issues, and then you can start setting policy in those areas."[110]

When he began his eighth term in the House at the outset of the 114th Congress, Ryan was regarded as the foremost Republican expert on budget policy in the House. Ryan used facts and analysis to draw the attention of his party and the nation to the national debt and the need for entitlement and tax reform. A staunch conservative, he has also worked across party lines on several occasions to develop feasible and practical policy alternatives. For example, in 2013 Ryan negotiated a two-year budget agreement with Senate Budget Committee Chair Patty Murray (D-Wash.) that avoided a debt ceiling crisis. Since the negotiation was between two committee chairs, the process did not include broad participation, but it did have all of the key elements of "deliberative negotiation" between the parties: nonpartisan fact-finding, repeated interactions, penalty defaults, and private meetings.[111]

Former Democratic Representative Henry Waxman (D-Calif.), who served as chair of the Subcommittee on Health and the Environment and ranking member and chair of the Committee on Government Oversight and Reform, used oversight and legislative power to challenge misinformation deployed by powerful corporate interests. Reflecting on forty years in the House, Waxman described the long, tedious, and ultimately satisfactory process of lawmaking: "despite the setbacks and frustrations, what Congress has achieved during my time has made clear to me that if you organize the right people, follow the facts, and force the issue, it is possible, and even likely, that good work can make a difference in the lives of millions of Americans—which, in the end, is a lawmaker's highest purpose."[112]

Of course not every member of Congress spends time becoming a policy expert, gathering facts, focusing on national problems, listening to arguments from both sides, and seeking ways to resolve differences. But some members do, evidence that deliberation continues to compete with political forces. In spite of party polarization group advocacy, and institutional reforms that have weakened committees, committee chairs continue to engage in deliberative aspects of lawmaking. Craig Volden and Alan Wiseman find that legislative effectiveness varies among committee chairs.[113] As Madison himself envisioned, the deliberative qualities of committee chairs also vary along a continuum, from narrow self-seeking interests on one extreme end to high-minded pursuit of national interests on the other.[114]

Deliberation on the Floor

Deliberation on the floors of the House and Senate depends on the capacity for amendments and the extent and quality of debate. The rise of interest advocacy, increased partisan polarization, and strong party leadership has adversely affected deliberation on the floors of the House and Senate, particularly in terms of the number and range of policy alternatives. The role of deliberation in floor debate is more difficult to assess.

Floor Amendments

For a short period of time, from the 92nd (1971–72) to the 95th Congress (1977–78), the number of floor amendments in the House doubled, giving more members the opportunity to participate in the lawmaking process.[115] Ironically perhaps, emphasis on one form of deliberation may have detracted from another; when voting on amendments became the primary activity on the floor, "fewer [members] attended floor sessions to listen to debate."[116] Since the 1980s, majority party leaders of both parties, operating through the Rules Committees, restricted the number of floor amendments on major bills.[117] In the context of party polarization, the House floor is rarely the setting for broad participation and consideration of policy alternatives. The one positive effect of restrictive rules is that they protect committee bills from being altered on the floor by a less informed and less deliberative body.[118]

Senate rules give individual senators and the minority party far more opportunities to offer floor amendments, yet partisanship has had several adverse effects on floor deliberation in the Senate. Since the 1980s, up until the recent Congress, overall amendment activity on the Senate floor had declined, while the portions of amendments from minority party members and ideologically extreme members have increased.[119] Partisan polarization has contributed to a substantial increase in the number of filibusters and cloture votes.[120] Filibusters on major legislation increased from 10 percent in 1969–71 to about 70 percent by the 110th Congress (2007–08).[121] Votes to invoke cloture were also rare before 1970, but rose to about fifty per congress by the 1990s and reached 112 by the 110th Congress.[122] The minority has used its leverage to force cloture on nearly every important bill that divides the parties, and bills that are filibustered and/or subject to cloture are less likely to pass the Senate and be enacted into law.[123]

Although the minority party has been mostly responsible for the changes in floor activity, the Senate Majority Leader has also used the power of preferential recognition to limit amendments. The Majority Leader can kill motions by the minority party members to amend bills[124] and block amendments by filling the amendment tree.[125] In seven years as Majority Leader, Senator Harry Reid (D-Nev.) filled the amendment tree eighty times, twice as many as the previous twenty-two years combined.[126] The majority leader can also keep bills off the floor that are opposed by a majority of the party. The Keystone XL Pipeline Act is a recent example; when the Democrats held a majority in the Senate, Majority Leader Harry Reid blocked efforts to vote on the bill, but after the Republicans gained control of the Senate in the 2014 midterm elections, the bill passed with sixty-two votes.

Floor Debate

Floor debate serves several deliberative functions: 1) an "important means for legislators to obtain information about the merits of policy," 2) a "source of information for media, the public and other constituencies," and 3) a "constraint on information and misinformation."[127] The form of floor debate in the House appears to meet the basic expectations of deliberation. A representative group of members from both parties are given time to argue for or against a bill, and they routinely speak to the merits of their position, cite studies or other information, and conclude their remarks with an appeal to others to support their position. Yet in most cases individual floor speeches are too brief, the process offers few opportunities for exchange or debate between opponents, and the total time for "debate" is not long enough to do justice to important matters. During floor debate, most members "seek only to advertise their positions, not to learn or reconsider the merits of issues."[128]

Nonetheless, "Floor debates vary considerably . . . in their value for deliberation."[129] In their extensive analysis of deliberation on a range of issues within each of three policy areas—welfare reform, estate tax repeal, and telecommunications deregulation—Mucciaroni and Quirk ranked floor debate along a continuum from very good to very poor.[130] They found that much of the information shared on the floor is misleading or inaccurate, yet the quality of information and debate varied according to several factors: partisanship, issue salience, interest group involvement, and chamber. The quality of deliberation in both the House and Senate was better on telecommunications and estate tax repeal, both of which were less salient and less partisan than welfare reform. In debates with high levels of partisan and ideological conflict, "legislators offer more extreme claims, distort their opponents' positions, and withhold individual concessions."[131] Debates on issues with bipartisan coalitions had the "least amount of distortion."[132]

Party polarization and interest group advocacy have made Senate floor debate more acrimonious.[133] Yet, Mucciaroni and Quirk found that, compared with the House, debate was more informative in the Senate for all three issues they studied.[134] Senate debates were much longer and allowed more opportunities for members to support their claims and offer rebuttals of unsupported claims.[135] Thus even on the most salient issue in the study, welfare reform, the context for floor debate in the Senate induced senators to make fewer bold or unsubstantiated claims.

As noted, party polarization has encouraged message politics and enabled obstructionist tactics on the Senate floor. Although floor speeches designed to gain political advantage contain exaggerations and distortions, they usually include some element of the truth.[136] Moreover Barbara Sinclair argues that a partisan debate is "often directly focused on policy, and it has the virtue of involving the public—at least the attentive public—in the process."[137]

The Framers and the Future of Deliberation

To what extent does deliberation in the contemporary Congress meet the expectations of the Framers? What reforms might improve deliberation in Congress? The answers to those questions depend on the capacity of institutions and leaders to control the worst effects of factions and build deliberative majorities. Party polarization, advocacy groups, and institutional reforms have made it increasingly difficult for Congress to achieve the ideals of deliberative democracy in committees and on the floors of the House and Senate. Narrow majorities and electoral competition for majority party control further intensify factionalism and partisanship.

Thus the contemporary Congress has a more difficult time serving as an effective medium whereby representatives can work to "refine and enlarge the public views,"[138] and for laws to reflect the "mild voice of reason, pleading for the cause of an enlarged and permanent interest."[139] Debates could be more civil and grounded in neutral information; processes could provide more ways for members to offer and vote on viable alternatives to problems; and members could focus more on the broad concerns of the public and be more committed to addressing the nation's challenges. Institutional dysfunction has prompted reformers, beginning with Woodrow Wilson, to advocate institutional changes to make the policy process more "efficient" and more responsive to both public opinion and presidential leadership.

Yet, such reforms would not necessarily make Congress more deliberative or better able to control factions. The Constitution's institutional structure was designed to manage the factionalism that naturally thrived in a republican form of government; parties and groups have always been features of American democracy and often rivals of deliberation. Separation of powers, bicameralism, and staggered electoral terms continue to mediate public opinion and work roughly as the Federalists' intended.[140] The Constitution permits a variety of governing arrangements, and laws are passed by various types of coalitions.[141]

To improve deliberation, I suggest considering reforms designed to restore and strengthen the role of committees, which are the most appropriate institutions for deliberation in either the House or the Senate. First, the House and Senate should schedule five-day workweeks and meet for three consecutive weeks[142] or two weeks on and two weeks off.[143] More concentrated time in Washington would give committees greater latitude to hold hearings and mark up bills and allow members to have repeated interaction, which improves deliberative negotiation.[144] Second, the Senate should reduce the number of committees senators may serve on.[145] For the 113th Congress, senators had an average of three committee assignments and seven subcommittee assignments. Fewer assignments would enable senators to increase policy expertise and perhaps incentivize the Senate to defer more often to committees. Third, committees should work more often in executive committee session; greater secrecy would improve the chances of free flowing debate and genuine consideration of alternatives.[146] Finally, all major bills should be subject to committee review, be accompanied by a committee report, and be reported at least three days before consideration on the floor.[147]

Enactment of those reforms will depend on the consent of the stakeholders and, as Paul Quirk has pointed out, "Congress rarely makes important institutional changes mostly to improve deliberation."[148] Moreover, such reforms would need to anticipate the effects on representation, majority formation, and the ability to oversee the executive. As Eric Schickler has argued, reform "involves superimposing new arrangements on top of preexisting structures intended to serve different purposes."[149] Reforms often fail to achieve their intended objective and often produce "a set of institutions that work at cross-purposes."[150] Most important, we should keep in mind that the contemporary Congress is "rooted in a constitutional framework and electoral system that help to produce members for whom multiple collective interests are likely to be salient."[151] Advocacy groups and polarized parties may overwhelm institutional reforms designed to improve deliberation. Yet so long as Congress is not entirely dysfunctional[152] and most bills that pass Congress are subjected to significant debate and analysis,[153] deliberation will continue to compete with politics in the lawmaking process. Meanwhile, modest reforms can improve deliberation. Ultimately, though, the quality and degree of deliberation will continue to vary by issue, institutional setting, and the choices of leaders.

Notes

1. Joseph M. Bessette, *Deliberative Democracy & American National Government* (University of Chicago Press, 1994), pp. 20–28.

2. Ibid., pp. 13–15, 26; Frances E. Lee, *Beyond Ideology: Politics, Principles, and Partisanship in the U.S. Senate* (University of Chicago Press, 2009), pp. 1–2.

3. Randall Strahan, "Personal Motives, Constitutional Forms, and the Public Good: Madison on Political Leadership," in *James Madison: The Theory and Practice of Republican Government*, edited by Samuel Kernell (Stanford University Press, 2003), pp. 72–75.

4. Bessette, *The Mild Voice of Reason*, p. 66.

5. Paul J. Quirk, "Deliberation and Decision Making," in *The Legislative Branch*, edited by Paul J. Quirk and Sarah A. Binder (Oxford University Press, 2005), pp. 314–15.

6. Charles O. Jones, *The United States Congress: People, Place, and Policy* (Homewood, Ill.: Dorsey Press, 1982), p. 26.

7. Quirk, "Deliberation and Decision Making," pp. 321–32; Thomas E. Mann and Norman J. Ornstein, *The Broken Branch: How Congress Is Failing America and How to Get It Back on Track* (Oxford University Press: 2006), pp. 7–13.

8. Lee, *Beyond Ideology*, pp. 10–12.

9. E. Scott Adler and John D. Wilkerson, *Congress and the Politics of Problem Solving* (University Press, 2012), chapter 1.

10. Laurel Harbridge, *Is Bipartisanship Dead? Policy Agreement and Agenda-Setting in the House of Representatives* (Cambridge University Press, 2015), pp. 51–54.

11. Regarding the size of the majority, see Steven S. Smith, *Party Influence in Congress* (Cambridge University Press, 2007), pp. 207–08. Regarding presidential leadership, see Lee, *Beyond Ideology*, chapter 4.

12. John B Gilmour, *Strategic Disagreement: Stalemate in American Politics* (University of Pittsburgh Press, 1995), chapter 1.

13. Mann and Ornstein, *The Broken Branch*, pp. 226–38; Gary Mucciaroni and Paul J. Quirk, *Deliberative Choices: Debating Public Policy in Congress* (University of Chicago Press, 2006), chapter 8; Bipartisan Policy Center Commission on Political Reform, *Governing in a Polarized America: A Bipartisan Blueprint to Strengthen Our Democracy* (Washington D.C.: Bipartisan Policy Center, 2014), pp. 56–69 (http://bipartisanpolicy.org/library/governing-polarized-america-bipartisan-blueprint-strengthen-our-democracy).

14. Bessette, *The Mild Voice of Reason*, p. 5.

15. *Federalist* No. 10 (http://teachingamericanhistory.org/library/document/federalist-no-10).

16. Ibid.

17. *Federalist* No. 63 (http://teachingamericanhistory.org/library/document/federalist-no-63).

18. *Federalist* No. 62 (http://teachingamericanhistory.org/library/document/federalist-no-62).

19. *Federalist* No. 63.

20. Bessette, *The Mild Voice of Reason*, pp. 20–26.

21. *Federalist* No. 73 (http://teachingamericanhistory.org/library/document/federalist-no-73).

22. *Federalist* No. 48 (http://teachingamericanhistory.org/library/document/federalist-no-48).

23. *Federalist* No. 10.

24. James Madison, *Vices of the American Political System*, April 1787 (http://teachingamericanhistory.org/library/document/vices-of-the-political-system).

25. Strahan, "Personal Motives, Constitutional Forms, and the Public Good," p. 64.

26. *Federalist* No. 10.

27. *Federalist* No. 50 (http://teachingamericanhistory.org/library/document/federalist-no-50).

28. Lee, *Beyond Ideology*, chapters 1 and 8.

29. Sarah A. Binder, *Stalemate: Causes and Consequences of Legislative Gridlock* (Brookings Institution Press, 2003), chapter 2.

30. Mucciaroni and Quirk, *Deliberative Choices*, 4–5; Edward L. Lascher, Jr., "Assessing Legislative Deliberation: A Preface to Empirical Analysis," *Legislative Studies Quarterly* 21 (1996), pp. 505–07.

31. Bessette, *The Mild Voice of Reason*, pp. 46, 49–55.

32. Ibid., pp. 56–60.

33. Mucciaroni and Quirk, *Deliberative Choices*, p. 4.

34. Ibid.

35. Steven S. Smith, *Call to Order: Floor Politics in the House and Senate* (Brookings Institution Press, 1989), p. 239.

36. Bessette, *The Mild Voice of Reason*, pp. 49–51; Mucciaroni and Quirk, *Deliberative Choices*, p. 5.

37. Smith, *Call to Order*, p. 239.

38. Ibid.

39. Randall Strahan, *New Ways and Means: Reform and Change in the Congressional Committee* (University of North Carolina Press, 1990), p. 7.

40. Bessette, *The Mild Voice of Reason*, pp. 52–55.

41. Mucciaroni and Quirk, *Deliberative Choices*, pp. 5–10.

42. Smith, *Call to Order*, pp. 239–40.

43. Quirk, "Deliberation and Decision Making," pp. 318–21.

44. *Federalist* No. 10.

45. Quirk, "Deliberation and Decision Making," p. 322.

46. Andrew Rich, *Think Tanks, Public Policy, and the Politics of Expertise* (Cambridge University Press 2004), p. 15.

47. Donald F. Wolfensberger, *Congress and the People: Deliberative Democracy on Trial* (Johns Hopkins University Press, 2000), p. 278.

48. Jonathan Rauch, *Demosclerosis: The Silent Killer of American Government* (New York: Times Books, 1994), chapter 3.

49. Rich, *Think Tanks, Public Policy, and the Politics of Expertise*, p. 148.

50. Theda Skocpol, *Diminished Democracy: From Membership to Management in American Civic Life* (University of Oklahoma Press, 2003), pp. 200–04.

51. Both quotations are from Morris P. Fiorina with Samuel J. Abrams, *Disconnect: The Breakdown of Representation in American Politics* (University of Oklahoma Press, 2009), p. 135.

52. Alan I. Abramowitz, *The Disappearing Center: Engaged Citizens, Polarization, and American Democracy* (Yale University Press, 2010), chapter 3.

53. Skocpol, *Diminished Democracy: From Membership to Management in American Civic Life*, pp. 232–36.

54. Sean T. Theriault, *Party Polarization in Congress* (Cambridge University Press, 2008), chapters 7 and 8; Sean T. Theriault, *The Gingrich Senators: The*

Roots of Partisan Warfare in Congress (Oxford University Press, 2013), chapters 8 and 9.

55. Patrick Sellers, *Cycles of Spin: Strategic Communication in the U.S. Congress* (Cambridge University Press, 2010), chapter 3; Roger H. Davidson, "Senate Floor Deliberation: A Preliminary Inquiry," in *The Contentious Senate: Partisanship, Ideology and the Myth of Cool Judgment*, edited by Colton C. Campbell and Nicol C. Rae (Lanham, Md.: Rowman and Littlefield, 2001), pp. 38–42; C. Lawrence Evans and Walter J. Oleszek, "Message Politics and Senate Procedure," in *The Contentious Senate: Partisanship, Ideology and the Myth of Cool Judgment*, edited by Colton C. Campbell and Nicol C. Rae (Lanham, Md.: Rowman and Littlefield, 2001), pp. 108–13.

56. Lee, *Beyond Ideology*, chapter 5.

57. James M. Curry, *Legislating in the Dark: Information and Power in the House of Representatives* (University of Chicago Press, 2015), pp. 199–204. In chapter 6, Curry uses the American Clean Energy Act of 2009 and the REAL ID Act of 2005 to show how committee chairs restrict information during the bill drafting process.

58. Barbara Sinclair, *Unorthodox Lawmaking*, 4th ed. (Washington, D.C.: CQ Press, 2012), chapter 2 and p. 147; John H. Aldrich and David W. Rohde, "Congressional Committees in a Continuing Partisan Era," in *Congress Reconsidered*, 9th ed., edited by Lawrence C. Dodd and Bruce I. Oppenheimer (Washington, D.C.: CQ Press, 2009), pp. 224–25.

59. William Bendix, "Bypassing Congressional Committees: Parties, Panel Rosters, and Deliberative Processes," *Legislative Studies Quarterly* (forthcoming).

60. Stanley Bach and Steven S. Smith, *Managing Uncertainty in the House of Representatives: Adaptation and Innovation in Special Rules* (Brookings Institution Press, 1988), pp. 71–74; Sinclair, *Unorthodox Lawmaking*, pp. 148–51.

61. James I. Wallner, *The Death of Deliberation* (Lanham, Md.: Lexington Books, 2013), chapters 2 and 7.

62. Barbara Sinclair, *Party Wars: Polarization, and the Politics of National Policy Making* (Oklahoma University Press, 2006), p. 359.

63. John H. Aldrich and David W. Rohde, "The Consequences of Party Organization in the House: The Role of the Majority and Minority Parties in Conditional Party Government," in *Polarized Politics: Congress and the President in a Partisan Era*, edited by Jon R. Bond and R. Fleisher (Washington, D.C.: CQ Press, 2000), pp. 41–42.

64. Christopher J. Deering and Steven S. Smith, *Committees in Congress*, 3rd ed. (Washington, D.C.: CQ Press, 1997), pp. 189–90.

65. Quirk, "Deliberation and Decision Making," p. 331.

66. Joseph Cooper, "From Congressional to Presidential Preeminence: Power and Politics in the Late Nineteenth-Century America and Today," in *Congress*

Reconsidered, 9th ed., edited by Lawrence C. Dodd and Bruce I. Oppenheimer (Washington, D.C.: CQ Press, 2009), pp. 379–83.

67. Lee, *Beyond Ideology*, chapter 4.

68. Mann and Ornstein, *The Broken Branch*.

69. Frances E. Lee, "Interests, Constituents, and Policy Making," in *The Legislative Branch*, edited by Paul J. Quirk and Sarah A. Binder (Oxford University, 2005), pp. 288–90.

70. Mucciaroni and Quirk, *Deliberative Choices*, pp. 150–52.

71. Bessette, *The Mild Voice of Reason*, pp. 177–79.

72. Harbridge, *Is Bipartisanship Dead?*, chapter 2.

73. Nolan McCarty, "The Policy Effects of Political Polarization," in *Transformation of American Politics: Activist Government and the Rise of Conservatism*, edited by Paul Pierson and Theda Skocpol (Princeton University Press, 2007), pp. 232–34, 237–40.

74. Joseph Cooper and Garry Young, "Partisanship, Bipartisanship, and Crosspartisanship in Congress since the New Deal," in *Congress Reconsidered*, 6th ed., edited by Lawrence C. Dodd and Bruce I. Oppenheimer (Washington, D.C.: CQ Press, 1997); Adler and Wilkerson, *Congress and the Politics of Problem Solving*, pp. 202–03.

75. Harbridge, *Is Bipartisanship Dead?*, chapter 5.

76. Adler and Wilkerson, *Congress and the Politics of Problem Solving*, p. 12.

77. David W. Brady and Hahrie C. Han, "Polarization Then and Now," in *Red and Blue Nation? Consequences and Correction of America's Polarized Parties*, edited by Pietro S. Nivola and David W. Brady (Brookings Institution Press, 2006); William F. Connelly Jr., *James Madison Rules America: The Constitutional Origins of Congressional Partisanship* (Lanham, Md.: Rowman and Littlefield, 2010), chapter 7.

78. "Questions for Speaker Candidates," in Jake Sherman, "Freedom Caucus Suggests House Rules Changes," *Politico*, October 8, 2015 (www.politico.com/blogs/the-gavel/2015/10/house-freedom-caucus-rules-change-214591).

79. Mike DeBonis, "Elected House Speaker, Ryan Calls for Reform," *Washington Post*, October 30, 2015 (www.washingtonpost.com/news/powerpost/wp/2015/10/29/paul-ryan-set-to-be-elected-62nd-house-speaker).

80. Charles O. Jones, "Joseph G. Cannon and Howard W. Smith: An Essay on the Limits of Leadership in the House of Representatives," *Journal of Politics* 30 (1968), pp. 617–46.

81. Bessette, *The Mild Voice of Reason*, pp. 146–48.

82. Adler and Wilkerson, *Congress and the Politics of Problem Solving*, p. 16 and chapter 6.

83. Charles O. Jones, *The Presidency in a Separated System*, 2nd ed. (Brookings Institution Press, 2005), chapter 7.

84. Richard F. Fenno Jr., *Congressmen in Committees* (Boston, Mass.: Little, Brown, 1973), p. xiii.

85. Fenno, *Congressmen in Committees*, p. 172.

86. Charles Stewart, III, "Congressional Committees in a Partisan Era: The End of Institutions as We Know It?," in *New Directions in Congressional Politics*, edited by Jamie L. Carson (New York: Routledge, 2012), pp. 104–08; John H. Aldrich, Brittany N. Perry, and David W. Rohde, "Richard Fenno's Theory of Congressional Committees and the Partisan Polarization of the House," in *Congress Reconsidered*, 10th ed., edited by Lawrence C. Dodd and Bruce I. Oppenheimer (Thousand Oaks, Calif.: Sage/CQ Press, 2013), pp. 195–99.

87. C. Lawrence Evans, "Congressional Committees," in *The Oxford Handbook on the American Congress*, edited by George C. Edwards III, Frances E. Lee, and Eric Schickler (Oxford University Press 2011).

88. Barry R. Weingast and William J. Marshall, "The Industrial Organization of Congress," *Journal of Political Economy* 96 (1988), pp. 123–63.

89. Keith Krehbiel, *Information and Legislative Organization* (University of Michigan Press, 1991), chapter 3.

90. Gary W. Cox, and Mathew D. McCubbins, *Setting the Agenda: Responsible Party Government in the U.S. House of Representatives* (Cambridge University Press, 2005), chapter 2.

91. David W. Rohde, *Parties and Leaders in the Post Reform House* (University of Chicago Press 1991), p. 31.

92. Aldrich, Perry, and Rohde, "Richard Fenno's Theory," pp. 200–15.

93. Aldrich and Rohde, "Congressional Committees in a Continuing Partisan Era," p. 226.

94. Adler and Wilkerson, *Congress and the Politics of Problem Solving*, p. 139.

95. Rich, *Think Tanks, Public Policy, and the Politics of Expertise*, p. 147.

96. Martha Derthick and Paul J. Quirk, *The Politics of Deregulation* (Brookings Institution Press, 1985), p. 238.

97. Andrew Rich found that policy experts played significant roles in defining problems and proposals for welfare reform (Rich, *Think Tanks, Public Policy, and the Politics of Expertise*, pp. 147–48), though Gary Mucciaroni and Paul Quirk rated the floor debates on various aspects of the welfare reform from "poor" to "fair," with the Senate debates better than the House (Mucciaroni and Quirk, *Deliberative Choices*, chapter 3).

98. Rich, *Think Tanks, Public Policy, and the Politics of Expertise*, pp. 180–96; Mucciaroni and Quirk rated the debates on telecommunications policy slightly better than the debate over welfare reform, with more informed debates in the Senate than the House and on issues that involved interest group competition (Mucciaroni and Quirk, *Deliberative Choices*, chapter 5).

99. Daniel J. Palazzolo and Fiona R. McCarthy, "State and Local Government Organizations and the Formation of the Help America Vote Act," *Publius: The Journal of Federalism* 35 (2005), pp. 515–35.

100. Mucciarini and Quirk, *Deliberative Choices*, pp. 187–88.

101. Dana Milbank, "Good Riddance to the Worst Congress Ever," *Washington Post*, December 19, 2014 (www.washingtonpost.com/opinions/dana-milbank-good-riddance-to-the-worst-congress-ever/2014/12/19/1f25b99e-8796-11e4-9534-f79a23c40e6c_story.html).

102. Bipartisan Policy Center, *Some Returns to Regular Order, Some Departures in 2015* (Washington, D.C.: Bipartisan Policy Center, 2016) (http://bipartisanpolicy.org/blog/some-returns-to-regular-order-congress-2015).

103. Evans, "Congressional Committees."

104. Quirk, "Deliberation and Decision Making," p. 342; Connelly, *James Madison Rules America*, p. 42. For a recent study of one-party deliberation, see William Bendix, "Neglect, Inattention, and Legislative Deficiencies: The Consequences of One-Party Deliberations in the U.S. House," *Congress and the Presidency* 43 (2016), pp. 82–102.

105. Bessette, *The Mild Voice of Reason*, p. 151. Italics is in the original.

106. Sarah Binder and Frances E. Lee, "Making Deals in Congress," in *Solutions to Political Polarization* in America, edited by Nathaniel Persily (New York: Cambridge University Press, 2015), pp. 243–44.

107. Bessette, *The Mild Voice of Reason*, pp. 135–36.

108. Gregory J. Wawro, *Legislative Entrepreneurship in the U.S. House of Representatives* (University of Michigan, 2000), chapter 1.

109. Paul Ryan, *The Way Forward: Renewing the American Idea* (New York: Twelve/Hachette Book Group, 2014), p. 75.

110. Ryan, *The Way Forward*, p. 76. Italics in the original.

111. Jill Lawrence, *Profiles in Negotiation: The Murray–Ryan Budget Deal* (Brookings Center for Effective Public Management, 2015), pp. 1–13 (www.brookings.edu/~/media/research/files/papers/2015/02/profiles-negotiation-murray-ryan-lawrence/brookingsmurrayryanv421315.pdf).

112. Henry Waxman, *The Waxman Report: How Congress Really Works* (New York: Twelve/Hachette Book Group, 2009), p. 224.

113. Craig Volden and Alan E. Wiseman, "Legislative Effectiveness and Representation," in *Congress Reconsidered*, 10th ed., edited by Lawrence C. Dodd and Bruce I. Oppenheimer (Thousand Oaks, Calif.: Sage/CQ Press, 2013), pp. 245–46.

114. Bessette *The Mild Voice of Reason*, p. 136.

115. Smith *Call to Order*, pp. 24–35.

116. Ibid., p. 32.

117. Bach and Smith, *Managing Uncertainty in the House of Representatives*, pp. 116–17; Sinclair, *Unorthodox Lawmaking*, pp. 150–51.

118. Sinclair, *Unorthodox Lawmaking*, p. 270.

119. Frances E. Lee, "Individual and Partisan Activism on the Senate Floor," in *The U.S. Senate: from Deliberation to Dysfunction*, edited by Burdett A. Loomis (Washington, D.C.: CQ Press, 2012), pp. 113–19.

120. Sarah A. Binder and Steven S. Smith, *Politics or Principle? Filibustering in the United States Senate* (Brookings Institution Press, 1997), pp. 105–06.

121. Walter J. Oleszek, 2014, *Congressional Procedures and the Policy Process*, 9th ed. (Thousand Oaks, Calif.: Sage, 2014), p. 306.

122. Sarah A. Binder, "How We Count Senate Filibusters and Why It Matters," *Washington Post*, May 15, 2014 (www.washingtonpost.com/blogs/monkey-cage/wp/2014/05/15/how-we-count-senate-filibusters-and-why-it-matters).

123. Sinclair, *Party Wars*, pp. 358 and 360.

124. Chris Den Hartog and Nathan W. Monroe, *Agenda Setting in the U.S. Senate: Costly Consideration and Majority Party Advantage* (Cambridge University Press, 2011), chapter 8.

125. Oleszek, *Congressional Procedures and the Policy Process*, p. 194.

126. Bipartisan Policy Center Commission on Political Reform, *Governing in a Polarized America*, p. 59.

127. Mucciaroni and Quirk, *Deliberative Choices*, p. 6.

128. Quirk, "Deliberation and Decision Making," p. 316.

129. Ibid., p. 335.

130. Mucciaroni and Quirk, *Deliberative Choices*, chapters 3–5.

131. Ibid., p. 188.

132. Ibid., p. 198.

133. Davidson, "Senate Floor Deliberation: A Preliminary Inquiry."

134. Mucciaroni and Quirk, *Deliberative Choices*, chapters 3–5.

135. Ibid., p. 194.

136. Sellers, *Cycles of Spin: Strategic Communication in the US Congress*, pp. 220–21.

137. Sinclair, *Party Wars*, p. 354.

138. *Federalist* No. 10.

139. *Federalist* No. 42 (http://teachingamericanhistory.org/library/document/federalist-no-42).

140. Connelly, *James Madison Rules America*, chapter 9.

141. Jones, *The Presidency in a Separated System*, pp. 25–30.

142. Bipartisan Policy Center Commission on Political Reform, *Governing in a Polarized America*, p. 53.

143. Mann and Ornstein, *The Broken Branch*, p. 232.

144. Binder and Lee, "Making Deals in Congress," pp. 255–56.

145. Bipartisan Policy Center Commission on Political Reform, *Governing in a Polarized America*, p. 57.

146. Binder and Lee, "Making Deals in Congress," pp. 252–53.

147. Bipartisan Policy Center Commission on Political Reform, *Governing in a Polarized America*, p. 59.

148. Quirk, "Deliberation and Decision Making," p. 341.

149. Eric Schickler, *Disjointed Pluralism: Institutional Innovation and the Development of the U.S. Congress* (Princeton University Press, 2001), p. 252.
150. Ibid., p. 267.
151. Ibid., p. 268.
152. Sinclair, *Party Wars*, pp. 360–61.
153. Evans, "Congressional Committees."

Changing House Rules

From Level Playing Field to Partisan Tilt

DONALD R. WOLFENSBERGER

It is much more material that there should be a rule to go by than what that rule is; that there may be a uniformity of proceeding in business not subject to the caprice of the Speaker, or captiousness of the members. It is very material that order, decency, and regularity be preserved in a dignified public body.

THOMAS JEFFERSON

If the majority do not govern, the minority will and if the tyranny of the majority is hard, the tyranny of the minority is simply unendurable. The rules, then, ought to be so arranged as to facilitate the action of the majority.

THOMAS B. REED

One can only imagine what Thomas Jefferson might say if he observed the U.S. House of Representatives in session today: "Where's the uniformity?" What Jefferson feared, "the caprice of the Speaker or captiousness of the members," are on display almost daily as new rules are adopted to handle each major bill. Jefferson would surely wonder just how and why Congress had gotten so far off the uniform procedural track.[1]

House Speaker Thomas Brackett Reed of Maine would provide the justification for such changing rules a century later, after decades of interminable debates punctuated by hundreds of votes on dilatory motions.[2]

At the beginning of the republic, the House and Senate adopted a similar set of standing rules. However, both bodies have since spun off from the mother ship and hurtled into separate orbits in which the only rules that count are the rules of the day. The elaborate set of twenty-nine House standing rules are now preempted routinely by so-called special rules or order of business resolutions reported by the House Rules Committee, setting the terms of debate and amendment for each major piece of legislation.

The purpose of this chapter is to briefly trace the Founders' intended role for the legislative branch and the rules necessary to fulfill that role. Given space constraints, the chapter will focus on the House and, particularly, on more recent procedural developments in an increasingly polarized and partisan environment. Finally, the chapter will trace the nexus between a theory of partisan rules development and the progressive critique of the Constitution and Congress over time.

The Founders' Congress and Its Rules

The central challenge running through the Constitutional Convention in 1787 was how to create and maintain a representative form of government that would be strong enough to be effective yet not so democratic that it could easily become a tyranny of the majority, trampling the rights of minorities. James Madison, principal architect of the Constitution, attempted to allay concerns about a potentially out-of-control Congress in several essays in the *Federalist*, the most oft-cited being No. 10. He opens the essay by alluding to concerns that Congress might end up on the same bad path as some state governments: "Complaints are everywhere heard . . . that our governments are too unstable; that the public good is disregarded in the conflicts of rival parties; and that measures are too often decided, not according to the rules of justice, and the rights of the minor party, but by the superior force of an interested and overbearing majority."[3]

As political scientist Greg Weiner explains, what Madison meant by "justice" in that passage "was a procedural standard guaranteeing that decisions would be made according to known rules." Madison was not arguing against the right of a majority to rule, says Weiner: "The problem arose when majorities did so arbitrarily, unpredictably, or on the basis of sheer force." Weiner goes on to note that in Madison's writings, "justice is generally associated with fairness and rules rather than the substance of political decisions." The important thing to Madison, says Weiner, was that majorities reach substantive outcomes in a fair rather than arbitrary manner, and that "they consented to this arrangement because securing a stable and predictable environment was the very reason political society was instituted to begin with."[4]

It is within this procedural context that Madison proceeds in *Federalist* No. 10 to explain Congress's central role as a deliberative assembly that would "refine and enlarge the public views by passing them through the medium of a chosen body of citizens whose wisdom may best discern the true interest of their country and whose patriotism and love of justice will be least likely to sacrifice it to temporary or partial considerations."[5]

For such deliberation to take place requires a set of rules and procedures that enable all legislators to present their views and alternatives. With such procedural protections, Congress could control Madison's greatest fear, that the republic might devolve into a direct democracy in which a majority faction would "invade the rights of other citizens." Since factions are inevitable in a free society, he wrote, the "principal task of modern legislation" is the "regulation of these various and interfering interests" by involving "the spirit of party and faction in the necessary and ordinary operations of government."[6] Put another way, the dangers of faction can best be mitigated by ensuring the full and fair representation of all factions in the regular decision-making processes of Congress. That requires a body of rules that is impartial and does not allow a single party to dominate the rulemaking or legislative processes.

Jefferson shared Madison's concern about the dangers a majority faction could pose to minority rights. In his *Manual of Parliamentary Practice*, written for the guidance of the Senate while he was vice president, Jefferson cites a maxim former House of Commons Speaker Arthur Onslow said he often heard as a young member: "nothing tended more to throw power into the hands of administration . . . than a neglect of, or departure from, the rules of proceeding" which provide "a shelter and protection to the minority, against the attempts at power."[7]

In the preface to the *Manual*, Jefferson expresses the hope that future generations will build on his work, "till a code of rules shall be formed for the use of the Senate, the effects of which may be *accuracy in business, economy of time, order, uniformity, and impartiality* [emphasis added]."[8]

For the purposes of this chapter, we will use Jefferson's and Madison's concepts of parliamentary rules as a measuring rod against which to judge the contemporary House: Do the rules provide a fair and predictable system in which decisions can be made in a timely and efficient manner, while respecting the rights of the minority?

Not surprisingly, the rules the first House adopted in April 1789 bore a striking resemblance to the rules adopted by the Senate and, before that, by various colonial and state legislatures, the Continental Congress, the Congress of the Confederation, and the Constitutional Convention itself. All were drawn from the rules of the British House of Commons. The colonies may have broken away from their colonial father, King George III, but the rules of parliamentary procedure, learned at the knee of the "Mother of Parliaments," had not been abandoned by her runaway offspring.

The set of twelve House rules spelled out such things as: 1) the duties of the Speaker to preside over the House, preserve order and decorum, decide on points of order, announce the results of votes, and appoint committees of three or fewer members (the House soon extended the Speaker's appointment powers to all committees); 2) the rules of decorum and debate; 3) the introduction and disposition of bills; 4) the right of members to speak no more than twice on the same subject (later changed to once); 5) the operation of committees of the whole House; and 6) the use of motions for the previous question, to amend, commit or adjourn.[9] They were adopted without substantial controversy.

A Partisan Rules Theory and the Progressive Critique

The set of neutral rules adopted by the first House did not last long. Political scientist Sarah Binder, in her book *Minority Rights, Majority Rule*, puts forward a "theory of the partisan basis of procedural choice," tracing the emergence of party-driven rules to disputes over the previous question motion during the run-up to the War of 1812.

Binder makes a convincing, evidence-based case that procedural changes in the House ever since have been driven primarily by partisan considerations and strength: "majority parties are more likely to change the rules in their favor if they believe such changes will increase their chances of legislative success." This is especially the case "when minority obstructionism hampers the achievement of the majority party's legislative goals," leading to the further suppression of minority rights. Conversely, when majority parties are weak and cross-party coalitions emerge, minority rights are expanded, at least until majorities grow stronger and take back those rights.[10]

Binder later notes that, even after numerous House rules changes in the 1970s that eliminated most minority opportunities to obstruct, new ways were found to further suppress the minority party, mainly through special rules from the Rules Committee. What differentiates the House of the 1980s to the present from earlier partisan Houses from 1890 to 1910 has been the use of special rules to specifically disadvantage individuals and minority parties from full participation in the legislative process rather than simply to overcome minority obstructionism. It will be argued here that this has put the institution on a dangerous new path that may not be as reversible as past patterns of alternating dominance either by committees or by parties.

What we will call "the progressive critique" of the Constitution and Congress was initially laid out by a young graduate student at Johns Hopkins University named Woodrow Wilson in his classic work *Congressional Government* (1885). Wilson later updated his work in a series of lectures later published in 1908 as *Constitutional Government*, which recognized the emergence of stronger presidents, Speakers, and parties since his earlier work.

At the center of Wilson's thinking was his dismissal of the Constitution's system of checks and balances as obsolete and detrimental to the nation's growth and social and economic development: "No living thing can have its organs offset each other as checks and live. . . . Government is not a body of blind forces; it is a body of men, with highly differentiated functions . . . but with a common task and purpose."[11]

Wilson was originally critical of Congress for its fragmented committee system chaired by "petty barons" with no central policy direction or accountability. An Anglophile at heart, Wilson thought the only answer was a form of party government, not unlike the Westminster system, which he considered the most perfect of all: "parties may be said to have been our real body politic . . . the discipline and zest of parties has held us together, has made it possible for us to form and to carry out national programs." Wilson saw the president as leader of his party and the nation: "If he leads the nation, his party can hardly resist him. His office is anything he has the sagacity and force to make it."[12] Wilson's notion of responsible party government was operational for at least the first two years of his presidency (1913–14), when he successfully worked with Congress to enact his New Freedom platform.

The Reed Revolution and the Cannon Revolt

An early chronicler of the House, former Representative De Alva Stanwood Alexander (R-N.Y.), notes in his 1916 history that "obstruction very early took its rise in unlimited debate," invoked for party advantage or by individuals for selfish purposes. "It proceeds on the theory that the effort of a minority to defeat the majority is as legitimate and patriotic as the majority's use of its greater number." Whenever the majority cut off one avenue of obstruction, the minority would find another. "This constant warfare, waged for a century, resulted in limiting the rights of the minority and entrenching the power of the majority."[13]

Initially, the pushback from majorities was gradual and incremental on such things as periodic reassertions of the previous question motion to force an immediate vote on the pending question (as opposed to simply setting off a new debate over whether the motion should be adopted). But majority assertiveness culminated with the election of Representative Thomas B. Reed (R-Maine) as Speaker. Much has been written about the House revolution Reed wrought when Republicans regained control of the chamber in 1889 and he became Speaker. The majority was still frustrated in its efforts to call up its bills due to minority party obstruction—forcing repeated votes on procedural motions and blocking action by refusing to help make a quorum (the "disappearing quorum" problem). Except for a few privileged bills, like appropriations measures, the only way to bring up bills out of the order in which they had been reported was by unanimous consent or by suspending the rules, which required a two-thirds vote.

Reed knew for some time what he would do as Speaker and how best to accomplish it. He did not keep his intentions secret. In an essay published in *Century Magazine* several months before the new House convened, Reed spelled out the responsibility of the new majority: "The rules, then, ought to be so arranged as to facilitate the action of the majority." Reed did not dismiss the value of "debate and for due and careful consideration" but, after such debate, "there ought to be no hindrance to action except those checks and balances which our Constitution wisely provides."[14]

Instead of having the Rules Committee, which he chaired, report a set of rules when the new House convened, Reed waited until the most opportune moment to act first from the dais as Speaker. As the springboard for action, Reed chose a resolution to seat the Republican candidate in a contested election case, knowing that would rally and unify his Republican colleagues. When Democrats tried to use a disappearing quorum to block consideration of the resolution, Reed told the clerk to take down the names, as he called them, of those Democrats present who had refused to respond to their names. That caused a great uproar among Democrats.

Reed then proceeded to rule against various dilatory motions, holding that "The object of a parliamentary body is action and not stoppage of action." Reed then proceeded to the Rules Committee, where he asked his colleagues to incorporate his rulings in the resolution to adopt the standing rules of the House. The Republicans supported him in committee and on the floor, and the Reed Rules were born.[15]

Just as important, Reed institutionalized the practice of the Rules Committee's reporting order of business resolutions or special rules providing for the consideration of specified legislation, out of their order on the calendar. Such resolutions required only a majority vote for adoption. The special rules could also call for a limitation on debate time and even on the amendment process. The Reed Rules, combined with special rules, ushered in the modern House of the twentieth century. Reed's innovative Republican 51st Congress was rewarded by being turned out of power by voters in 1890.

When Republicans regained control of the House in the 54th Congress (1895), they reelected Reed as Speaker. He promptly inaugurated a new practice of having the resolution adopting House rules considered by the House before the Rules Committee even met—even though the package changed the rules of the previous Congress back to the Republican rules of 1890. They were considered under the hour-rule instead of under an open amendment process, and adoption of the previous question blocked any minority amendments. This was Reed's final procedural coup, giving the majority complete control over House rules.[16]

Reed retired in 1898 after serving two more terms. After the next Speaker, Republican Representative David Henderson of Iowa, retired, Representative Joseph Cannon of Illinois became Speaker in 1903. Cannon served four terms before he was toppled in a floor coup by Democrats and a group of forty-some insurgent Republicans favoring more progressive legislation. While Reed was proactive legislatively, Cannon was of the view that "no new legislation is needed; everything is just fine back in Danville [his hometown]."

The revolt against Cannon was a revolt of the progressives of both parties, anxious to get at new legislation they thought the country needed. It stripped him of his membership and chairship of the Rules Committee and his power to appoint its members. When the Democrats came to power in 1911, they completed the revolution by providing for the election by the House of all committees, and they replaced "Czar Speaker" with "King Caucus" under the leadership of their Majority Leader and Ways and Means Committee chair, Representative Oscar Underwood of Alabama. Important committee legislation, like tariff bills, was first considered by the Democratic Caucus, where it could be amended. The caucus then voted binding instructions on both members of the relevant committee and on all House Democrats to support the caucus-approved bill in committee and on the floor. As one scholar has shown, the binding caucus rules were used sparingly during Democratic control in this period, saved for only the most important bills, primarily during Wilson's first term as president.[17]

Return of the Progressive Critique and Reforms

The progressive critique of Congress and proposals for reform resurfaced among liberal politicians and academics in the 1940s through the early 1960s after Congress turned away from the New Deal in 1937. A conservative coalition of southern Democrats and Republicans formed a majoritarian block that could stymie many of the liberal policy proposals of presidents Truman and Kennedy. The three main targets of the progressive reformers were the House Rules Committee, the legislative traffic cop that put up more stop signs than yield signs; the seniority system of elevating to committee chairships the most senior member of a committee (usually a southerner); and the Senate filibuster that was used to block civil rights bills and other liberal programs.

The progressive congressional reform platform was reiterated in reports like the 1945 American Political Science Association report on "The Reorganization of Congress," which, in turn, led to the 1946 Legislative Reorganization Act (with political scientist George B. Galloway writing both reports); the 1950 American Political Science Association report, "Toward a More Responsible Two-Party System"; and a similar APSA report in 1964.

The critique and reforms would later appear in influential books like James MacGregor Burns's *The Deadlock of Democracy: Four Party Politics in America* (1963) and Missouri Democratic Representative Richard Bolling's two books, *House Out of Order* (1963) and *Power in the House* (1968).

The latter two books would become bibles to the Democrats' 1974 freshman class of 1975 "Watergate Babies."[18] The progressive reform agenda was later reiterated by many witnesses before the Joint Committee on the Organization of Congress in 1965, leading to the Legislative Reorganization Act of 1970 and subsequent reforms adopted by the Democratic Caucus to complete the revolt against committee chairs.

The congressional reform revolution of the 1960s and 1970s was engineered by the Democratic Study Group, an informal caucus of liberal members founded in the late 1950s. The 1970 Legislative Reorganization Act established a "committee bill of rights" that ensured greater majority rule within committees and provided for the first time for recorded votes on amendments in the committee of the whole. The caucus rules changes abolished the seniority system for choosing committee chairs, replacing it with separate, automatic votes in the caucus on each chair. Three incumbent southern chairs were ousted in 1975, putting the rest on notice. Another caucus rule created a subcommittee bill of rights that empowered subcommittee chairs to set their own agendas and hire their own staff. The House Rules Committee was returned to the leadership fold by giving the Speaker authority to nominate its Democratic members directly to the full caucus.[19]

When the new democratization of the House became somewhat chaotic, the postreform Congress turned to the leadership to help draw things together. The reformers had always intended, as recommended by Bolling's book, "for a distillation, impervious to abuses, of the best in the historical caucus and the best in the historical speakership."[20] The leadership had wisely held back until asked by the junior members to step in.

A Significant Departure from Past Practices

As Binder points out, Democrats imposed barriers against minority dilatory tactics "continuously from 1975 through 1979" so that by the early 1980s they had fine-tuned House rules to eliminate most minority obstructionism. At that point, Binder continues, "Democratic majorities turned to procedural innovations to limit minority influence over the agenda," mostly in the form of restrictive special rules from the Rules Committee.[21]

The early tipoff to this new direction came in the form of a letter sent in 1979 by Representative John LaFalce (D-N.Y.), and cosigned by over forty colleagues, to Speaker Thomas P. ("Tip") O'Neill and Rules Committee

Chairman Richard Bolling (D-Mo.) requesting more "modified open" rules "limiting the number of . . . amendments" that can be offered, "and the time permitted for debate" on them. They conceded that some might cry "gag rules," but they claimed to be interested only in greater institutional efficiency "for the good of the House, its membership, and the country." However, it was obvious to most observers that they were reacting to politically embarrassing amendments being offered by Republicans who took full advantage of the rules authorizing recorded votes in the committee of the whole and establishing a new House television broadcasting system that had gone live to the public earlier in 1979.[22]

Bolling, who some said had put LaFalce and friends up to writing the letter, was more than happy to oblige and, shortly thereafter, restrictive amendment rules were being granted on more than just tax bills as had previously been the case. Data compiled by Stanley Bach and Steven S. Smith confirms this. Whereas, in the 94th Congress (1975–76), 84.3 percent of all special rules were open, 11.3 percent were structured (allowing only specified amendments), and only 4.4 percent were closed; by the 96th Congress (1979–80), only 71.2 percent were open and 31.1 percent were structured or closed. Their table ends with the 99th Congress (1985–86), with only 55.4 percent of the rules open, and the rest structured or closed.[23]

A Rules Committee minority compilation of open versus restrictive rules published in January 1993 picks up from there, showing 54 percent open rules in the 100th Congress (1987) and, by the 102nd Congress (1991–92), only 34 percent open rules and 66 percent restrictive.[24]

This author has compiled a table on special rules from the 103rd Congress (1993–94) through the current 114th Congress (2015–16). It shows the trend toward more restrictive rules continuing both under Republican majorities (104th–109th and 112th–114th Congresses) and Democratic majorities (110th and 111th Congresses).

Open rules under Republicans in the 104th Congress rose briefly to 58 percent of the total, compared to 44 percent under the Democratic majority in the previous Congress, while structured and closed rules were 42 percent of the total. In their last Congress in the majority, in the 109th Congress (2005–06), before a brief hiatus of Democratic rule, only 19 percent of the rules granted by Republicans were open, while 81 percent were structured or closed. When Democrats ended their two-Congress majority run in 2010, there were no open rules: 100 percent were structured or closed. And, by the 113th Congress, under a Republican majority, just

FIGURE 5-1. Open versus Restrictive Rules in the House of Representatives, 94th through 113th Congresses

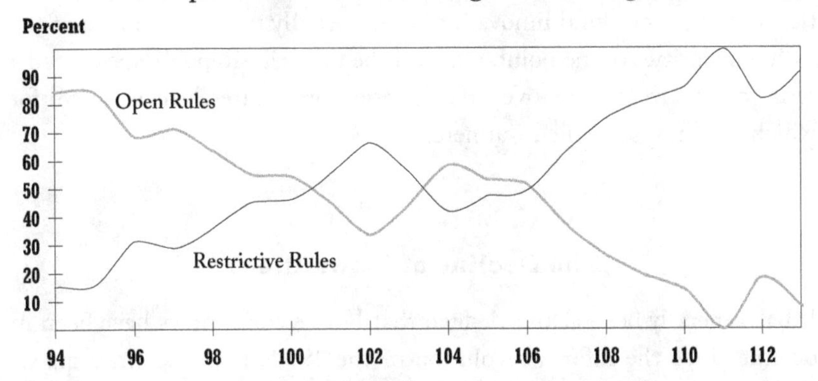

Sources: Steven S. Smith, Call to Order (Brookings Institution, 1989), table 3.1 (p. 75); Walter Oleszek, Congressional Procedures and the Policy Process (Washington, D.C.: CQ Press, 2007), table 4-3 (p. 129); and Donald R. Wolfensberger, Special Rules Providing for the Original Consideration of Legislation in the House, 103rd–114th Congress, table 1, Bipartisan Policy Center website.

8 percent of all rules were open, 43 percent were structured, and 48 percent were closed.[25] (See figure 5-1.)

In addition to an increasing reliance on restrictive amendment rules from the Rules Committee already mentioned, the special rules could also be used to waive House rules against any rules violations in bills and to provide for consideration only of omnibus substitutes for budget resolutions. Other devices invented included so-called self-executing rules, in which a leadership-preferred amendment to a bill would be considered adopted upon the adoption of a special rule for the bill, thereby avoiding a separate debate and vote on the amendment when the bill was called up.

More recently, the Rules Committee has simply substituted the language of a "Rules Committee Print" for committee-reported language, as the new base bill for amendment purposes. In so doing, it is sometimes inserting new leadership-blessed language without having to use the self-execution language or even to explain the changes.[26] Moreover, more and more major bills coming through the Rules Committee have bypassed committees altogether—running 37 percent of all special rules for bills in the 113th Congress.[27]

Finally, a device was invented, initially through language in special rules but eventually incorporated into the standing rules in 2003, that authorizes the chair to postpone and cluster floor votes, thereby separating debates on amendments from the final votes on them. As time went on, the possibilities for such procedural innovations grew, usually to the advantage of the ruling majority. At one point, while in the minority Republicans coined a term for this trend: "creative rule alteration procedures," the acronym for which need not be spelled-out here.

The Decline of Committees

It has generally been acknowledged that House committees have been in decline since the reform revolution of the 1970s removed their quasi-independent status and brought them under the firm "guidance" of the majority caucus and leadership, regardless of which party has been in the majority. A Republican leadership task force on committee reform chaired by Representative David Dreier concluded in 1995, "As party leadership becomes more powerful, committees become relatively weaker."

It is ironic that most of the Republican minority's reform proposals in the 1980s and early 1990s were aimed at restoring committees vis-à-vis the leadership. Moreover, much of the GOP Contract with America's congressional reforms were designed to foster greater deliberation and accountability in committees—rules that reduced members' committee and subcommittee assignments, limited the number of subcommittees per committee, abolished proxy voting, and required all roll call votes in committees to be published in committee reports.

It can be argued that limiting committee and subcommittee chairs to no more than three consecutive terms deprives committees of the continuity and expertise that seasoned committee chairs bring to a committee's power and prestige. But Republicans were wary of vesting too much power in one place for too long (just as earlier Democratic majorities were). The term limits on chairs were offset by a four-consecutive term limit on Speakers, though that was repealed in the 108th Congress (2003) with an eye to protecting the reign of Speaker Dennis Hastert (R-Ill.), though only in his third term at the time. In addition, the Republicans later removed the term limit on Rules Committee chairs.

What arguably did weaken committees' capacities was the Contract's one-third reduction in committee staff in the 104th Congress, from roughly

1,800 in the 103rd Congress to 1,171 personnel in the 104th. Recent research has shown that the one-third reduction in committee staff has been accompanied (since 1977) by a three-fold increase in leadership staff, from sixty-nine to 214.[28]

The ideal of greater committee deliberation gave way immediately in the new Republican majority's 104th Congress to a strict 100-day time limit for voting on all legislation mentioned in the ten-part contract, which amounted to some two dozen bills. Committees were required to report the bills as written in the contract, with no wiggle room for compromise or amendments. While the Speaker promised to get back to regular order thereafter, the die had been cast for a leadership-dominated system, both in the types of bills to be reported and in the type of floor process under which they would be considered.[29]

In their 2006 campaign platform, "A New Direction for America," House Democrats promised a return to the regular order, including "full hearings and open subcommittee and committee markups," and a floor procedure "that allows open, full, and fair debate consisting of a full amendment process that grants the minority the right to offer its alternatives."[30] The platform was a knock-off of the GOP's 1994 contract, the main difference being a pledge to complete votes on their "Six for '06" priority bills within 100 legislative hours instead of mimicking the Republicans' 100-day timetable.

Predictably, that promise ran up against their fair and openness promises; their opening-day rules package included closed rules on the first four of the "Six for '06" bills, with the final two bills considered a few days later under closed rules as well. Overall in the Democrats' comeback, 110th Congress (2007–08), only 14 percent of the special rules considered were open compared to 19 percent for the Republicans in the preceding Congress, while 36 percent of the Democrats' rules were completely closed, versus 32 percent for Republicans.[31]

To their credit, the Democrats' did not roll back the Republicans' 1995 rule guaranteeing the minority a motion to recommit bills with amendatory instructions, a right that majority Democrats had decimated in the 1980s and early 1990s.[32] In the 111th Congress the Democratic majority changed the rules to confine the guarantee to only straight motions to recommit (to send the bill physically back to committee) and to motions to recommit with amendatory instructions (to report back an amendment "forthwith"), thereby precluding general instructions (for example, to conduct a further study or develop an amendment on a certain topic).[33]

Why Do They Do It?

The recurring question that arises through each of the three changes in House party control over the last twenty years is: Why do minority parties always promise that if they win majority control they will be more open and fair, but then quickly revert to the same closed and unfair practices as their predecessors, the *Animal Farm* syndrome? A hard-boiled politico would answer, quite simply, "Because they can." But that's not a satisfactory explanation.

A major reason is the reality of a time-limited, two-year Congress and the majority's eagerness to fulfill as many of its campaign's policy promises as quickly as possible, knowing full well it could lose its majority status at the next election. The procedural promises take a back seat (or are locked in the trunk), with relative confidence that the public pays no heed to how things get done.

A related explanation is offered by political scientists John E. Owens and J. Mark Wrighton, drawing on Daniel Patrick Moynihan's "iron law of emulation." According to Owens and Wrighton, as polarization continues to increase in the House, "when one political party acquires a technique enhancing its power, the other party will likely adopt it as well in order to carry out election promises and to prevent potential dissidents from within its ranks from forming bipartisan coalitions with the minority." The authors say this tendency is especially evident when the two parties are in intense conflict and competition."[34] Obviously, this copycat tendency becomes much easier the second time around, when both the pot and kettle have been pre-blackened. By then it is not a heavy lift to ratchet up restrictive floor procedures.

Former House Parliamentarian Charles W. Johnson perhaps best summarizes the reason for the House Majority Leadership's procedural "circumvention of those cornerstones of legislative practice." It is, he says, "to assure the retention of a partisan voting majority, as well as to enhance the certainty of time and issue, the minimization of minority rights, and political 'cover' for majority members, all at the expense of a more open, informed and deliberative process."[35]

Does It Matter?

This chapter began by positing that the original rules of the House were designed to ensure the founders' ideal of a deliberative legislative body in which majority rule could prevail, while also protecting the rights of individual members and minority factions to fully participate in the process. Pure deliberation is an unrealizable ideal, but some form of it has characterized the House for most of its history, notwithstanding Speaker Thomas Reed's quip, "I thank God the House is no longer a deliberative body."[36]

To counter that flip quip (which Democrats used against him) Reed later wrote, in a more serious vein, of the value of both deliberation and debate: "to make laws wisely the body must be a deliberative body"; and, "real debate," he continued, is "speaking made and listened to for the purpose of elucidating the principles of a law proposed or of settling its details," but also "for the purpose of enlightening the outside world."[37]

If we judge the current system of special rules by the standards for legislative rules laid out in Jefferson's *Manual*, it might meet the standards of accuracy in business, economy of time, and order, but it fails the more important tests of regularity, uniformity, impartiality, and decency. Special rules, by their nature, are a departure from regularity, uniformity, and impartiality. And such rules tend to provoke anger and incivility from the minority rather than promote decency.

It does not speak well for the House that nearly half the special rules in the current 114th Congress and its predecessor have been completely closed to amendments, a radical departure from the Founders' vision of an inclusive and egalitarian body.

Beyond the increasingly restrictive floor procedures, the central control by majority party leaders over both legislative processes and substance has a crippling effect on the value of committee work. More and more, committees are imitating House floor behavior of perfunctory debates. That has been made possible by House adoption of a rule in 2005 that permits committees to postpone and cluster recorded votes on amendments during bill markup, a near replica of the 2003 House floor rule allowing postponed votes.

Just before Republicans recaptured the House in 2010, Representative John Boehner, soon to be elected Speaker, told an American Enterprise Institute audience about the need to return to the regular order: "the truth is, much of the work of committees has been co-opted by the leadership," he said. "In too many instances, we no longer have legislators; we just have voters. In my view," he continued, "if we want to make legislators legislate again, then we need to empower them at the committee level. If Members were more engaged in their committee work, they would be more invested in the final products that come to the floor."[38]

Representative Paul Ryan (R-Wisc.), upon his election to replace Boehner as Speaker five years later, offered a similar critique and commitment to restoring regular order: "The House is broken. . . . We need to let every Member contribute. . . . The committees should retake the lead in drafting all major legislation. . . . In other words, we need to return to regular order."[39] The rhetoric had not changed but neither, apparently, had actual practices under Boehner, or Ryan's remarks would not have been necessary.

Finally, one cannot ignore the parallel lines of decline in House deliberation on the one hand and citizen trust in and approval of Congress on the other. While it is true that most voters do not understand the nuances of legislative procedures, they do have a general sense that parties are engaged in bitter partisan battles for majority control, in political gamesmanship, in interest group favoritism, and in messaging, all at the expense of serious lawmaking and problem-solving.

Even the most essential work of Congress is being neglected. It is hard to hide six consecutive years of not even being able to complete on time its most basic duty of funding the government through regular appropriations bills while careening from one fiscal cliff to another. Such failures of Congress bring into question its very legitimacy. Madison reminds us that, "Duty, gratitude, interest, ambition itself are the cords by which [members] will be bound to fidelity and sympathy with the great mass of people."[40] What remains if those cords are severed?

What Can Be Done?

The steady ratcheting up of restrictive floor amendment procedures under both Democratic and Republican majorities, along with other innovative procedural devices favoring the majority, have transformed the nature of the legislative process from one of accommodation and compromise to one of majority party domination and minority party marginalization. The progressive reformers had come as close to party government as they might get by relegating minority party members to the role of "loyal opposition" instead of full participants (if not equal partners) in the legislative process as the founders intended. All this was aided and abetted by the increasing polarization between the parties, leaving little room for finding middle ground on which to compromise.

The Founders' fears of party factions governing through passions rather than reason is becoming a reality as genuine deliberation and debate recede into the chamber's woodwork.[41] The problem with the party government model is that a parliamentary system cannot be transplanted to U.S. soil and thrive. The attempt has, instead, produced a fruitless hybrid, a parliamentary system without accountability. That is because members of Congress are, first and foremost, loyal to their constituents (both geographic and economic), as opposed to their party. Moreover, they are not about to pay blind obeisance to a president. Members and their constituents still revere our Constitution's system of divided powers and checks and balances, even though they often deplore and decry its results.

Instead of total party government supplanting the Founders' government, Congress operates under what might be called "partisan governance," with the governance confined to the internal workings of each party in each chamber. That produces the paradox of unified party floor votes but an apparent incapacity for bicameral or interbranch governing.

The American people may be oblivious to the procedural peregrinations of Congress. However, they do hold the same basic ideals as members of the First Congress that the rules of the game should be fair, that the game should be played on a level playing field on which their elected representatives have the same right to participate as any other political player. The partisan tilt of the playing field that favors one team over the other only adds to the cynicism of the fans in the stands and, unless reversed, will eventually alienate them from the game altogether.

Before that happens, the leadership of the House should act to address the rising discontent voiced both by citizens and members of Congress alike. This can be done by shifting from a culture of campaigning to one of deliberative lawmaking. To start this process the leadership should take some simple steps to revalue committee work that, over time, has depreciated. Moving to five-day workweeks would give committees more time and space to deliberate and legislate. The current three-term limits on committee and subcommittee chairs should be either abolished or increased to five consecutive terms. Restoring trust and confidence in committees begins at the top with trusted and expert committee leaders that members will want to serve with.

The current rule that allows recorded votes in committees to be postponed and clustered at the end of a bill markup session should be repealed so that members can reengage in the important deliberative stages of argumentation and persuasion. Leaders should desist in scheduling unreported bills on the floor except in emergency situations. Likewise, closed amendment rules on the floor should be reserved only for emergency bills, while opening up most other bills to modified open rules with time caps on the amendment process. And finally leadership should refrain from substituting new bill language in the Rules Committee for that already agreed to by committees.[42]

To Speaker Paul Ryan's credit, during the first four months of his speakership (November 2015–February 2016), of the nineteen special rules reported by the Rules Committee only two (11 percent) have been closed to amendments, compared to 50 percent of the eighty rules reported prior to that in the 114th Congress. Moreover, of those same nineteen bills, only one (5 percent) was unreported, compared to twenty-five of the eighty bills (31 percent) given rules prior to that.[43] Clearly, at the outset of the Ryan speakership, at least, a conscious effort was being made to restore a regular order that is both more fair and open.

There are no procedural quick fixes that can instantly reverse the vice-like constrictions on members' individual rights and committees' deliberative role. But the steps outlined above can begin an incremental process of reestablishing a balance between responsible party agenda-setting and responsive committee lawmaking in the nation's interest.

Notes

1. Thomas Jefferson, *A Manual of Parliamentary Practice for the Use of the Senate of the United States*, 1st ed. 1801 (Washington, D.C.: Government Printing Office: 1993), p. 2 (hereafter referred to as Jefferson's *Manual*).

2. Thomas B. Reed, "Rules of the House of Representatives," *The Century Magazine* XXXVI-106 (April 1888 to April 1889), p. 795.

3. Alexander Hamilton, James Madison, John Jay, *The Federalist Papers* (New York: Mentor Books, 1961), p. 77.

4. Greg Weiner, *Madison's Metronome: Thee Constitution, Majority Rule, and the Tempo of American Politics* (University Press of Kansas, 2012), pp. 72, 79.

5. *Federalist* No. 10, p. 82.

6. Ibid.

7. Jefferson's *Manual*, p. 1. The House incorporated Jefferson's *Manual* as part of its rules in 1837; the Senate never has.

8. Ibid, p. xxix.

9. *Annals of Congress,* April 7, 1789, pp. 98–102 and April 13, 1789, pp. 121–22.

10. Sarah Binder, *Minority Rights, Majority Rule* (Cambridge University Press, 1997), pp. 8–11.

11. Woodrow Wilson, *Constitutional Government: A Study in American Politics* (New Brunswick, N.J.: Transaction Publishers, 2002; originally published by Columbia University Press, 1908), p. 56.

12. Ibid, pp. 218, 69.

13. De Alva Stanwood Alexander, *History and Procedure of the House of Representatives* (Boston and New York: Houghton Mifflin Company, 1916; BiblioLife, LLC, 2009), p. 184. Citation refers to the 2009 edition.

14. Reed, "Rules of the House of Representatives," *Century Magazine*, p. 795.

15. Binder, *Minority Rights, Majority Rule,* p. 127.

16. See Donald R. Wolfensberger, "Adopting House Rules in a New Congress: From Democratic Deliberation to Partisan Monopoly," *Congressional Record,* January 7, 1997, H-16 et seq.; also published in modified form by the Woodrow Wilson Center, January 4, 2007, and updated August 2014 (www.wilsoncenter.org/sites/default/files/rulesadoptonpaper.pdf).

17. Matthew N. Green, "Institutional Change, Party Discipline, and the House Democratic Caucus, 1911–19," *Legislative Studies Quarterly* 27, no. 4 (November, 2002), pp. 601–33.

18. As told to this author by one of those freshman Democrats.

19. For a fuller account, see Donald R. Wolfensberger, *Congress and the People: Deliberative Democracy on Trial* (Johns Hopkins University Press, 2000), pp. 86–101.

20. Richard Bolling, *Power in the House* (New York: E.P. Dutton & Co., 1968), p. 266.

21. Binder, *Minority Rights, Majority Rule,* pp. 161–64.

22. Steven S. Smith, *Call to Order: Floor Politics in the House and Senate* (Brookings Institution Press, 1989), pp. 40–45.

23. Stanley Bach and Steven S. Smith, *Managing Uncertainty in the House of Representatives: Adaptation and Innovation in Special Rules* (Brookings Institution Press, 1988), p. 57, table 3-3.

24. "Table 4. Open v. Restrictive Rules, 95th–102nd Congresses," *Congressional Record* 139, no. 1 (January 5, 1993), p. 71.

25. "Special Rules Providing for the Original Consideration of Legislation in the House, 103rd–114th Congresses (1993–2016), table 1 (http://bipartisanpolicy.org/wp-content/uploads/2013/02/House-Rules-Data.pdf).

26. For a further discussion of recent procedural devices employed by the House Rules Committee, see Megan S. Lynch and Mark J. Oleszek, "Recent

Innovations in Special Rules in the House of Representatives," in *The Evolving Congress*, Committee Print, Committee on Rules and Administration, U.S. Senate, 113th Congress, 2d Session (S. Prt. 113–30), 245 et seq.

27. Ibid, tables 2 and 5.

28. R. Eric Peterson and Lara Chausow, "Staffing Priorities in Congress: From Collective to Individualized Activities," Paper presented at the 2015 APSA Annual Meeting, San Francisco, Calif., September 3, 2015.

29. See Wolfensberger, *Congress and the People*, chapters 10 and 11, pp. 175–91.

30. "A New Direction for America" (www.washingtonpost.com/wp-srv/special/politics/political-rallying-cry/new-direction-for-america.pdf).

31. Wolfensberger, "Special Rules Providing for the Original Consideration of Legislation in the House," Bipartisan Policy Center (http://bipartisanpolicy.org/wp-content/uploads/2013/02/House-Rules-Data-114-Congress-BPC.pdf).

32. See Donald R. Wolfensberger, "The Motion to Recommit in the House: The Creation, Evisceration, and Restoration of a Minority Right" in *Party, Process and Political Change in the House: Further New Perspectives on the History of Congress*, vol. 2, edited by David W. Brady and Mathew D. McCubbins (Stanford University Press, 2007), pp. 271 et seq.

33. H. Res. 5, sec. 2(g), Adopting House Rules for the 111th Congress, January 6, 2009, p. 7.

34. John E. Owens and J. Mark Wrighton, "Partisan Polarization, Procedural Control, and Partisan Emulation in the U.S. House: An Explanation of Rules Restrictiveness Over Time," Paper Presented at the History of Congress Conference, George Washington University, May 29–June 1, 2008, unpublished paper.

35. William McKay and Charles W. Johnson, *Parliament and Congress: Representation and Scrutiny in the Twenty-First Century* (Oxford University Press, 2010), p. 8.

36. William A. Robinson, *Thomas B. Reed, Parliamentarian* (New York: Dodd, Mead and Company, 1930), p. 255.

37. Thomas B. Reed, "A Deliberative Body," *The North American Review* 152, no. 411 (February, 1891), pp. 149–53.

38. Representative John A. Boehner, "Congressional Reform and 'The People's House,'" Remarks delivered at the American Enterprise Institute, September 30, 2010 (www.aei.org/publication/congressional-reform-and-the-people-house/print).

39. Remarks of Representative Paul Ryan, *Congressional Record*, October 29, 2015, H 7339.

40. *Federalist* No. 57, p. 352.

41. See, for instance, Madison boasting in *Federalist* No. 38 that the Constitutional Convention "must have enjoyed . . . an exemption from the pestilential influence of party animosities—the disease most incident to deliberative bodies and most apt to contaminate their proceedings," yet Hamilton worrying in *Federalist* No. 1 about the likely effects of parties on the ratification debates that "noth-

ing could be more ill-judged than the intolerant spirit which has at all times characterized political parties," and which will let loose "a torrent of angry and malignant passions."

42. Some of these proposals are drawn from recommendations of the Bipartisan Policy Center's Commission on Political Reform in its report, "Governing in a Polarized America: A Bipartisan Blueprint to Strengthen Our Democracy" (http://bipartisanpolicy.org/search/Governing+in+a+Polarized+America).

43. Wolfensberger, "Special Rules Providing for the Original Consideration of Legislation in the House," Bipartisan Policy Center (http://bipartisanpolicy.org/wp-content/uploads/2013/02/House-Rules-Data-114-Congress-BPC.pdf).

6

Reclaiming Institutional Relevance through Congressional Oversight

MELANIE M. MARLOWE

Picture this—Senator Howard Baker asks, "What did the President know, and when did he know it?" in the Watergate hearings. Oliver North standing with perfect posture as he is sworn in before the House and Senate committees investigating the Iran-Contra scandal. Internal Revenue Service (IRS) official Lois Lerner says, "I have done nothing wrong," then takes the Fifth before the House Committee on Oversight and Government Reform.

These scenes from congressional oversight hearings might paint pictures of a responsible Congress that is constantly engaged in oversight, protective of the rule of law, and institutionally committed to maintaining its place in the constitutional system, but is this really the case? This chapter will look at the congressional oversight responsibility and consider its effectiveness, and will argue that strengthening this power can contribute to broader reform and revitalization of the branch as a whole. While the Framers of the Constitution did not lay out a rule for every political circumstance, and understood that the powers of each branch would increase and decrease depending on events, personality, and public opinion, they clearly expected each branch to defend its institutional prerogatives.

The examples presented at the beginning of this chapter are rather high-profile instances of Congress investigating matters of vast public importance, but adversarial hearings are just one of the ways Congress fulfills its oversight responsibilities. Oversight may take many forms. In the early stages of an inquiry,[1] members of Congress and majority and minority staff may exchange information, send letters, engage in negotiations, and take depositions. They may receive reports from inspectors general and others charged with evaluating particular aspects of government operations. They may contact executive branch officials, visit agencies, speak with constituents, and hold hearings.

The Exercise and Bases of Oversight Power

The oversight power may be exercised for a number of reasons, several of which are explained in House Rule X.[2] Congress must look at the implementation, enforcement, and effectiveness of laws and agency actions, and assess whether the executive branch is sufficiently carrying out legislative intent. It must consider the behavior of executive branch officials who are given discretion and tasked with writing rules. Congress must weigh the costs and benefits of programs, investigate fraud and mismanagement, and determine whether there are more responsible ways of providing services to the public. Members may wish to protect their constituents' favored programs from budget reduction and their personnel from criticism. Congress may also use its oversight powers to examine cooperation among federal, state, and local governments, respond to media stories, and investigate constituent complaints. It should be admitted that, in some sense, oversight powers are cumulatively used for the purpose of furthering the policy objectives of the majority.

Article I, Section 1, clause 1 of the United States Constitution gives Congress "all legislative Powers herein granted." While not a general legislative power, the authority of Congress to formulate laws and assess their effectiveness in the areas specified in Article I, Section 8 is broad.

Congress has exercised its oversight power since the earliest days of the Republic. In 1790, a select congressional committee undertook an investigation of Robert Morris to determine whether he had improperly expended public funds during his time as superintendent of finances in the Revolutionary period.[3] In 1792, Congress investigated the failed St. Clair military expedition. This episode is important because it reached questions of whether Congress could form an inquiry into a high-ranking executive official and the legitimacy of the president invoking executive privilege.

The Supreme Court has repeatedly recognized that, while the Constitution does not spell out an explicit congressional power of oversight, Congress has an inherent constitutional oversight role. In 1927, the Supreme Court took up a case involving a witness who refused to testify before a senate committee investigating the attorney general's actions in the Teapot Dome scandal.[4] The Court acknowledged that the Constitution does not specifically grant either the House or the Senate the power to hold investigations and compel testimony in furtherance of a wise legislative process, but stated that both houses have "not only such powers as are expressly granted to them by the Constitution, but such auxiliary powers as are necessary and appropriate to make the express powers effective."[5]

In *Quinn v. United States*, a case involving witnesses before the House Un-American Activities Committee, Chief Justice Warren stated: "There can be no doubt as to the power of Congress, by itself or through its committees, to investigate matters and conditions relating to contemplated legislation. This power, deeply rooted in American and English institutions, is indeed co-extensive with the power to legislate."[6]

Congress does not have broad power to force the disclosure of purely private information, but may only inquire about that which is essential to Congress fulfilling its legislative missions.[7] Congress must have information to make good laws, understand wrongdoing, and assess how the national government might be improved. Not surprisingly, Congress has passed laws supporting its oversight power,[8] including laws providing for the protection of whistleblowers[9] and creating various positions for greater financial oversight in departments and agencies.[10] Congress established the General Accounting Office in 1921 to be "independent of the executive departments" in its investigations of "all matters relating to the receipt, disbursement, and application of public funds."[11] The 1946 Legislative Reorganization Act charged standing committees to "exercise continuous watchfulness of the execution [of any laws] by the administrative agencies" and to "study all pertinent reports and data" submitted by the agencies to Congress.[12] It also established what would become the Congressional Research Service "to advise and assist [committees] in the analysis, appraisal, and evaluation of any legislative proposal."[13] The Inspector General Act of 1978 created offices of inspector general in cabinet departments, major agencies, and other prominent government bodies.[14]

House and Senate rules require all House and Senate standing committees, with the exception of the Senate Appropriations Committee, to fulfill oversight duties. The House Committee on Oversight and Government Reform (OGR) and the Senate Committee on Homeland Security and Government Affairs have particularly expansive oversight authority. For example, House Rule X provides OGR with the power to examine laws, programs, agencies, research, and forecasting. It also has power to "at any time conduct investigations of any matter. . . . Conferring jurisdiction over the matter to another standing committee,"[15] and the chair of OGR may issue subpoenas without the backing of a majority of the committee members.

The oversight power has been recognized by the executive branch: "It is beyond dispute that Congress may conduct investigations in order to obtain facts pertinent to possible legislation and in order to evaluate the effectiveness of current laws."[16] The power has also been conceded, to some degree, in the area of foreign affairs.[17] However, it has been argued that congressional oversight of solely executive powers, such as vetoes and pardons, would go beyond the scope of Congress's legitimate oversight authority.[18]

History has demonstrated that the branches of government do not always agree on how the oversight function is carried out in particular cases. But all three branches have confirmed that, on some level, Congress needs information to properly fulfill its constitutionally mandated legislative role; therefore, the constitutional structure must provide support for this power.

Tools of Congressional Oversight

We generally think of oversight as adversarial congressional investigations, and much of it is. Congressional hearings have become a favorite way for members to call attention to matters of public concern. In the last half-century, the expansion of the administrative state, a divided government, and the rise of television have all contributed to the increased use of hearings to conduct oversight.

When information is not forthcoming or witnesses are evasive or simply will not answer questions, the threat of a subpoena or an actual subpoena may be issued to force compliance. On occasions when an individual continues to refuse to give requested information to Congress, even when that material has been legally subpoenaed, Congress may cite that person for contempt in three different ways. Under Congress's inherent contempt power, the sergeant-at-arms of either the House or Senate may collect that individual, who is then tried before the corresponding house and, if found to be in contempt, may suffer the punishment of imprisonment. The time may be unspecified—until he complies with the subpoena—or for a particular period. In 1821 the Supreme Court agreed that this power was necessary to protect Congress from being exposed to every indignity and interruption that rudeness, caprice, or even conspiracy, may mediate against it."[19] The inherent contempt power was used at least eighty-five times between 1795 and 1934, but it has not been used since, possibly because of the burden of holding a congressional trial.

As an alternative to the inherent contempt power, in 1857 Congress enacted a statutory criminal contempt procedure.[20] This power makes failure to testify or produce documents under subpoena, or failure to completely answer questions, a misdemeanor with a maximum punishment of $100,000 fine and one year in prison. The contempt citation must be supported by a majority of the committee and of the entire House or Senate. Once the citation has been verified by the House Speaker or President of the Senate, the U.S. Attorney has a "duty" to submit the matter to a grand jury.[21] However, the U.S. Attorney, who works on behalf of the executive branch, may decline to do so, thus exposing a weakness of the statutory criminal contempt method that requires participation from all three branches. From the time of its passage until 1935 it was almost never invoked, but in the last eighty years has become the dominant means of punishing contempt.

Both Houses have established methods of civil enforcement of subpoenas involving federal courts. In 2014 Attorney General Eric Holder was held in contempt of Congress for refusing to turn over documents related to the Fast and Furious gun-trafficking matter, and the House voted to file suit against him in federal district court.[22] The action against Holder was the first time Congress had used this power against a sitting member of the cabinet.[23] Because the civil contempt method does not require participation by the executive branch, it has become a favored way for Congress to assert its oversight prerogatives against members of that branch.

Congress has other means of exercising its oversight authority. The appropriations power may be a formidable weapon to inspire cooperation. It may increase funding to an institute or force an agency division to make across-the-board cuts. Legislative authorizations can be an important tool for coercing compliance with oversight activity. This may include threatening to eliminate a position, alter the job description, relocate a departmental program to another agency, or cut a program altogether.

Congress has some constitutional authority over who will make up the executive branch. The Senate has the clear constitutional power to advise and consent to presidential nominations. Senators regularly hold up confirmation proceedings as a way of extracting information from the executive branch, even in nominations that are only tangentially related to the oversight target. Article II, S. 2 of the Constitution authorizes Congress to grant the president, courts, or department heads appointment power over "inferior officers."

The House may impeach and the Senate may remove executive branch officials who are guilty of "high Crimes and Misdemeanors."[24] While the meaning of "high Crimes and Misdemeanors" is debated, precedent set in the Watergate investigation affirms that failure to fully comply with an oversight investigation may give cause for impeachment. The third article of impeachment charged that: "Richard M. Nixon, substituting his judgment as to what materials were necessary for the inquiry, interposed the powers of the Presidency against the lawful subpoenas of the House of Representatives, thereby assuming to himself functions and judgments necessary to the exercise of the sole power of impeachment vested by the Constitution in the House of Representatives."[25]

While it should not be used except in cases of overwhelming political necessity, the impeachment and removal process is a legitimate oversight tool in appropriate circumstances.

What Is the Problem with Oversight Today?

The lack of proper oversight today is a problem of the administrative state. While Congress has the authority and tools, already discussed, to press for compliance in its oversight activities, the size, scope, and diffuse nature of government power and decision-making make it impossible for Congress to grasp what is going on in a coherent and productive way. Broad delegations of power go to an assortment of agencies. These delegations and their attending money, personnel, and discretion have reduced Congress's influence in the political system and increased the executive's. The *Federal Register* puts the number of agencies at 438[26] and notes an increase of about 160 major final rules during 2013–14.[27]

This author admits to being a partisan of the presidency and one who subscribes to the view that Article II of the Constitution grants all executive power to the president. The president's authority might be more open-ended than Congress's is, but it is not limitless, and he or she is required by oath to take care that the laws are faithfully executed.[28] The Framers intended a Congress that makes laws and a president who enforces them and acts in certain areas while administering the government. But they expected the members of the branches to have institutional jealousy and to protect and even attempt to enlarge their powers. As long as other institutional actors would push back against constitutional usurpations of power, political power might settle around the strongest public claims. It is interesting to note that by 1787, the Framers were concerned with legislative tyranny, not executive, expressing anxiety that "The legislative department is everywhere extending the sphere of its activity and drawing all power into its impetuous vortex."[29] In our case, however, Congress has been complicit in its own irrelevance, permitting and even inviting executive encroachment on its constitutional authority and preventing it from possessing substantive political influence. Let's look at a few recent examples of this.

One week after the terrorist attacks on September 11, 2001, Congress passed, and President Bush signed, the Authorization for the Use of Military Force.[30] At a time when opinion among both the public and political leaders was fraught with concern about the possibility of more attacks on U.S. soil, Congress authorized President Bush "to use all necessary and appropriate force against those nations, organizations, or persons he determines planned, authorized, committed, or aided the terrorist attacks that occurred on September 11, 2001, or harbored such organizations or persons, in order to prevent any future acts of international terrorism against the United States by such nations, organizations or persons." The law gives blanket authority to the president to assess who should be punished, when, and where, and has no sunset provision for this power. In the last fifteen years, this law has been the basis for the detention of suspected terrorists at Guantanamo Bay, drone strikes all over the Middle East, and hunting Islamic State terrorists in Syria and Libya in 2016. Although Congress may pass future legislation repealing the AUMF, it is unlikely to do so, and it is improbable that a president would sign such a restriction absent another authorization granting essentially the same powers.

The 2400-page Dodd–Frank bill, passed as a response to the financial crisis of 2008–09, provides a glaring example of Congress ceding its constitutional authority to an unaccountable bureaucracy.[31] The Consumer Financial Protection Bureau (CFPB), created in Title X of the act, is established as a bureau of the Federal Reserve. The act provides for a director appointed by the president and confirmed by the Senate. The director's term is five years, during which he or she may be removed only for cause, such as malfeasance in office or dereliction of duty. Because the CFPB's budget is an allocation of about 12 percent of the operating expenditures of the Fed (almost $600 million in 2013), there is little oversight by either Congress or the Federal Reserve. Federal courts are required to grant *Chevron* deference[32] to the CFPB's interpretation of relevant laws, and other agencies are bound by CFPB's interpretations as well. CFPB regulations are not reviewable by the Office of Management and Budget. The CFPB may regulate any item or product it considers to be "unfair, deceptive, or abusive," but "abusive" is nowhere defined and provides a roving warrant for bureau action. Only a two-thirds vote by the Financial Stability Oversight Commission may overturn a CFPB determination, and that is only if the action might affect the stability of the national financial system.

As part of the Patient Protection and Affordable Care Act of 2010 (PPACA),[33] Congress created the Independent Payment and Advisory Board (IPAB), which is tasked with managing (and even cutting) Medicare spending. The fifteen-member board will be appointed by the president and confirmed by the Senate. Board members may initially serve two six-year terms, but if there is not a successor to a seat, that member may continue in the position indefinitely. In some instances, the Secretary of Health and Human Services may act unilaterally on behalf of the board and appropriate funds for the board. The PPACA funds the IPAB in perpetuity, so there is no need to return to Congress to ask for funding. Unbelievably, Congress wrote the law so as to prevent itself from repealing it in the case that circumstances or popular sentiment so indicated; Congress may only rescind IPAB if it does so in the form of a joint resolution introduced between January 1 and February 1, 2017, and passed by a three-fifths vote of all members of both the House and Senate by August 15, 2017. The law also states "The Secretary shall" more than one thousand times, providing hundreds of opportunities for the Secretary of Health and Human Services to make policy determinations that are not subject to popular approval. The PPACA prohibits courts from reviewing the Secretary's implementation of IPAB recommendations.

These provisions are but a few of the many clear examples of Congress acting contrary to James Madison's expressed intentions. In both instances, public officials saw a real crisis and assumed that the best way to combat those problems was to set aside the constitutional obstacles to action and give government an unrivaled range of power and independence. In the name of good government and independence, Congress willingly gave away its essential constitutional power—that of *making laws*—to the president himself and executive branch bureaucracies. The ambition of one branch is no longer counteracting the ambition of another. Instead of forcing ongoing democratic deliberation and providing opportunities for improved services through a public competition of ideas, these anti-constitutional laws invite and entrench pressure from special interests and increase the risks of arbitrary policy. Vast bureaucracies of unelected, tenured officials have broad discretion to make policies that will have deep and lasting impacts on the lives of American citizens in very personal ways. It may be safe to say that most of these bureaucrats have good intentions and, possibly, expertise regarding their responsibilities. But that does not overcome the constitutional safeguards that protect each branch's prerogatives and individual liberty.

Although many in and outside of government might believe the president legitimately exercises more independent authority in national security matters, Congress, in passing the Authorization for the Use of Military Force, made it very difficult politically to make a case that the president had exceeded statutory authority in his decisions. Although courts eventually stepped in to curb executive power, Congress had demonstrated reluctance to be responsible for war powers. In the last two pieces of legislation, not to mention other bills, Congress ceded its own confirmation, budget, legislative, and oversight responsibilities. Congress did that. Congress eliminated the constitutional process for legislative action. It invited encroachment and facilitated its own irrelevance.

The inability or unwillingness of Congress to legislate clearly has also given openings for presidents (and their subordinates) to act on their own, with the stroke of a pen, in a number of policy areas. In just the last few years, President Obama raised the minimum wage federal contractors must pay those who work for them.[34] He signed an order allowing children who entered the United States illegally to remain without threat of deportation and with work rights,[35] and later approved another initiative protecting another four million adults from deportation.[36] His Clean Power Plan is designed to increase the use of solar and wind energy while dramatically cutting coal-fired electricity.[37]

While not contesting here the wisdom, popularity, or legality of the president's actions, the fact is that they have enormous financial costs in both the public and private sectors. They may affect due process and other rights of individuals. They certainly have great political consequences on the national, state, and local levels. The public deliberation and transparency required for democratic governance are largely missing. People who make most of the laws affecting ordinary Americans are unelected and anonymous. If something goes wrong, with the exception of perhaps a Lois Lerner, we don't know who did it.

Our national policy has expanded from economic to civil rights, to health and safety, and to what might be called lifestyle rights. There is virtually no area of life that is not under the watch of a member of an executive bureaucracy. We have gone from accepting only legislation laws enacted by Congress as binding, to recognizing formal rules submitted by agency heads and guidance letters issued by lower-level bureaucrats. By the time regulations are planned and implemented, Congress can only react in ways that may produce neither the most thoughtful reflection on public policy nor the will to make substantive changes. The time for deliberation is past. The diffusion of serious policymaking responsibility in dozens of agencies and among hundreds or thousands of individuals is not consistent with able oversight.

How Congress May Begin to Regain Its Proper Oversight Role

Congress has reduced its own power at the same time it has enlarged the scope and power of the presidency. Because bureaucratic size and interests have been developing for decades, it is unrealistic to think that a proper balance will be restored in the near future. But Congress already has sufficient constitutional and political means at its disposal to reclaim some of its proper oversight authority, if it chooses to do so. It will not be easy, because the Congress is divided between parties and within the parties themselves, and these remedies require a strong measure of institutional unity. Focusing on small steps that aim toward the larger goal of institutional strength is a good and necessary start.

Legislative ameliorations to the problem of congressional irresponsibility include the Congressional Review Act (CRA), a current law that permits Congress to disapprove "major" proposed and final rules (in this case meaning regulations that have an annual economic impact of more than $100 million). The problem with relying on the CRA is evident when one understands it has been successfully employed only once, in 1996. It is highly unlikely, especially in an era of divided government, that both houses of Congress and the president will come together again anytime soon. In addition, as a defensive rather than offensive measure, it is an ineffective way for Congress to reclaim its power. It simply allows Congress a place on the sidelines, and does little to encourage it to affirmatively resist encroachments on its legislative power.

A second possible legislative remedy is the Regulations from the Executive in Need of Scrutiny (REINS) Act, a rather awkwardly titled bill passed most recently by the House of Representatives in July 2015.[38] If signed into law, Congress would be required to affirmatively endorse all major regulations before they could go into effect. Because REINS would require congressional approval and not simply acquiescence before rules were binding, it would be preferable to the CRA from constitutional and democratic perspectives. However, the chances that it will gain the signature of a president or pass Congress over a president's veto are essentially zero.

If Congress wants to reassert its oversight authority, it must begin by making laws.

Congress must reduce delegations of authority to executive departments, agencies, and independent boards. Today, Congress passes good ideas and leaves it to the executive branch to fill in the details. Members of Congress don't want the hard work of policymaking when they see that constituent service and fundraising are more likely to perpetuate their terms than are reading reports and taking sides. Policymaking means accountability for consequences, explanations for not choosing alternatives, and, sometimes, making winners and losers out of constituents and donors. Delegating the lawmaking power means members can take credit for the good and shift the blame for the bad. Members should engage in the process of governing and write laws that limit the discretion and deference given to the executive branch. By so doing, they could provide standards for committee evaluation and language for courts to draw on when interpretations are challenged. Congress might also consider clearly defining terms in law and adding sunset provisions where possible. Acting on the front end of the legislative process means fewer agency actions to review and a less-dispersed administrative apparatus to keep track of.

This is not an argument for eliminating all executive discretion in policymaking, but it is one designed to refortify the legislative branch, especially against the executive. It is acknowledged that at least initially this probably means a legislative process that is slower and less ambitious than the policymaking we see today. This is not necessarily bad; paraphrasing the words of Alexander Hamilton, it's better to not pass good laws than it is to pass bad ones. It becomes virtually impossible to claw your way back to prelegislation conditions.[39]

Congress must reclaim its power over the national budget.

For the last several decades, Congress's fiscal irresponsibility has handed the executive branch great power and autonomy. High levels of borrowing and spending have permitted vast expansion of the administrative state. Failure to pass a budget, deficit and spending caps, and attempts to give the president various forms of a line-item veto are all examples of a Congress insufficiently interested in its power. Madison noted in *Federalist* No. 58 that "this power over the purse may, in fact, be regarded as the most complete and effectual weapon with which any constitution can arm the immediate representatives of the people, for obtaining a redress of every grievance, and for carrying into effect every just and salutary measure."[40] The fact that the bills' supporters were so insistent on removing CFPB and IPAB from the regular appropriations process provides great support to Madison's view. Why would they have worked so hard to do this? It is because once funding is no longer subject to review by another branch, there is very little that can be done to restrain those who exercise the relevant power.

In *Federalist* No. 78, Hamilton pointed out the great strength of the legislative branch is that it "commands the purse,"[41] and noted in *Federalist* No. 79 that "a power over a man's subsistence amounts to a power over his will."[42] Once Congress has given an entity an independent stream of income, serious accountability evaporates. While other agencies' budgets may not be as secure as those described here, when there is no perceptible threat of reduction or elimination, proper behavior is more difficult to obtain. Congress has also permitted entitlements to consume such a large share of the federal budget that there is little discussion and ranking of national priorities.

Congress should take seriously its authority over the terms and tenure of executive officials.

This includes both the confirmation and removal processes. As we saw in the CFPB and IPAB cases, while appointments to those boards are initially confirmed, terms may be indefinite. When there are vacancies, whether by Congress's refusal to confirm or the president's refusal to appoint, authority reverts to the executive branch. A cynical observer might wonder if a president would purposefully let nominations slip by the wayside to have a direct subordinate (such as the Secretary of Health and Human Services) formulating policy that would be nearly impossible to be overturned.

It is too much to hope that Congress will stop creating independent boards and commissions. As long as it continues to do so, making shorter terms and demanding (perhaps by refusing appropriations) that only those confirmed to those positions may exercise policymaking authority would at least be a step in the right constitutional direction. Congress might also work with the executive branch on legislation to reduce the number of positions that are required to be confirmed by the Senate. Although this might appear to be excessively deferential to the president, this proposal, along with Congress's reassertion of its legislative power, would mean less diffuse accountability from the executive branch and would provide more time for senators to fully vet the nominations of those with the most public authority.

Congress might also specify more clearly reasons for removal, and not be afraid to use its impeachment and removal powers in appropriate circumstances. Doing so would send a signal that might encourage good behavior and interdepartmental cooperation.

The impeachment and removal process is a serious one and should not be undertaken except in cases of extraordinarily clear and belligerent intransigence. It takes the place of the president's removal power when used against executive branch officials, and overturns the will of the people when the targets are the president or vice president. It is a time-consuming and energy-sapping process that has high political costs, especially for the losing branch. However, it is a constitutional process put in place by people who understood it to be a necessary feature of a peaceful and competent regime.

In early September 2015, Representative Paul Gosar (R-Ariz.), initiated a resolution calling for the impeachment of Gina McCarthy, the administrator of the EPA.[43] Gosar, a member of the House Committee on Oversight and Government Reform, charged her with lying during the previous seven months when she testified about the creation of a rule expanding the

EPA's ability to regulate waterways. "Administrator McCarthy committed perjury and made several false statements at multiple congressional hearings, and as a result, is guilty of high crimes and misdemeanors—an impeachable offense."

The IRS was also in the crosshairs of congressional Republicans. In the ongoing investigation into whether or not that agency illegally targeted conservative organizations in the run-up to the 2012 election, John Koskinen, the IRS Commissioner, has testified at several hearings before various committees. Republican members of Congress sent President Obama a thirty-page letter demanding that he fire Mr. Koskinen, accusing him of obstructing congressional investigations and misleading Congress as they questioned him about missing emails and other "lost" documents.[44] In June 2016, OGR voted, along party lines, to censure Koskinen.[45] Representative Jason Chaffetz, Chairman of OGR, has indicated that impeachment of Koskinen was being considered.[46]

Though not without political risks, impeachment and removal are legitimate weapons in Congress's arsenal. If used in appropriate circumstances, they may serve as a threat and an inducement to proper behavior.

Congress must regain control of hearings.

Congress uses hearings as an effective way to educate themselves and the public on policy matters and to hold executive branch officials accountable for ongoing and future actions. While hearings have not always been common or even noticed events,[47] today congressional hearings may be the most visible public means of oversight. Unfortunately, oversight hearings are in a sorry state today. They are filled with testy exchanges as members of Congress repeatedly scream questions at flustered and sometimes evasive and petulant witnesses. Committee members don't show up for hearings and chairs are unable to force members to be present. Members come late and ask questions that have already been put to the witnesses by other members. Members forego serious preparation and are obviously unfamiliar not only with their personal statements and questions for witnesses, but sometimes even the specific topic as well. Members use their question time to further a campaign strategy, not to elicit information for legislative evaluation. The usefulness of the hearing to raise a member's or party's short-term visibility takes precedence over demonstrating a long-term capacity to govern. Too many hearings, especially by several committees on the same subject, may make them less compelling and less substantive.

The rise of television and social media, including YouTube, has created an atmosphere where the public relations aspect of an issue is more important than understanding the policy substance. In an age where all information is for immediate public consumption, it becomes difficult for members of Congress to honestly acquire and assess information. For example, in 2013 OGR undertook a lengthy evaluation of the Social Security Disability Insurance (SSDI) program, which is in dire financial straits. If changes are not made to the program immediately, benefits will be cut. This is a fiscal reality that members of both political parties understand. However, garnering member support for even modest alterations in the SSDI program was impossible to secure. Concerns of media reports of wheelchair-bound citizens storming the halls of Congress in opposition to any SSDI changes effectively preempted the possibility of legislative changes that might have saved full benefits for those who are truly in need.

In January 2013, the House Committee on Foreign Affairs held a hearing on the September 11, 2012, attacks on the U.S. Consulate in Benghazi, Libya.[48] While the hearing could have been an occasion for Congress to find out what happened in Libya that evening, what administration officials there and in United States did at that time and in subsequent weeks, what may have led to a breakdown in security at the consulate, and how to prevent attacks like this in the future, it most certainly was not. Committee Democrats used their time to praise the accomplishments of the sole witness, former Secretary of State Hillary Clinton, and express gratitude for her work. Instead of asking direct questions that required a direct response, most Committee Republicans used almost all their time for making political statements about the failure of the administration to adequately protect the four Americans who lost their lives there, and to condemn officials for blaming an anti-Islam video for inspiring the attacks. The few who did ask questions simply repeated ones that had already been asked. Questions were asked so quickly that Clinton was able to evade responding to many of them.

Chairs are relatively weak, compared to those of three or more decades ago. This is particularly true in the Republican Party, where a seniority system has given way to term limits. Thus, chairs have little direct authority over individual members and cannot compel attendance at hearings, let alone write the questions for individual members or force the committee to adhere to a unified theme. Maintaining a seniority system, at least for OGR, might have far-reaching effects in terms of member education and contributions in policy and style. The more frequently members are exposed to the hearing atmosphere, the more likely they are to get a sense for what a successful hearing would be, including how to treat witnesses and how to get meaningful responses from them.

The failure of committee members to attend hearings indicates that other things—such as constituent service, fundraising, and travel home—are prioritized over governing. Hearings should not be held simply to advertise outrage at executive branch wrongdoing. Consistent with the purposes of oversight described above, hearings should be held to monitor ongoing executive branch activities and to make suggestions for legislation. If initial hearings on a particular policy can be held in a bipartisan fashion, even knowing that as particulars are developed the majority and minority will become more divided, so much the better for substance and appearance.

Whether one likes it or not, congressional hearings are an important instrument in Congress's oversight toolbox. Calling for hearings at the beginning of the legislative process is an especially essential step in Congress reclaiming its constitutional authority. Committees have a responsibility to move beyond the superficial style currently employed in holding hearings and move to a model in which substance and coherence are key.

Congress must invest in the professionalization of its members and staffs.

Executive branch employees frequently have specialized degrees or particular skills that lead to their jobs. They have time to develop greater expertise as they consistently work on issues related to their field. They have civil service protection and good benefits, which provide strong incentives to remain in the bureaucracy.

Members of Congress are not tenured. They must fundraise and campaign relentlessly. They sit on many committees and subcommittees, each covering its own particular slice of the national policy pie. While there may be some overlap in policy jurisdiction, the ultimate aims, personalities, and processes of each committee vary, so information may not be directly applicable across them. They may use four days a week traveling to and from home, working in the district office on constituent issues, but not boning up on the deeper and long-term aspects of policy that is incredibly complex legally, technologically, and socially.

Staff members are often young. They have little institutional memory. They are assigned several policy issues and may be familiar with them only superficially—possibly whatever a Google search might turn up—and temporarily, until they pick up the next file. The information they transfer to their bosses is often similarly paltry, so unless they are highly motivated, their knowledge is also low and temporary. They move from office to office regularly, are not paid well,[49] and live in one of the most expensive cities in the United States.

After nearly tripling congressional policy support in the 1970s, 1980 marked the beginning of Congress cutting back, including at the General Accounting Office and the Congressional Research Service. Today, there are 20 percent fewer staffers in those offices than there were in 1979. The number of federal bureaucrats has decreased about 10 percent during a similar period. But in the last few decades, the number of lobbyists, interest groups with a presence in Washington, and think tanks employing private policy analysts rose exponentially.[50] When information deficiencies are recognized, policymakers have turned with more regularity to these elite organizations to supply them with expertise and help raise their profiles.

How can Congress compete with an executive branch of full-time tenured experts and a private sector that provides high salaries and generous perks? Congress must invest in itself. Instead of cutting back staff and poorly paying those it has, expert staff should earn salaries (but not perks) that are competitive with mid-level, private policymaking opportunities in the D.C. area. Lower pay is probably appropriate for younger, more transient employees who focus on constituent service. Committee staff numbers should be increased and more emphasis should be placed on staff working directly with members who should not be the policy amateurs they often are. Hiring and retaining capable personnel who have experience and institutional memory is essential to the long-term effectiveness of Congress. It is admitted that this will be a hard sell for members to make to the American people, especially in a time when the public is feeling severe economic pressure, but it is a case that should be made.

Strengthen committees by allowing effective chairs to retain their positions. Those who are doing a good job shouldn't be forced out because of a time limit. Experienced, professional chairs who can take a long view of oversight and governing should be kept. This might also help with staff knowledge and retention, since the turnover that usually accompanies a change of chair would be reduced. This is especially valuable when cordial working relationships between the majority and minority have been developed.

Congress should increase the funding of its support organizations, including the Congressional Research Service, the Congressional Budget Office, and the Government Accountability Office. When members and staffs don't have internal information, they must look outside the halls of Congress. Lobbyists frequently provide the services congressional support agencies are too poorly staffed to offer. This might provide a connection that is welcome by both parties, but it is too often one in which the public interest takes a back seat to private opportunity. Clearly there is reluctance by members of Congress to have their proposals scored and possibly negative reports issued. But it could tend toward honesty and forthrightness in legislation.

Conclusion

In the current administrative state, effective legislative oversight is nearly impossible. An entrenched and byzantine executive branch with diffuse responsibilities and little immediate accountability, combined with unprofessional committees, weak leadership, and low policy interest in Congress, create conditions for confusion, not clarity.

The executive is partially at fault. Presidents interpret regulations and their discretion in the largest possible sense. The more the government acts, the more citizens and interest groups expect, and the more pressure is put on government to do something more. The executive suggests it and Congress subsequently funds it.

Federal courts also bear some responsibility for the decline in congressional power. By deferring to agency interpretations of rules as long as they are at all reasonable, courts are abdicating their responsibility to use independent judgment. One might feel some sympathy with courts that are reluctant to interfere in policymaking without clear legislative standards and definitions.

As much as possible, Congress must reclaim its oversight role at the front end of the legislative process, not in post-action sniping. While Congress has various ways to compel testimony and investigate wrongdoing, its efforts would be well spent on the hard work of writing tighter, clearer laws, thereby holding the executive branch and itself to higher standards, and becoming more professional. If Congress wants to be taken seriously, it must behave seriously. Although it's a long game, institutional relevance can only be regained through proper constitutional steps.

Notes

1. While members of Congress may independently engage in what might be called oversight activities (such as reading reports, assessing the effectiveness of legislation, and communicating with agency officials on behalf of constituents), we are generally concerned here with oversight undertaken by congressional committees.

2. John V. Sullivan, "Jefferson's *Manual* and Rules of the House of Representatives," Rule X(4)(c)(1) (Washington, D.C.: Government Printing Office, 2011), p. 491 (www.gpo.gov/fdsys/pkg/HMAN-112/pdf/HMAN-112.pdf).

3. "Investigations and Oversight" (http://history.house.gov/Institution/Origins-Development/Investigations-Oversight).

4. *McGrain v. Daugherty*, 273 U.S. 135, 161 (1927).

5. Ibid.

6. 349 U.S. 155, 160 (1955).

7. *McGrain v. Daugherty*, 273 U.S. 135, 173 (1927).

8. For a comprehensive overview, see Alissa Dolan and others, *Congressional Oversight Manual* (CRS Report RL30240) (Washington, D.C.: Congressional Research Service, 2014), pp. 6–10 (www.fas.org/sgp/crs/misc/RL30240.pdf).

9. Ibid., 6.

10. *Chief Financial Officers Act of 1990*, Public Law 101-576, *U.S. Statutes at Large* 107 (1990), p. 2838.

11. *1921 Budget and Accounting Act*, Public Law 67-13, *U.S. Statutes at Large* 42 (1921), pp. 23, 26.

12. Public Law 79-601 *U.S. Statutes at Large 60* (1946), p. 832.

13. Ibid., p. 836.

14. U.S. Code 5 (1978), Appendix 3.

15. Jefferson's *Manual*, p. 492.

16. Ralph W. Tarr, "Memorandum Opinion for the Attorney General," March 22, 1985, p. 60 (www.justice.gov/sites/default/files/olc/opinions/1985/03/31/op-olc-v009-p0060.pdf). This memo made clear, however, that in the administration's view, Congress could not carry out oversight investigations "for the purpose of managing Executive Branch agencies or for directing the manner in which the Executive Branch interprets and executes the laws."

17. Gerald R. Ford, "Special Message to the Congress Proposing Legislation to Reform the United States Foreign Intelligence Community," February 18, 1976 (www.fordlibrarymuseum.gov/library/speeches/760110.asp).

18. Gordon Crovitz, "Congressional Control of the Administration of Government: Hearings, Investigations, Oversight, and Legislative History," *Washington Law Review* 68 (1990), p. 600.

19. *Anderson v. Dunn*, 19 U.S. 204, 228 (1821).

20. U.S. Code 2 (2012), s. 192.

21. Ibid., s. 194.

22. House Committee on Oversight and Government Reform, *U.S. House of Representatives v. Holder*, 973 F. Supp. 2d 1 (D.D.C. 2013).

23. John Bresnahan and Seung Min Kim, "Holder Held in Contempt," *Politico*, June 28, 2012 (www.politico.com/story/2012/06/holder-held-in-contempt-of-congress-077988).

24. U.S. Const. art. II, S. 4.

25. H.R. Reports No. 93-1305 (1973), p. 4.

26. See www.federalregister.gov/agencies.

27. U.S. Library of Congress, Congressional Research Service, *Counting Regulations: An Overview of Rulemaking, Types of Federal Regulations, and Pages in the* Federal Register, by Maeve P. Carey, R43056 (2015), p. 8 (https://fas.org/sgp/crs/misc/R43056.pdf). The 113th Congress enacted 296 laws. Bills by Final Status, govtrack.us (www.govtrack.us/congress/bills/statistics).

28. U.S. Constitution art. II, s 1, cl. 8.

29. *Federalist* No. 48, in *The Federalist Papers*, edited by Clinton Rossiter (New York: Signet, 2003), p. 306.

30. "Joint Resolution to authorize the use of United States Armed Forces against those responsible for the recent attacked launched against the United States," Public Law 107-40, *U.S. Statutes at Large* 115 (2002), p. 224.

31. *Dodd–Frank Wall Street Reform and Consumer Protection Act*, U.S. Code 12 (2010).

32. *Chevron* deference is a principle of administrative law that compels courts to yield to government agencies' interpretations of ambiguous statutes, except in cases where the interpretation is unreasonable (defined as "arbitrary, capricious, or manifestly contrary to the statute"). As long as the interpretation is reasonable, a court may not prefer another reasonable or better agency judgment. The principle was established in *Chevron USA, Inc. v. National Resources Defense Council, Inc.*, 467 US 837 (1984).

33. *Patient Protection and Affordable Care Act*, U.S. Code 42 (2011).

34. Reid J. Epstein, "Obama Signs Minimum Wage Order," *Politico*, February 12, 2014 (www.politico.com/story/2014/02/miniumum-wage-executive-order-barack-obama-103450).

35. Julia Preston and John H. Cushman Jr., "Obama to Permit Young Migrants to Remain in U.S.," *New York Times*, June 15, 2012 (www.nytimes.com/2012/06/16/us/us-to-stop-deporting-some-illegal-immigrants.html).

36. Justin Sink, "Obama's Sweeping Action on Immigration," *The Hill*, November 20, 2014 (http://thehill.com/homenews/administration/224930-obama-to-protect-5-million-illegal-immigrants).

37. Jeff Mason and Valerie Volcovici, "Obama Issues Challenge on Climate Change with Power Plant Rule," *Reuters*, August 11, 2015 (www.reuters.com/article/2015/08/11/us-usa-climatechange-idUSKCN0Q820I20150811).

38. Neil Seifring, "The REINS Act Will Keep Regulations and Their Costs in Check," *The Hill*, August 4, 2015 (http://thehill.com/blogs/pundits-blog/economy-budget/250178-the-reins-act-will-keep-regulations-and-their-costs-in).

39. "The injury which may possibly be done by defeating a few good laws, will be amply compensated by the advantage of preventing a number of bad ones." *Federalist* No. 73, p. 442.

40. *Federalist* No. 58, p. 357.

41. *Federalist* No. 78, p. 464.

42. *Federalist* No. 79, p. 471.

43. H. Res. Impeaching Regina McCarthy, Administrator of the United States Environmental Protection Agency, for High Crimes and Misdemeanors, 114th Cong., 1st sess., 2015 (http://gosar.house.gov/sites/gosar.house.gov/files/Text%20of%20Legislation%20to%20Impeach%20EPA%20Administrator%20McCarthy.pdf).

44. Letter from Jason Chaffetz, Chairman, Committee on Oversight and Government Reform, to President Obama, July 27, 2015 (https://oversight.house.gov/wp-content/uploads/2015/07/2015-07-27-JC-to-Obama-WH-Koskinen-Resignation.pdf).

45. Laura Litvan, "House Committee Votes to Censure U.S. IRS Chief Koskinen," *Bloomberg.com*, June 15, 2016 (http://www.bloomberg.com/politics/articles/2016-06-15/irs-chief-faces-rare-censure-vote-by-u-s-house-committee).

46. Charles S. Clark, "House Oversight Republicans Call for IRS Chief's Head," *Government Executive*, July 27, 2015 (www.govexec.com/oversight/2015/07/house-oversight-republicans-call-irs-chiefs-head/118636).

47. Lance Cole and Stanley Brand, *Congressional Investigations and Oversight* (Durham: Carolina Academic Press, 2011), chapter 1.

48. House Committee on Foreign Affairs hearing on Benghazi, *The Secretary of State's View*, 113th Cong., 1st sess., 2013 (http://foreignaffairs.house.gov/hearing/terrorist-attack-benghazi-secretary-state%E2%80%99s-view).

49. Lee Drutman and Steven Teles, "Why Congress Relies on Lobbyists Instead of Thinking for Itself," *The Atlantic*, March 10, 2015 (www.theatlantic.com/politics/archive/2015/03/when-congress-cant-think-for-itself-it-turns-to-lobbyists/387295).

50. Ibid.

The Other End of Pennsylvania Avenue

GARY J. SCHMITT AND REBECCA BURGESS

A core tenet of courses in American government and civics, repeated from elementary school through college, and generation after generation, is that the Framers of the U.S. Constitution intended to create three equal branches of government. But for the past five decades the charge has regularly been made that the constitutional system is out of whack—that one end of Pennsylvania Avenue is far more powerful than intended or expected, that the federal government is dominated by an "imperial presidency."

That this charge has been leveled against presidents of both parties does not, of course, prove it is true; partisanship may generate claims that exaggerate or color the facts. However, it is also the case that the persistence of such claims across time and administrations suggests there may be more here than mere party politics. Even self-interested partisans need some ties to reality if they are going to convince the majority of their claims.

The fact that the first branch of government has slipped in relative importance to the executive branch may be easy to see today, but understanding why the phenomenon persists requires examining the various core elements that have given rise to it and maintain it. A congressional reform agenda intended to redress the balance of power, or, short of that, enhance those legislative capacities that make the current order more responsible and effective, will need to take account of why the governing system has evolved as it has.

Seeds of an Imperial Executive

Not surprising, the great analyst of the American regime, Alexis de Tocqueville, provides a road map for understanding the rise of the imperial presidency in his first volume of *Democracy in America* (1835), even though he wrote at a time when, for the three preceding decades, American presidents had been anything but imperial.[1]

In discussing the American chief executive Tocqueville begins by comparing the powers of the U.S. president with those "of a king in one of the constitutional monarchies of Europe" and, in particular, comparing the American office with that of the king of France. Setting the formal authorities side-by-side, Tocqueville makes what appears to be the obvious point that "the executive power is less strong in America." But he then immediately notes that "one must attribute the cause of it perhaps more to circumstances than laws."

Tocqueville's point is that, at the time, the federal government's dominant concerns were domestic. If that should change, so would the relative sway of the presidency, since "it is principally in relations with foreigners that the executive power of a nation finds occasion to deploy its skill and force." Indeed, he goes on to make the startling comment that "the president of the United States possesses almost royal prerogatives which he has no occasion to make use of." Properly understood, and contrary to our first impression, Tocqueville concludes "the laws permit him to be strong, circumstances keep him weak."

The potential for a more powerful chief executive, however, is not simply tied to whether or not the country undertakes or is forced to undertake a more active role in world affairs. Tocqueville notes that the French monarchy's authority is enhanced because the government in Paris is sovereign over all of France. At the time of *Democracy in America*'s publication, its author could still write that "sovereignty in the United States is divided between the Union and the states," hence, the president's writ "is limited and exceptional, like the sovereignty in whose name it acts." In contrast, "in France," the executive authority "extends to everything just like the sovereignty." But what if the division of governance in the United States is continually reduced in favor of the federal government over that of the states, as has happened? Doesn't the executive sphere, in administrating that expanded federal power, grow commensurately as well?

Finally, Tocqueville visited the United States at a time of transition in the American political order. Specifically, his travels to the United States coincided with the election of Andrew Jackson to the White House and the ascendency of national party politics. Presidents were no longer simply constitutional officers whose authorities and duties were defined by the specifics of Article II. "Energy in the executive" now had a second source, one more closely aligned with the general public through a specific party. As Tocqueville notes, instead of the presidential selection process producing an executive capable of resisting the tide of simple majoritarian politics, the growth of party politics turns that system on its head. It leads to what we might today refer to as a national mandate or, in Tocqueville's words, an election process intended to show by the candidate's election that the party's "doctrines have acquired a majority."

As Tocqueville might have put it, "this was no longer your [founding] father's presidency." But we now need to examine how each of these three elements that pulled the executive into greater prominence—foreign affairs, the administrative state, and popular politics—combined with the original institutional design to create the relationship between the two branches we see today. For while the founding generation would probably be surprised by the power and sway of the modern executive, more likely than not they would appreciate how they had also planted the seeds that made that growth possible.

The National Security Presidency

When the Constitutional Convention opened and the Virginia Plan was tabled to start the delegates' deliberations, the plan called for a separate executive branch vested with both the "general authority to execute the laws" and the power to exercise those "executive rights vested in the Congress by the Confederation."[2] To be sure, there were questions about exactly what those "executive rights" might be. In addition, there were questions about how they conformed with what James Wilson called the "purely republican" manners of the country.[3] Nevertheless, as the notes to the convention debate make clear, what James Madison in another context had called "the great powers . . . properly executive," were implicitly understood to fall in line with the foreign and defense powers as outlined by Locke, Montesquieu, and Blackstone.[4] Not surprisingly, from this Alexander Hamilton concluded that "as the participation of the Senate in the making of treaties, and the power of the Legislature to declare war, are exceptions out of the general 'executive power' vested in the President, they are to be construed strictly, and ought to be extended no further than is essential to their execution."[5]

Add to this understanding of executive authority the potential contribution of a largely independent, unitary executive to act, in the words of Publius, with "decision, activity, secrecy, and dispatch," and one can see the office's potential for expanding its role as security matters took a more prominent role in the country's policy agenda.[6] This potential was quickly exhibited by President Washington's unilateral decision to issue the Neutrality Proclamation in May 1793—a decision about which the president assumed he had the authority to interpret a treaty's obligations, issue legally-binding measures to enforce, and do so in spite of the possibility that the decision might well impinge on the Congress's authority to "declare war."[7]

Of course, it was Congress's prerogative to declare war and, as early practice and Court decisions make clear, it was also Congress's right to authorize more limited offensive military campaigns, what at the time were called "imperfect" wars.[8] Yet, from the first, it was also understood to be the executive's responsibility to use the armed forces to defend the nation and protect citizens and American commerce abroad. Indeed, as Abraham Sofaer notes in his analysis of early precedents, even while "outspoken advocates of executive power" assumed that the president's actions in this regard "had to be 'defensive,' or within the limits allowed by international law," protecting the country's rights under international law "left him with broad discretion, analogous to the royal prerogative described by Blackstone."[9]

Policing the Neighborhood and the Globe

What it meant to defend the nation and protect its rights grew as the country's sights expanded both geographically and strategically. Perhaps the first significant expansion was Roosevelt's Corollary to the Monroe Doctrine, which put newly established American military muscle behind the policy that European intervention in the Western Hemisphere would be seen as a threat to U.S. vital strategic interests. Reinforced by a network of treaties with both Latin American and Caribbean states that gave Washington conditioned rights of intervention and enhanced by the acceptance of the strategic view that the oceans were sea lanes of direct military and commercial importance rather than simply barriers to foreign intervention, presidents came to view their policing power as an inherent constitutional authority, one that Congress largely acquiesced to.[10]

The next great leap occurred in the wake of World War II, amid the rising confrontation with the Soviet Union and the palpable sense of failure among American statesmen over post–World War I policies to attempt to isolate the United States from crises abroad. In ratifying the United Nations Charter, the "greatest lesson of our generation," according to Senate Foreign Relations Chair Tom Connally, was that "world peace is indivisible."[11] In contrast to British Prime Minister Neville Chamberlain's prewar dismissal of Hitler's predatory ambitions toward Czechoslovakia as a "quarrel in a far-away country between people of whom we know nothing," American politicians now postulated that "a threat to international security and peace occurring anywhere on earth constituted a direct threat to the security and peace of the United States."[12]

Although the high-water mark of this strategic view as a justification for presidential action was Truman's decision to respond to the North Korean invasion of the South, the practice of presidents acting to address crises to the international order continues to this day. And while most of the major American military campaigns arguably were sanctioned in one fashion or another by Congress—Vietnam with the Tonkin Gulf Resolution (August 1964); the First Gulf War with the "Authorization for the Use of Military Force Against Iraq Resolution" (January 1992); Afghanistan and al Qaeda via the "Authorization for Use of Military Force" (September 2001); and Iraq by the "Authorization for Use of Military Force against Iraq Resolution" (October 2002)—presidents have routinely sent U.S. forces into harm's way without congressional sanction, even when American lives were not at stake, such as in Panama (1989), Grenada (1983), and "Desert One" (1980). These include Ronald Reagan's deployment of marine and naval forces to Lebanon in 1982; Reagan's 1987 decision to reflag Kuwaiti tankers and give them naval escorts in the Persian Gulf; George H. W. Bush's and Bill Clinton's respective decisions to send U.S. ground forces to Somalia in 1992 and 1993; Clinton's use of military assets in Bosnia and Haiti; the Clinton-directed air campaign against Yugoslavia in

1999; the follow-up deployment of peacekeeping forces in Kosovo; the Bush and Clinton administrations' enforcement of the no-fly zones in Iraq following the First Gulf War; and Barack Obama's use of air and naval forces against Libya in 2011.

With Congress having provided for a military capable of acting decisively across the globe, presidents have both the instrumental and the institutional capacity to act as "first decider" when it comes to responding to events they believe impinge on key national security interests. It is worth noting that Congress has largely conceded this position, either by failing to cut off funds for an operation they are in disagreement with or by giving the decision about when to intervene to the White House. Even under Dwight D. Eisenhower, perhaps the most deferential of postwar presidents to Congress, Congress passed joint authorizing resolutions on Formosa (1955) and the Middle East (1957) that left it up to the Oval Office to determine "the necessity" of using U.S. armed forces to protect, respectively, Taiwan and the independence of the states in the Near East.[13] In that regard there is continuity between those resolutions and the War Powers Resolution (1973), whose terms accept that a president may deploy forces into hostilities for two months without Congress asserting its own "war powers."[14] Putting aside that the resolution's mandates have been routinely ignored by presidents of both parties,[15] it is nevertheless revealing that a law intended to rein in the exercise of presidential war-making actually gives license to, even if only temporarily, a form of executive prerogative.

The Administrative Presidency

Motivated by the administrative failures of the Articles of Confederation and the weak performance of the typical state chief executive in the decade following independence, the delegates to the Constitutional Convention worked to disentangle the business of administration from legislative deliberation and to establish a largely independent office with the charge of the "faithful execution of the laws."[16]

During the convention, the delegates decided that to meet such a charge, a unitary executive was preferable to a plural executive or a single executive encumbered with an advisory council for appointments. As James Wilson argued, only a single chief magistracy would have the requisite "energy, dispatch and responsibility to the office" to ensure a much-needed constancy in government administration.[17] In this manner, the unitary executive precluded a ministerial council sharing in the president's powers. Vesting executive power, "ostensibly in one man, subject, in whole or in part, to the control and cooperation of others in the capacity of counselors to him," would only undermine the executive's ability to fulfill his obligations.[18] Having put aside the "privy council" model, the convention settled on a separate executive branch, headed by a president vested with "the executive power" and the supervisory right to require the written advice of "the principal Officer in each of the Executive Departments."[19]

With the broad outlines of separate executive power in place, it was left to the First Congress to spell out the precise administrative composition of the executive branch.[20] During that Congress's first days, Madison proposed three almost identical bills to establish a Department of Foreign Affairs, of War, and of the Treasury. Each would have a principal officer, the secretary, appointed by the president with the Senate's advice and consent. Each bill contained language noting that the department heads were to be directly responsive to the president's commands. And each assumed, tied to the majority of the members' appreciating the presidents' role in administrating the government, that those department heads served at the president's pleasure.[21]

The bill establishing the Treasury Department, however, did differ from the other two acts in one key aspect. Reflecting the constitutional delegation of power over appropriations and other financial matters to Congress, the bill laid several charges on the Treasury Secretary and his inferior officers to render written or oral reports to either legislative house—a construction that would seem to bear on the president's control over the department. And indeed, unlike the two other bills, which explicitly designated the departments of War and Foreign Affairs as "executive," the adjective was not included in the Treasury bill's title.[22] But with the removal power and a reporting power still tied to the president, the absence of the word "executive" seemed not to matter in practice. Soon after the "Decision of 1789," the Treasury Secretary was pointedly included in an appropriations bill designating executive officers' salaries. The not-so-subtle point: the president was still the guiding hand in administrating even those areas not deemed exclusively "executive" in nature.[23]

Early clashes between Alexander Hamilton, Washington's Federalist Treasury Secretary, and Republican Congressman (and future Treasury Secretary) Albert Gallatin over official appropriations illustrate how the advent of political parties brokered further understandings of the executive branch's administrative role. Congress at all times jealously guarded its right to appropriate funds, but by 1793 congressional Republicans sought to constrict the scope of executive power through a tighter control over funds' expenditure.[24] Aiming to curtail department heads' discretion, Gallatin explicitly proposed to end the practice of open-ended lump sum grants and force the Treasury to spend monies as specifically directed. The Treasury, he argued, did not have the power "to appropriate to one object, money that had been specifically appropriated for any other object." It was the legislature's "most sacred and important trust" from the people to apply appropriations, and any Treasury official who usurped such a trust by using funds at his own discretion was guilty of a power grab.[25]

Hamilton himself did not contest that "disbursements, finally, must no doubt be regulated by the laws of appropriation," but he countered with a fundamental point about the unpredictability of life: "provisory measures will often be unavoidable."[26] Joined by his fellow Federalists, Hamilton showed that unforeseeable circumstances forced the need for anticipatory appropriations, especially in the areas of foreign policy and the military. And if "cases of sufficient urgency" occurred, it was precisely the function of the executive to determine if the situation justified an exception to the rule. Who else could do so and be held adequately responsible in their republican system?

Gallatin and his fellow Republicans Madison and Thomas Jefferson ultimately, if quietly, admitted the point. Although Gallatin believed itemized appropriations were the only efficient legislative check on "executive prodigality," he agreed that there were limitations due to necessity requiring that the executive be allowed a "reasonable discretion."[27] Congress itself voted to revert to its lump sum formula after 1797—an implicit conferral of discretion on the executive's deputies to shift funds, at least in explicitly executive arenas such as foreign policy. The larger point: Even in the case of what ostensibly was the policy area closest to the heart of the legislature's capacity to check and control policies, the Constitution's architects had established an executive who wielded a broad, if not fully anticipated, say over the public purse.

Nor of course was Alexander Hamilton, as the first Secretary of the Treasury, shy about using the discretion accorded him by the separation of the executive branch from the legislature, even when undertaking his statutory obligation to report to Congress. It was Hamilton's three great reports to Congress in 1790 (the "Report on Public Credit," the "Report on a National Bank," and the "Report on Manufactures") that first set off constitutional alarm bells about the capacities of the executive to set the nation's deepest agenda and do so from within a department with ostensibly the closest ties to the legislature; hence, Madison's accusation that it was Hamilton who, as one of the coauthors of the *Federalist* papers, had "deserted" him with his effort to "administer the government . . . into what he thought it ought to be."[28]

From Administration to the Administrative State

By 1936 the complexity of the chief executive's administrative position famously prompted the Brownlow Commission to declare "the president needs help." The success of Franklin D. Roosevelt's New Deal agenda was contingent on an expansive federal bureaucracy handling the enlarged scope of the federal government's activities and responsibilities, an enlarged field statutorily sanctioned by Congress. Success in fulfilling these responsibilities rested on the president's ability to marshal all aspects of a now professional bureaucracy that now also included independent regulatory agencies.[29] To ensure the president's successful disbursement of his office, the Brownlow Commission articulated an ambitious program that refashioned the executive branch as the Executive Office of the Presidency. By providing new assistants to the president to strengthen the managerial control of administration, and giving the president the power to initiate government reorganizations, the president acquired new powers and tools to exert a portion of managerial control with the establishment of what became the Office of Management and Budget (OMB).[30]

The Brownlow Commission, however, was itself a reflection of the progressive thought that had been growing in political prominence since Woodrow Wilson. Pointing to the economic conditions created by the complexities of the Industrial Revolution and the early advent of the school of "scientific management," Wilson had announced that "the age of enlightened administration had come."[31]

Under this view, the administration of government could be separated from politics and entrusted, in good measure, to a bureaucracy composed of experts in specialized fields. Composed of nonpolitical administrators, the nonpartisan civil service would be shielded from heavy-handed oversight by both political branches. Court decisions as wide ranging as *Humphrey's Executor* (1935) and *Morrison v. Olson* (1988) have seemingly reinforced such administrative freedom of movement at the president's expense. However, the president retains a specific policymaking advantage over the professional bureaucracy due to the substantial number of political appointments within the administration that he can dispense to like-minded actors. The independence of the professional civil servant is narrowed in practice to such things as job security, since he is shielded by statutes and precedents from being fired by the chief executive in most instances. Outside of that, the civil servant will still be directed to execute his agencies' affairs by his department head, a presidential appointee. The heads of departments, in turn, are assisted by thousands of lower level Schedule C appointees spread throughout the whole executive branch, who have policymaking or policy-related duties in service to the executive's agenda.[32] It's a level of political penetration into the bureaucracy not found in any other major democracy, all of which reinforces the White House's advantage when it comes to how the laws are "to be faithfully executed."

The modern president retains a further advantage in policymaking over the modern Congress. Congressional action requires majorities (or more, in the case of the Senate) at all moments; and in cases of gridlock, it requires a supermajority to enact legislation. In contrast, the president can exercise his unilateral powers to issue executive orders, proclamations, and other kinds of directives to help define the federal policies on contentious matters such as civil rights, the environment, health care and social welfare, and immigration that Congress finds itself hard pressed to attend to or reverse.[33] As Congress's checks on the executive subside, presidential power takes advantage of its new opportunities to satisfy the public demand for action. Given the broad and complex field in which the federal government now operates, it is hardly any wonder that modern presidents use their administrative powers to greater and greater advantage.

President as National Leader

Teddy Roosevelt was hardly shy in publicizing his opinion that American presidents had a deplorable habit of failing to exercise the office's potential. Suggesting his predecessors had applied the Constitution as a protective napkin over the executive branch, Roosevelt acted to transform the institutional space and public expectation of the president as a national leader.[34] The silences in the Constitution were not to be read as signaling lack of power but, rather, opportunities for the exercise of power in the public interest. The president properly ought to be in the daily headlines of the nation, an active and visible leader.

Roosevelt was not simply indulging his imagination by invoking the Constitution to legitimate his view of the chief executive as also the nation's leader. From the outset, structural elements of the executive branch as well as the overall arrangement of powers within the Framers' Constitution have lent the president a national stature. His independent electoral base, spread throughout every state, immediately differentiates him from members of Congress with their particular, local constituencies and interests. Delegates at the Constitutional Convention consciously designed the presidential election process to improve the probability of a national figure enjoying majority support upon being elected.[35]

The Electoral College they established frees the president from the institutionally inferior position of owing his appointment to the legislature, reinforcing the separate importance of his office. Once elected, he is explicitly charged to provide information "from time to time" to Congress on the state of the nation, to "recommend . . . measures," and "on extraordinary occasions, convene both Houses," all of which suggests it is the president who provides the governing system with the "energy" to overcome the potential policy inertia that might result from separated powers.

Even the president's qualified veto power, as Martin Diamond and Harvey Mansfield have noted, can be understood to be more than just the negative mechanism found in the checks and balances scheme.[36] More broadly, when used, it provides an additional role for the president to set broad national guidelines on what are acceptable and unacceptable policies and laws.

But leadership within the constitutional order is not to be confused with leadership over and above that order. In that regard, the Constitution makes no provisions for permanent political parties, and when the nascent struggles of Federalists and Republicans became a political commonplace during his administration, George Washington labored to distance himself as president from the appearance of partisanship. He firmly believed that the president was the officer for the whole of the American people, a trust that would be jeopardized if he were to act in his official capacity as the captain of a particular party as well. By contrast, from his presidential campaign to his retirement, Thomas Jefferson was undeniably the Republican Party leader.[37]

Yet, even Jefferson attempted to keep partisanship tied to the constitutional order. He would not go over Congress's head to appeal directly to the public for support of his policy agenda. By working through party members in the House and the Senate, Jefferson arguably increased the executive's effective power and leadership role. The innovation of establishing a floor leader, recognized as the president's spokesman, was crucial to Jefferson's success in this regard, as Jefferson made frequent use of the floor leader to introduce executive-drafted bills. The party caucus was likewise crucial, Leonard White argues, as it facilitated conclaves of leaders from the legislative and executive branches in formulating policy.[38]

From Constitutional to Popular Leader

Jefferson, like Washington, had not thought that political parties would be a permanent aspect of the American political system.[39] The Republican Party's collapse due to its own success during the "Era of Good Feelings" seemed to vindicate this view. But on the heels of John Quincy Adams' presidency, Martin Van Buren argued that the lack of political parties with distinct, competing policy positions harmed rather than benefitted the executive as well as the republic. Presidential contests seemed set on the path toward being permanently decided by the House, severely damaging the executive's institutional independence. At the same time, presidential candidates felt encouraged to sponsor a personal factionalism among potential clients in the absence of clearly defined policy competition. By establishing distinct parties tied to developed policy positions, Van Buren sought to make presidential ambition safe and constructive for democracy while avoiding demagoguery. Party competition, he argued, would institutionalize a more active role for the voice of the majority in determining national policy. Elections would be contests between competing groups in which the victorious party could claim authority for carrying out its program, rather than being contests between personalities.[40]

Andrew Jackson seized on the claim of popular authority during his presidency, becoming the first president to claim that his election equaled a mandate from the people in support of his policy.[41] He steadfastly held the view that the president was the direct, special representative of the people. After his veto of the national bank became a central issue of the 1832 election, Jackson as well as his contemporary observers regarded his reelection as proof of the popular ratification of his policy. Furthermore, his association with Van Buren and the new Democratic Party cemented the union between the ideas of the popularly elected presidency and the president as head of the majority party. To fulfill those dual roles, Jackson made liberal use of the veto, justifying its use not so much as a protection against unconstitutional legislation but as a defense of his and his party's policies.[42]

Political parties expanded considerably the constitutional range of the executive branch when the president's party commanded majorities in both legislative houses. That situation showed the potential of the reverse as well—how easily a president could be made to look ineffective on the national stage once his party did not command a legislative majority. But it wasn't until Woodrow Wilson expanded Teddy Roosevelt's conception of the president as active leader with a constitutionally allowed "bully pulpit" into an image of a president empowered by the "mystique of the mandate" from the people of the United States to "be as big a man as he can" that the president's role as popular leader became canonical.[43]

Wilson established the foundations of the modern popular presidency in arguing that it was the president's especial responsibility to ensure a positive public good, which could only be attained by transcending the operation of formal institutions working within the constitutional confines of delegated and separated powers. The popular leader's or statesman's task was not simply to overcome the inertia of institutional rule that was no match for the compounding social problems of the industrial age, but to interpret for the people the policies called for by the progressive principles of the era.[44] Wilson's behavior in office then made his arguments tangible in such things as delivering the State of the Union message in person before Congress—reversing a 100-year precedent—and by taking it on himself not only to recommend specific measures but set out the broader policymaking agenda of the nation. In pursuing the latter objective, Wilson insisted that presidents should be judged for their legislative successes, thereby setting up the expectation of the people for presidential action. This naturally paved the way for Franklin D. Roosevelt's frenetic expansion of government programs and administration, which he justified on the grounds of meeting the nation's needs brought on by severe economic duress. "In their need, the people have registered a mandate that they want direct, vigorous action. . . . They have made me the present instrument of their wishes. In the spirit of the gift I take it."[45]

Wilson had argued that the president had "no means of compelling Congress except through public opinion."[46] FDR expertly navigated the new technologies of mass communication to bring his voice and policy initiatives directly to the American public. And he had no qualms in urging the public to pressure their congressmen to support his initiatives. Presidents after FDR, now expected to provide leadership from the office, have followed suit; in the sunset of Jimmy Carter's presidency, he was making national addresses on the state of the national consciousness, in the spirit of a "leader of the people" rather than as "head of the government" or even "head of a party."[47] The rhetorical presidency of today sustains itself on a speech that sets forth ever grander views of society and government, using mass media to enable a president to be constantly before the public gaze, literally talking above Congress rather than at it.[48]

From Rhetorical to Legislative Leader?

The rhetorical presidency's vast scope has had its practical effects, visible in the overtly legislative role that presidents in recent administrations have assumed. When President Obama commented publicly in 2011 that his administration would govern by "going . . . ahead and do[ing] it ourselves" whenever "Congress is not willing to act," he trumpeted an understanding of the president's legislative ability surpassing FDR's imaginings.[49] And when he announced the policy known as Deferred Action for Parents of Americans (DAPA) in November 2014, his use of executive action to circumnavigate Congress on immigration policy was just the latest of illustrations of the president using his authority to "faithfully" execute the laws to, in effect, act legislatively. But in moving toward making legislation about immigration, healthcare, and the environment through sheer declaration, independent of or, to his opponents, contrary to statutory law, the Obama administration's behavior is also just the latest—if perhaps most forward—expression of modern presidential administrations' exercise of lawmaking powers over against those of Congress.[50] Obama's executive actions arguably follow in the train of George W. Bush's controversial use of signing statements as an opportunity to participate more actively in the creation of legislation (beyond merely signing or vetoing bills transmitted from the

Congress). Bush's behavior, in turn, reflected actions taken by both the Reagan administration and the Clinton administration to reassert power over the direction of the administrative state through the regulatory apparatus. As then-Harvard Law School Dean Elena Kagan wrote, "President Clinton treated the sphere of regulation as his own." Building on "the legacy Reagan had left him," he devised a new way of "setting the policy direction of agencies—of converting administrative activity into an extension of his own policy and political agenda."[51]

Back to the Future?

Pierre L'Enfant's plan for the nation's capital captured the fundamental equality between the two political branches by having the Capitol and what was originally called the President's Palace be the two cornerstones for the city's eventual development. From the Congress's home and the president's house, the main thoroughfares of the capital were to flare out, with only Pennsylvania Avenue connecting the two. And indeed that is how the city developed, with those concerned with the business of the legislature largely residing south of the Capitol's front and those in the administration living north of what became the White House.[52]

Initially, all of the executive office buildings—War, Navy, State, and Treasury—resided neatly in front of the White House. But just as the president has gained immense resources to coordinate policy implementation, set out legislative agendas, manage the country's foreign and defense affairs, and administer the government more broadly, so, too, has the executive branch expanded its footprint in an ever increasing sprawl of buildings across the capital and neighboring suburbs.

Of course the line between the "energetic executive" of the Founders and today's quasi-imperial presidency has not been a straight one. As Stephen Griffin notes, much had to change between the Quasi-War with France in 1798 and the Korean War in 1950. In the former, President John Adams had little if any existing "military or state capacity on which he could draw" to assert his war-making authority, while in the latter case, President Harry Truman's unilateral decision to wage a significant war in Korea could call upon "a preexisting military capacity" created during World War II and sustained during the early days of the Cold War.[53] The fact is, throughout the majority of the nineteenth century, presidents, with some notable exceptions such as Andrew Jackson and Abraham Lincoln, were hardly heads of a dominating branch of government. With domestic issues, internal development, and the continental expansion in self-government attracting much of the federal government's attention, it was perhaps natural that Congress would be first among equals when it came to the other branches of government.

This state of play is a reminder that the Constitution's system of separated powers and checks and balances is not, as the progressives wanted to portray it, an inert, static system. It was designed to adapt to circumstances and respond to new contingencies, just as it was also designed to make sure those responses were kept within bounds by the other branches. Even today, as powerful as presidents have become, there have been instances (Vietnam in 1973; Somalia in 1993; and Impoundment in 1974) when Congress has used its authorities to bring presidents to heel. Similarly, in the late 1970s it created new select committees to help reign in an area—intelligence—once thought to be solely the prerogative of the executive. Indeed, one of the interesting paradoxes of the American constitutional system is that, while the American president is often described as the globe's most powerful democratically elected chief executive, it can also be argued that the Congress remains the most powerful legislature in the world.[54]

That said, it would be difficult to imagine a fundamental change in the relative status of the two branches absent an equally fundamental change in the modern scope of the federal government, America's role in the world, and the role of the presidency as *the* popular leader. Perhaps the key question then becomes less about Congress regaining "lost turf" and more about ensuring that the authority it does wield is properly directed.

Broadly speaking, this might mean checking the presidency's Wilsonian tendency to assert and ground its leadership on the basis of a populist national mandate. Certainly many of the key founders hoped that the presidency would act as a curb on an unreasoned majoritarianism that might arise from the legislature and, in turn, provide wise and decent policy ballast to the system. But for reasons outside of the Constitution proper, the home of that simple majoritarian instinct lies more with the executive today than with Congress.

Flipping the system on its head, but retaining the spirit of Madison, one might pursue a reform agenda for Congress where the principle of "ambition to counteract ambition" brings forth the first branch's capacity for deliberation and oversight to check an energetic executive further fueled by the steroids of populism. In practice, this might mean rolling back previous "reforms" that seem to have had the effect of reducing the influence of once strong, autonomous committees and powerful chairs in favor of creating more cohesive party caucuses.[55] At the extreme, it means making Nancy Pelosi's statement as House Speaker to members that "we have to pass the bill so that you can find out what is in it, away from the fog of the controversy" unacceptable to those same members who care about the Congress as an institution with constitutional responsibilities of its own.

Admittedly, checking the president's bully pulpit by resurrecting the deliberative capacities of the Congress is no easy political task if, in the attempt to do so, it is couched in institutional terms alone. There are reasons why the congressional reforms of the recent past were undertaken, not the least of which was to make the institution appear more open and more democratic. Accordingly, a first step would be to develop a case for reform that pits the Congress's claim to represent a wider-ranging and deeper majority against that of the once-in-four-years, slice-in-time, popular vote that selects the president. In short, Congress needs to formulate and promote a view of sound representative rule that challenges both the simple populism of the modern executive and Congress's own recent accounts of itself. Until then, it will have an increasingly difficult time keeping up with the house down the street.

Notes

1. See Alexis de Tocqueville, *Democracy in America,* translated, edited by Harvey C. Mansfield and Delba Winthrop (University of Chicago Press, 2000), vol. 1, part 1, chapter 8, "On the Federal Constitution," subsections: "How the Position of the President of the United States Differs from that of a Constitutional King in France," "Accidental Causes that Can Increase the Influence of the Executive Power," and "Crisis of the Election."

2. *The Records of the Federal Convention of 1787*, edited by Max Farrand, vol.1 (Yale University Press, 1937), p. 21.

3. Ibid., p. 71.

4. "Madison to Caleb Wallace, August 23, 1785," in *The Writings of James Madison*, vol. 2, pp. 166–77. The letter was written two years prior to the Constitutional Convention, discussing what a constitution for a possible new state of Kentucky might entail. Madison wrote that the federal character of the United States had the effect of reducing the authorities exercised by state chief executives, limiting their powers largely to the administration of the laws.

5. *The Pacificus–Helvidius Debates of 1793–1794: Toward the Completion of the American Founding*, edited by Morton Frisch (Indianapolis, Ind.: Liberty Fund, 2007), "Pacificus Number 1," p. 16.

6. Charles Kessler, introduction to *The Federalist Papers*, edited by Clinton Rossiter (New York: New American Library, 1999), p. xx.

7. See Gary J. Schmitt, "President Washington's Proclamation of Neutrality," in *The Constitutional Presidency*, edited by Joseph M. Bessette and Jeffrey K. Tulis (Johns Hopkins University Press, 2009), pp. 54–75.

8. See Robert Scigliano, "The War Powers Resolution and the War Powers," in *The Presidency in the Constitutional Order: An Historical Examination*, edited by Joseph M. Bessett and Jeffrey K. Tulis (Transaction Publishers, 2010), pp. 124–25. See also, Abraham D. Sofaer, *War, Foreign Affairs and Constitutional Power: The Origins* (Cambridge, Mass.: Ballinger, 1976), pp. 118, 123, 129, 139, 161–64, 166.

9. Sofaer, *War, Foreign Affairs and Constitutional Power*, p. 165.

10. Roosevelt's announcement of the policy was contained in his State of the Union address, *Message of the President of the United States,* 1904 (www.presidency.ucsb.edu/ws/index.php?pid=29545). For analysis of this era and the roles of the president and Congress in widening the country's "defensive" parameters, see Mariah Zeisberg, *War Powers: The Politics of Constitutional Authority* (Princeton University Press, 2013), pp. 96–124.

11. *Congressional Record*, vol. 91, p. 10,968.

12. Ibid., p. 8059. Senator Warren Austin, a Republican, was a member of the Foreign Relations Committee and served as the second U.S. ambassador to the United Nations.

13. "Joint Resolution Authorizing the President to Employ the Armed Forces of the United States for Protecting the Security of Formosa, the Pescadores and Related Positions and Territories of that Area," January 29, 1955 (www.govtrack.us/congress/bills/84/hjres159/text), and "Joint Resolution to Promote Peace and Stability in the Middle East," March 9, 1957 (www.govtrack.us/congress/bills/85/hjres117/text).

14. Sec. 5(b) of the War Powers Resolution (50 U.S.C 1541-1548) (http://avalon.law.yale.edu/20th_century/warpower.asp).

15. For an overview of the War Powers Resolution's implementation, see Richard F. Grimmett, "The War Powers Resolution After Thirty-Six Years," April 22, 2010 (Congressional Research Service, Library of Congress).

16. For a pithy sample of this argument, see Alexander Hamilton to James Duane, September 3, 1780, in *The Founders Constitution*, vol. 1, chapter 5, document 2 (University of Chicago Press) (http://press-pubs.uchicago.edu/founders/documents/v1ch5s2.html). For extended narratives of how state and national governments played out under the Articles of Confederation specifically in regard to the administration and execution of government, see, among others, Charles C. Thach Jr., *The Creation of the Presidency, 1775–1789* (Indianapolis, Ind.: Liberty Fund, Inc., 2007); Richard J. Ellis, editor, *Founding the American Presidency* (Lan-

ham, Md.: Rowman & Littlefield Publishers, Inc., 1999); Leonard D. White, *The Federalists: A Study in Administrative History* (New York: The Macmillan Company, 1956), pp. 13–25; Forrest McDonald, *The American Presidency: An Intellectual History* (University of Kansas, 1994), pp. 125–81.

17. See the debates on June 2 and June 4. James Madison, *Debates in the Federal Convention of 1787*, edited by Gordon Loyd (Ashbrook Center at Ashland University, 2014) pp. 24–38.

18. *The Federalist Papers*, pp. 391–99.

19. U.S. Constitution, Article II, Sec. 2.

20. For detailed treatments of the executive branch debates, including debates over the removal power, during the First Congress as a result of establishing the administrative departments, see White, *The Federalists*; Henry Barrett Learned, *The President's Cabinet: Studies in The Origin, Formation and Structure of an American Institution* (Yale University Press, 1912); Mary L. Hinsdale, "The Cabinet and Congress: An Historical Inquiry," in *Proceedings of the American Political Science Association*, vol. 2 (1905), pp. 126–48; John A. Fairlie, "The President's Cabinet," *American Political Science Review* 7 (February 1913), pp. 28–44.

21. See The Congressional Register (June 17, 1789) reprinted in *Debates in the House of Representatives*, First Session: June–September 1789; *Documentary History of the First Federal Congress,* 1789–1791, AT 904, 921, edited by Charlene Bangs Bickford and others, 1992.

22. See *Documentary History of the First Federal Congress of the United States of America,* edited by Charlene Bickford and others (Columbia, S.C.: Model Editions Partnership, 2002). XML version based on the *Documentary History of the First Federal Congress of the United States of America,* edited by Charlene Bickford and others, vol. 6 (Johns Hopkins Press, 1986), pp. 1975–91; 2028–32 (http://adh.sc.edu).

23. The tag "Decision of 1789" for Congress's 1789 decision regarding the removability of the Secretary of Foreign Affairs by the president has been in currency since at least 1835. See *Myers v. United States*, 272 U.S. 52, 151 (1926) (quoting Daniel Webster's speech of February 1835, which referred to the debate over the removal power as the "decision of 1789"). The Decision of 1789 was the first significant legislative construction of the Constitution, remarkable not only because Congress confronted a difficult constitutional question, but because it sided with its "rival" the executive in its decision. For a detailed examination of how the bills to establish the major administrative departments materialized the chief executive as chief administrator, see Saikrishna Prakash, "New Light on the Decision of 1789," 91 *Cornell L. Rev.* 1021 (2006) (http://scholarship.law.cornell.edu/clr/vol91/iss5/2).

24. See White, *The Federalists*, especially pp. 222–36, 323–58, and 507–16, and Leonard D. White, *The Jeffersonians: A Study in Administrative History 1801–1829* (New York: The MacMillan Company, 1951). For further perspectives on the Gallatin–Hamilton feud as it related to the larger Federalist–Republican divide over the proper bounds of executive and legislative power, see Jeremy

D. Bailey, *Thomas Jefferson and Executive Power* (Cambridge University Press, 2007); Louis Fisher, *The Law of the Executive Branch: Presidential Power* (Oxford University Press, 2014); Louis Fisher, "Presidential Spending Discretion and Congressional Controls," *Law and Contemporary Problems* 37 (1972), pp. 135–72; Gerhard Casper, "Appropriations of Power," *University of Arkansas at Little Rock Law Journal* 13 (1990).

25. White, *The Federalists*, pp. 323–34.

26. Ibid, p. 333.

27. Ibid, p. 331.

28. Madison, quoted in Memoranda by N. P. Trist, September 27, 1834, reprinted in *Records of the Federal Convention of 1787*, edited by Max Ferrand (Yale University Press, 1966), p. 534.

29. The literature on the birth of the administrative state with the explosion in government agencies that occurred in the first few decades of the twentieth century, arguably due to the combination of a shift in political ideology and the social and economic effects of the industrial revolution and Great Depression, is vast and contentious. For an overview of the dramatic shift, see Eldon J. Eisenach, *The Lost Promise of Progressivism* (University Press of Kansas, 1994); Sidney M. Milkis, "The Roots of New Deal Reform," in *The President and the Parties: The Transformation of the American Party System Since the New Deal* (Oxford University Press, 1993), pp. 21–51; Ronald J. Pestritto and William J. Atto, "Introduction to American Progressivism," in *American Progressivism: A Reader* (Lanham, Md.: Lexington Books, 2008), pp. 1–32; Eric R. Claeys, "The National Regulatory State in Progressive Political Theory and Twentieth-Century Constitutional Law," in *Modern America and the Legacy of the Founding*, edited by Ronald J. Pestritto and Thomas G. West (Lanham, Md.: Lexington Books, 2007), pp. 35–74. For the theoretical underpinnings, see Herbert David Croly, *Progressive Democracy* (New York: The Macmillan Company, 1915); John Dewey and James Tufts, "Social Organization and the Individual," in *Ethics* (New York: Henry Holt and Co., 1908), pp. 427–85; Charles Edward Merriam, "Recent Tendencies," in *A History of American Political Theories* (New York: The MacMillan Company, 1915), pp. 305–33; Frank Johnson Goodnow, *Politics and Administration: A Study in Government* (New York: The MacMillan Company, 1900). For examinations of the effects on government policy and behavior, see Gary Lawson, "The Rise and Rise of the Administrative State," *Harvard Law Review* 1231 (1993–94); Chris DeMuth, "The Regulatory State," *National Affairs*, no. 12 (2012) (www.nationalaffairs.com /publications/detail/the-regulatory-state).

30. See Donald R. Brand, "Progressivism, the Brownlow Commission, and the Rise of the Administrative State," in Pestritto and West, *Modern America and the Legacy of the Founding*.

31. See, in particular, Woodrow Wilson, "The Study of Administration," in *Political Science Quarterly II* (1887), pp. 197–222.

32. William G. Howell, *Power Without Persuasion: The Politics of Direct Presidential Action* (Princeton University Press, 2003).

33. See Terry M. Moe, "The Presidency and the Bureaucracy: The Presidential Advantage," in *The Presidency and the Political System*, 4th ed., edited by Michael Nelson (Washington, D.C.: CQ Press, 1995), pp. 408–39; William G. Howell and David E. Lewis, "Agencies by Presidential Design," *Journal of Politics* 64 (2002), pp. 1095–114. Compounding this advantage until recently has been the so-called *Chevron* Doctrine, in which the Supreme Court ruled that federal administrative agencies are to be presumed to have broad authority to interpret congressional acts unless Congress anticipated a particular dispute by providing in law a particular answer or unless the agency interpretation of a statute is discernably unreasonable. Given the generality of many of the country's regulatory laws, the Court's deference to the agencies in such instances has given those agencies significant governing advantages. See *Chevron U.S.A., Inc. v. Natural Resources Defense Council, Inc.*, 467 U.S. 837 (1984) (www.law.cornell.edu/supct/html/historics/USSC_CR_0467_0837_ZS.html).

34. Theodore Roosevelt, "The Presidency: Making an Old Party Progressive," in *An Autobiography* (New York: The MacMillan Company, 1913), pp. 379–99.

35. Martin Diamond, "The Electoral College and the American Idea of Democracy," in *As Far as Republican Principles Will Admit: Essays by Martin Diamond*, edited by William A. Schambra (Washington, D.C.: AEI Press, 1992), pp. 186–205.

36. See Diamond, "The Separation of Powers and the Mixed Regime," in *As Far As Republican Principals Will Admit*, pp. 58–67; see also Harvey Mansfield, *Taming the Prince: The Ambivalence of Modern Executive Power* (New York: The Free Press, 1989).

37. See White, *The Jeffersonians*; Dumas Malone, "Presidential Leadership and National Unity: The Jeffersonian Example," *Journal of Southern History* 35 (1969), pp. 3–17.

38. White, *The Jeffersonians*, p.28.

39. For an account of Jefferson's presidency and Jeffersonianism, see "The Triumph of Jeffersonianism," in Sidney M. Milkis and Michael Nelson, *The American Presidency: Origins and Developments, 1776–2011* (Washington, D.C.: CQ Press, 2012), pp. 100–25.

40. James W. Ceaser, "Political Parties and Presidential Ambition," *Journal of Politics* 40 (1978), pp. 708–39.

41. Robert A. Dahl, "Myth of the Presidential Mandate," *Political Science Quarterly* 105 (1990), pp. 355–72.

42. See James W. Ceaser, "Martin Van Buren and the Case for Electoral Restraint," in *Presidential Selection: Theory and Development* (Princeton University Press, 1979), pp. 123–69; see, also, Martin Van Buren, *Inquiry into the Origin and*

Course of Political Parties in the United States, ed. by his sons (New York: Hurd and Houghton, 1867).

43. See especially chapters 3 and 8 in Woodrow Wilson, *Constitutional Government in the United States* (Columbia University Press, 1908), pp. 58–81, 198–222.

44. See, for example, Woodrow Wilson, *The New Freedom* (New York: Doubleday, Page and Company, 1913).

45. As cited in *The Power of the Presidency*, edited by Robert S. Hirschfield, 2nd ed. (Chicago: Aldine, 1973), p. 165.

46. Wilson, *Constitutional Government*, p. 184.

47. James W. Ceaser, Glen E. Thurow, Jeffrey Tulis, and Joseph M. Bessette, "The Rise of the Rhetorical Presidency," *Presidential Studies Quarterly* 11 (1981), pp. 158–71.

48. See Andrew Rudalevige, "The 'Foetus of Monarchy' Grows Up," in *The New Imperial Presidency: Reviewing Presidential Power after Watergate* (University of Michigan Press, 2009), pp. 19–56; and Lester G. Seligman, "The Presidential Office and the President As Party Leader," *Law and Contemporary Problems* 21 (1956), pp. 724–34.

49. See Adam J. White, "Obama's Regulatory Rampage," *Weekly Standard*, January 28, 2013, p. 24; see also Josh Blackman, "Gridlock and Executive Power," Working Paper (http://papers.ssrn.com/sol3/papers.cfm?abstract_id=2466707).

50. Christopher DeMuth Sr., "Congress Incongruous," *Library of Law & Liberty* (August 3, 2015) (http://www.libertylawsite.org/liberty-forum/congress-incongruous).

51. Elena Kagan, "Presidential Administration," 114 *Harv. L. Rev.* 2245, 2281–82 (2001).

52. See James Sterling Young, *The Washington Community: 1800–1828* (Columbia University Press, 1966).

53. Stephen M. Griffin, "The Executive Power," in *Oxford Handbook of the United States Constitution*, edited by Mark Tushnet, Mark A. Graber, and Sandford Levinson (Oxford University Press, 2015), p. 345.

54. See William G. Howell and Jon C. Pevehouse, *While Dangers Gather: Congressional Checks on Presidential War Powers* (Princeton University Press, 2007); and Douglas L. Kriner, *After the Rubicon: Congress, Presidents, and the Politics of Waging War* (University of Chicago Press, 2010). Even in the case of war powers, see two recent volumes that argue that, while control of a war's initiation has, in many respects, slipped out of the Congress's hands, Congress's influence over war making is not negligible.

55. See Kathryn Pearson's "The Constitution and Congressional Leadership" in this volume for an explication of the changes undertaken by Congress internally that effected its ability to "fulfill its Constitutional responsibilities" of oversight and deliberation.

8

The Constitution and Congressional Leadership

KATHRYN PEARSON

The U.S. Constitution intentionally starts with the U.S. Congress. In *Federalist* No. 51, James Madison observed: "In a republican government, the legislative authority necessarily predominates."[1] The Framers of the Constitution sought a strong and effective legislature in the wake of the failure of the Congress of the Confederation. In Article I, they designed Congress to be the branch of government closest to the people, to make national policy, and to protect the nation from executive branch overreach.

The Constitution established three separate branches of government sharing power. They created a large, bicameral legislature to counteract majority and minority factions and to provide checks and balances to prevent tyranny. By design, the Framers created several veto points with the potential to stall the legislative process. While the Framers provided the means and incentives for the three branches to defend themselves against encroachment from the others, they overestimated the dominance of the legislative branch and members' incentives to protect the institution's standing relative to the other two branches.

In essence, the Framers created an obstacle course for legislating. Additional veto points, such as the Senate filibuster, developed over time.[2] From the outset, party and committee leaders were critical actors in coordinating policymaking within and across parties, helping Congress fulfill its constitutional role. Parties and committees structure congressional organization in the House of Representatives. Majority party leaders and committee chairs set the agenda, set the rules, and structure debates. The balance of power between committee and party leaders has varied over time, however, with important implications for governing and congressional power. During periods of both committee and party dominance, political scientists and political commentators alike have bemoaned the outsized influence of committee and party leaders and the resulting legislative biases.

In the contemporary era, the two parties have grown increasingly competitive and polarized. Members have largely centralized power in the hands of majority party leaders, who enjoy considerably more power than House committee chairs do, with important implications for the legislative process, members' legislative autonomy, and representation.

In this chapter, I compare committee and party leadership during the "textbook" era (1937 through the 1960s) and the "postreform" era (1975 to the present), assessing the transfer of power away from committee chairs into the hands of party leaders. I analyze contemporary intraparty factions and the ways in which they have hindered party leaders. I conclude with a discussion of the challenges of congressional leadership in a highly competitive and highly polarized era and a call for institutional reforms.

The Development of Committee and Party Leadership

The Constitution was largely silent on the subject of congressional organization and leadership, except to stipulate in Article I, Section 2 that the "House of Representatives shall choose their Speaker and other Officers," and in Section 3 that "The Vice President of the United States shall be President of the Senate, but shall have no Vote, unless they be equally divided. The Senate shall choose their other Officers, and also a President pro tempore, in the Absence of the Vice President, or when he shall exercise the Office of President of the United States."

As the House's only constitutional officer, from the outset the Speaker had both partisan and nonpartisan responsibilities as the leader of the chamber and his party inside Congress.[3] The speakership of Henry Clay from 1811 to 1825 fostered significant institutional development. Clay established the speakership as the central leadership institution in the House and institutionalized the standing committee system.[4] Prior to the establishment of the standing committee system, temporary committees were created only after specific bills were considered on the House or Senate floor. Once action was completed on a bill, the temporary committees were dissolved. In the decades that followed, as committees developed expertise and authority, they gained significant autonomy.

Republican Speakers Thomas Reed (1889–91, 1895–99) and Joseph Cannon (1903–11) stand out as powerful Speakers; indeed, their leadership is often referred to as "Czar rule." They determined members' committee assignments and controlled the Committee on Rules, using it to shape the agenda in the House, and they punished those who did not follow the party. As the political landscape changed and members grew resentful of Cannon's overreach, House members voted to dramatically weaken Cannon's power in the "revolt" of 1910. A coalition of insurgent, progressive Republicans and minority party Democrats resentful of being shut out of the process voted to oust Cannon from the Rules Committee and to expand the Rules Committee, subjecting it to election by the House.[5] Members resented Cannon's tight control over the levers of power in the House that stripped them of opportunities to exert influence, and Cannon's overreach cost him his job and cost the speakership many of its tools.[6]

The "Textbook Congress"

From 1937 to the late 1960s, Democrats held the majority in the House for all but four years, yet Democratic party leaders wielded relatively little power compared to committee chairs. Political scientists describe this period as the "textbook Congress," because powerful, largely autonomous committee chairs exerted control over the agenda, sometimes blocking legislation favored by majority party leaders from reaching the House floor.[7]

A strict seniority system determined committee chairs during the textbook era: chair positions automatically went to the committee's longest-serving majority party member. Conservative southern Democrats held a disproportionate number of chairs, as they typically represented districts that generated no real Republican competition and, thus, tended to hold safe seats that allowed them to serve for long periods of time.[8]

A conservative cross-party coalition of southern Democrats and Republicans in the House often voted against most non-southern Democrats on the House floor and in key committees, stopping initiatives proposed by

Democratic presidents and majority party leaders.[9] Southern Democratic committee chairs, with the support of southern Democrats and Republican committee members, dominated key committees, including the Rules Committee. The Rules Committee not only blocked legislation favored by Democratic leaders by refusing to report special rules, they also pushed their own agenda to the floor over the objections of Democratic leaders. Eric Schickler and Kathryn Pearson (2009) identify more than forty conservative initiatives during this era that were brought by the Rules Committee to the House floor even though they were opposed by the Democratic White House, the Rules Committee chair, and in nearly all cases, by a majority of northern Democrats.[10] During the textbook era, non-southern Democrats were more likely to sign discharge petitions to bring bills automatically to the House floor, circumventing committee gatekeeping, than minority party Republicans or southern Democrats were, illustrating northern Democrats' lack of control over the legislative agenda despite their majority party status.[11]

Majority party Democratic leaders lacked the power to discipline their members.[12] In his book *House Out of Order* (1965), Richard Bolling (D-Mo.) wrote that the Speaker was "something like a feudal king—he is the first in the land; he receives elaborate homage and respect; but he is dependent on the powerful lords, usually committee chairmen, who are basically hostile to the objectives of the national Democratic Party and the Speaker."[13] The most prominent Speaker during this time period, Democrat Sam Rayburn of Texas (1940–61), lacked the influence over his caucus that Reed and Cannon had enjoyed. Rayburn was forced to plead with chairs to report bills favored by most Democrats, and he generally lacked the power to bypass the powerful, often conservative, committee chairs.[14]

Bolling and other liberal Democrats grew increasingly frustrated by conservative Democrats' institutional advantages, especially the disproportionate number of committee chairs held by southern Democrats relative to their share in the Democratic Caucus and the success of the conservative coalition. Liberals formed the Democratic Study Group (DSG) in 1959. The DSG, ranging from 115 to 170 members during its early years, met regularly, elected leaders, created policy task forces, provided information about legislation and campaign services to members, and created a whip system to coordinate and mobilize legislative coalitions.[15] The DSG was a key driver of the institutional reforms that followed, illustrating the importance of an intraparty faction whose efforts greatly strengthened the power of party leaders to induce responsiveness to the Democratic Caucus as a whole.

Institutional Reforms

The DSG spearheaded efforts to reform party practices to enhance the influence of liberals in the Democratic Caucus. Political changes outside Congress in the late 1960s and early 1970s were also critical to the institutional reforms that shifted power in the House from committee chairs to party leaders.[16] As the Republican Party became viable in more areas in the South, southern conservatives were increasingly likely to run and win as Republicans. The number of southern Democrats decreased, and the remaining southern Democrats' constituencies became more liberal over time.[17] Non-southern Democratic victories in the 1964 and 1974 elections further increased support for liberal policies and institutional reforms. The 1974 elections added seventy-five new, largely liberal Democrats, for a net gain of forty-eight Democratic seats who helped DSG members agitating for reform. Junior members seeking power, combined with liberal Democrats intent on greater agenda control, enabled Democrats to adopt several reforms to enhance the power of party leaders at the expense of committee chairs' power, while at the same time allowing junior members to exert some power through their subcommittees and votes in the Democratic Caucus.[18]

In 1973 Democrats reformed the rules to require an automatic secret ballot on committee chairs at the start of each Congress. The incentives for party loyalty were clear to prospective committee chairs, and the effects were significant: Democrats voted to oust three committee chairs after the 1974 elections. Not only did sitting committee chairs become more loyal to the party in their voting records in the years immediately following the passage of the restrictions on the seniority system, but so did those who were fairly close to obtaining committee chairs, particularly those members who were the next in line to become chair under the seniority system.[19]

The 1970s reforms endowed party leaders with power not possessed by a leader since Speaker Joe Cannon (R-Ill.) in 1910.[20] The Ways and

Means Committee no longer doubled as the "Committee on Committees," determining Democratic members' committee assignments and committee transfers. In 1975, Democrats empowered the leadership-controlled Steering and Policy Committee to make committee assignments. Chaired by the Speaker, the Democratic Steering and Policy Committee was composed of party leaders and eight members appointed by the Speaker.

The reforms gave the Speaker much more control over the legislative agenda. In 1975, the Speaker was authorized to select the chair and Democratic members of the House Rules Committee. With a nine to four supermajority of hand-picked, loyal Democrats, the Rules Committee would no longer thwart the leadership's legislative agenda by simply refusing to report a rule governing the consideration of legislation or granting favorable rules to legislation opposed by majority party leaders. The Speaker also gained the power to refer legislation to more than one committee, to set time limits on committee consideration, and to expedite the consideration of legislation in committee and on the House floor.

Congress also reformed the budget process in 1974, creating budget committees in each chamber, outlining the congressional budget process and providing the possibility for annual reconciliation bills to bring about the specific tax and spending changes required to meet the budget resolution targets. The Budget Act also limited the power of the president to impound funds and created the Congressional Budget Office as a source of expertise independent from the executive branch. Members of both parties supported the changes to give Congress more power relative to the executive branch in budget policy.[21] Although the new budget process reflected a tension between the fragmentation caused by several overlapping committees making budget decisions and the centralization provided by the reconciliation process, it soon became clear that the budget reforms strengthened party leaders.[22] Ultimately, the budget process continued to shift more power to party leaders relative to committee chairs and rank-and-file members in negotiating must-pass legislation and budget summits with the president.

The reforms of the 1970s were critical in shifting power from committee chairs to party leaders. Throughout the next two decades, a series of party reforms, House reforms, an increasingly homogeneous Democratic Caucus, and leadership innovations continued to increase party leaders' power, even if the trajectory was uneven at times, as leaders differed in their willingness to use and extend their power.[23]

Democratic Leaders in the Postreform Era

In January 1987, James (Jim) Wright (D-Tex.) succeeded Tip O'Neill (D-Mass.) as Speaker of the House. Rank-and-file Democrats had sought a powerful Speaker to challenge President Reagan.[24] O'Neill had not expanded the power of the speakership; indeed, his famous adage "all politics is local" emphasizes his attention to constituency, rather than party, issues. By contrast, Wright promulgated a partisan legislative agenda. Over the objections of minority party Republicans, Wright used procedural maneuvers to block Republican-supported alternatives and ensure the passage of Democratic legislation.[25] Wright's use—or, in the view of Republicans, abuse—of partisan procedural tactics, particularly on the House floor, prompted complaints and fueled Republicans' pursuit of ethics charges against Wright. Newt Gingrich (R-Ga.) spearheaded the attacks on Wright's ethics, eventually leading to Wright's resignation.

House Democrats responded by nominating Thomas (Tom) Foley (D-Wash.) as Speaker, viewing him as the antidote to Wright. Foley had risen through the ranks as a committee chair, party whip, and Majority Leader, and he had a reputation for prioritizing governance over partisan politics. Members, however, soon became dissatisfied with his leadership and inability to pass a legislative program, particularly in the context of unified Democratic Party control after the election of President William Clinton in 1992. When Foley was defeated for reelection in 1994 and Democrats lost their House majority for the first time in forty years, Democrats had failed to pass two of their biggest agenda items, health care reform and welfare reform. Like Wright, Foley had struggled to balance his dual role as the institutional leader of the House and the leader of his party. Whereas Wright had overreached in his partisan (and ethical) behavior, Foley did not deliver policy achievements Democrats had hoped for during a Democratic administration.

With large margins in the late 1980s and early 1990s, Democratic leaders did not question the durability of their majority party status. With an increasingly homogeneous Democratic Caucus and weakened committee chairs, the influence of the cross-party conservative coalition declined. Democrats were less likely to seek Republican support in committee and on the House floor. Shut out of the process, Republicans responded by criticizing Democrats and increasing partisan conflict, but not without internal division over their strategy.[26]

Republican Party Control and the Expansion of Party Leaders' Power

When Republicans gained fifty-two seats in 1994, giving Republicans a majority in the House of Representatives for the first time in forty years, a sea change in Congress occurred. It was clear that majority party status was not guaranteed after the next election, ushering in an era of dramatically increased electoral and policy competition between the parties, rendering the two parties into competitive teams.[27]

Republicans' victory catapulted Newt Gingrich into the speakership, and both parties replaced their conciliatory leaders with partisan leaders who had little interest in seeking bipartisan compromise. Speaker Gingrich not only benefited from Democratic reforms, he took active steps to increase his own power in the 104th Congress. New Republican committee chairs were term-limited to six years, making it clear that party leaders, not committees, were in charge, as no committee chair would serve long enough to establish autonomy over policy or their committee members. Rather than relying on a Speaker-dominated Steering Committee, as Democrats had done, Gingrich hand-picked committee chairs, violating seniority on key committees. New rules gave committee chairs the power to appoint subcommittee chairs instead of relying on seniority, but the chairs had to consult with the Speaker.

Party leaders, not committee chairs, determined the legislative agenda, the first 100 days of which were outlined in the "Contract with America." Yet there was little grumbling. Republicans, including committee chairs, were grateful to Gingrich for his role in the 1994 elections, as they had never experienced life in the majority. When committee chairs did resist, Gingrich simply circumvented them by creating task forces to consider specific legislation.

After Republicans lost congressional seats in the 1998 mid-term elections, Gingrich stepped down as Speaker. After Speaker Gingrich's initial would-be replacement, Robert Livingston (R-La.), withdrew from the contest and resigned from the House after his extramarital affairs were exposed, Deputy Whip Dennis Hastert (R-Ill.) emerged as the party's choice for Speaker. Hastert's reputation as a serious and low-profile legislator established him as an antidote to Gingrich. Despite the expectation that he would restore civility in the House and be more willing to work with Democrats, he further centralized party leaders' power and continued to shut Democrats out of the legislative process.[28]

When George W. Bush was elected president in 2000, Hastert focused on advancing their shared conservative policy agenda. Despite the separation of powers, the Republican president and Republican Speaker worked as a team during President Bush's first term, demonstrating that, in a polarized era, a shared partisan identification and electoral competition promotes teamwork across the branches to a greater extent than an institutional connection brings the two congressional parties together to defend the institution.

The extent to which term limits on committee chairs bolstered party leaders' power became even clearer six years after they were enacted, when many chairs opened up. An interview process for prospective committee chairs by the leadership-dominated Steering Committee—on which the Speaker and the Majority Leader controlled seven of the twenty-eight votes—gave party leaders considerable control over the process. The rules changes also provided ambitious members with incentives to demonstrate their party loyalty, their ability to work with the leadership, and their legislative skills. Party leaders rewarded loyal voters and fundraisers for the party with committee chairs, skipping the most senior committee members in several cases.[29]

With power centralized in the hands of party leaders, it was evident that the party median rather than the floor median was typically pivotal in the policymaking process. Despite their narrow majorities from 1995 to 2006, Republican leaders relied on their own members' votes to pass their legislative program instead of trying to attract support from centrist Democrats, even rebuffing the Blue Dog Democrats who initially expressed great interested in working with Republicans.[30] Speaker Hastert admitted that he was not interested in passing legislation that required significant Democratic support in a speech at a Congressional Research Service-sponsored conference in the Cannon House Office Building in October 2003. This practice became dubbed the Hastert rule after Hastert explained that he would not bring a bill to the House floor for a vote unless a majority of Republicans approved. Although the Hastert rule receives media attention from time to time (particularly when leaders occasionally violate it), it is not a rule, nor is it a new practice in the postreform era. As party leaders accrued more power and electoral competition intensified during the twelve years of GOP control, scholars and journalists alike bemoaned the rise of partisan polarization and highlighted the partisan acrimony.[31]

Democrats' Continued Expansion of Party Leaders' Power in the House

Democratic victories in the 2006 elections translated into a net gain of thirty House seats and majority party control, advancing Nancy Pelosi (D-Calif.) from her position as Minority Leader to Speaker of the House. Pelosi inherited the tools accrued by her Democratic predecessors and greatly benefited from the leadership centralization during the preceding twelve years of GOP control. She wielded significant influence over the legislative agenda and over the careers of rank-and-file members, and she used her position to pursue partisan policy initiatives, fundraise for her colleagues, exclude the minority party from decision-making, and relentlessly attack Republicans. Under Pelosi's leadership, minority party Democrats voted together at the highest rate in fifty years, averaging 92 percent support in both 2007 and 2008, according to *CQ Weekly*. Democratic committee chairs grateful to be in the majority—including some of whom had chaired their committees twelve years earlier—were willing to cede more power to party leaders than Democratic chairs had in the past.[32] After Democrats vociferously criticized GOP committee chair term limits, it took Democrats two years to repeal term limits on committee chairs once in the majority.

The conflict between Speaker Pelosi and John Dingell (D-Mich.) illustrates the extent to which party leaders had gained power. In the 110th Congress, Pelosi and Energy and Commerce Committee Chair John Dingell disagreed over important party legislative priorities. Dingell was a living (congressional) legend. The most senior member of the House, Dingell had been either the chair or ranking minority member on the Energy and Commerce Committee since 1981—six years before Speaker Pelosi was elected to Congress. Yet, as a committee chair, Dingell was the gatekeeper blocking Democrats' environmental policy, refusing to move Democrats' energy policy proposals through his committee because of his concerns about protecting the auto industry in his home district. To circumvent Dingell, Pelosi created a new Select Committee on Energy Independence and Global Warming and brought its legislation directly to the Democratic Caucus, much to Dingell's ire. By the 111th Congress, rank-and-file Democrats had enough of Chairman Dingell's refusal to move energy legislation, especially with a newly elected Democratic President Obama in the White House. In a violation of the seniority system, by a 137 to 122 vote, House Democrats replaced him with the committee's second most senior Democrat and Pelosi ally, Henry Waxman (D-Calif.). Not just any loyal Democrat, Waxman had played a key role shaping and passing Democrats' health and consumer protection agenda for decades, and he had been a fierce and partisan chair of the Government Reform and Oversight Committee in the 110th Congress.[33]

The role of the House Rules Committee during Pelosi's speakership shows just how significantly the power of party leaders has increased relative to that of congressional committees and committee chairs. When Democrats gave the Speaker the authority to appoint the majority party members of the Rules Committee with Caucus approval in 1975, that significantly bolstered the responsiveness of Rules Committee members to party leaders and increased the agenda setting power of the majority party leadership.[34] In the years that followed, the Rules Committee evolved to manage the "uncertainty" generated by an increasingly disgruntled minority and provide critical advantages for the majority party by limiting the number of open rules and preventing the minority party from amending legislation at the expense of majority party policy preferences.[35] However, once considered an "exclusive committee" that members sought out, by 2007 Speaker Pelosi needed to appoint an unprecedented number of freshmen, four, to the Rules Committee to fill its vacancies, and the committee dropped its "exclusive" designation so that all its members could add an additional committee assignment.[36] As the number of members' amendments permitted by special rules declined, it seemed the powerful "arm of the leadership" had become a rubber stamp for the leadership instead, lacking enough autonomy to make its exclusive service worthwhile to its members.

After the 2008 elections, the Democratic Caucus expanded its majority in the 111th Congress, and, most significantly, had the opportunity to work with a Democratic president, Barack Obama. To pass many elements of President Obama's agenda, Pelosi balanced satisfying the most liberal and conservative wings of her caucus, including members in the Blue Dog Coalition, a group of centrist and conservative Democrats, and the Progressive Caucus, a group of liberal Democrats. Pelosi frequently met with subgroups of Democrats, including the freshmen, to seek consensus on the party agenda.[37] Perhaps even more striking than Democrats' record-breaking level of party unity in the 110th Congress was the high level of Democratic unity in the 111th Congress, 91 percent in 2009 and 89 percent in 2012, when the Democratic majority was more heterogeneous than it had been in the previous Congress and Pelosi faced the challenge of passing, rather than attacking, the president's legislative program.

When it came to President Obama's most important legislative priority, health care reform, Pelosi's role in its passage can hardly be overstated. She started the process in the House before President Obama became intricately involved. Although three House committees marked up the bill, Pelosi put it together. When key House Democrats threatened to withdraw their support over disagreements related to abortion funding, Pelosi worked out a deal in her office to appease both sides. And when it seemed that the House and Senate would not be able to reconcile their versions of reform after Senate Democrats lost their filibuster-proof majority, Pelosi's leadership was critical in crafting and executing a complicated legislative strategy that resulted in the bills that President Obama ultimately signed into law.

Intraparty Factions and the Limits of Strong Party Leadership

Since the 2010 elections, factions within the Republican majority party have threatened majority party leaders' ability to govern and to protect the institutional standing of Congress. The challenges that GOP Speaker Boehner confronted, and that his successor Speaker Ryan confronts, demonstrate the difficulty of leading a majority party divided over strategy and institutional loyalty. With strong majority party leaders, committees and their chairs have fewer incentives to develop expertise and produce legislation than they did in the past.

Republicans gained sixty-four seats to win a 242 to 193 majority in the 2010 elections, their best showing since 1946. Republicans elected Boehner as Speaker, and he presided for nearly five tumultuous years until he announced his resignation on September 22, 2015, and handed the gavel to Paul Ryan (R-Wis.) on October 29, 2015. While the enthusiasm generated by the Tea Party movement and their anti-government rhetoric likely increased excitement in the electorate that bolstered Republicans in the 2010 elections, the newly elected Tea Party members of the House hindered Boehner's ability to lead the GOP Conference.

Boehner initially won the speakership with no opposition, as he had served as Minority Leader during Pelosi's speakership. First elected to the House in 1990, Boehner's path to leadership started with his ties to Newt Gingrich and his strategy of confrontation. As a freshman, Boehner was one of the "gang of seven" that urged GOP leaders to aggressively criticize Democratic leaders.[38] During Gingrich's speakership, Boehner served as Republican Conference Chair, but was defeated by J. C. Watts (R-Okla.) over his presumed involvement in a coup attempt against Gingrich.[39] Boehner turned to committee work as chair of the Education and Workforce Committee until 2006, when he was elected Majority Leader after Tom DeLay (R-Tex.) stepped down.[40]

In a departure from his recent predecessors, Boehner did not immediately extend the Speaker's power, and he promised to give more deference to committee chairs than Pelosi had. However, Boehner started off the 112th Congress by adhering to the party rule that limits chairs to six years, counting their time as chair and, importantly, their time as ranking member. Committee chairs complained that Boehner negotiated deals without them, cutting them out of the process.[41]

An intraparty Republican faction made it very difficult for Speaker Boehner to forge budget compromises with President Obama and Senate Majority Leader Harry Reid. In April 2011 Tea Party Republicans objected to a bill Boehner proposed to avert a government shutdown because they deemed the spending cuts insufficient. Forty percent of Tea Party Caucus members voted against its passage, compared to 19 percent of the remaining Republicans.[42] A few months later, Tea Party members again defected at higher rates (47 percent) than their Republican colleagues (21 percent) when Boehner brought a bill to the floor to raise the debt ceiling and establish a "supercommittee" to identify $1.5 trillion in budget cuts.[43] In the final budget showdown of 2011 on New Year's Eve, Boehner was forced to violate the Hastert rule by passing a budget bill that the majority of his party opposed, as 63 percent of Republicans voted against the deal extending the Bush-era tax cuts for most earners and postponing scheduled budget cuts that he negotiated with the president and Senate Democrats. Only 15 percent of Tea Party Caucus members supported the compromise, compared to 42 percent of other Republicans.[44] Three other bills Boehner brought to the floor in the 112th Congress also violated the Hastert rule.[45]

After the bruising 112th Congress, Boehner showed more willingness to exert power in the 113th Congress. He increased his own votes on the party's Steering Committee to five, decreasing the number of votes for the class of 2010, in turn, decreasing the influence of the Tea Party members. In a rare move, Boehner also removed four members from their powerful committees—three Tea Party members who often caused problems for Boehner, and one moderate who also defected too frequently.[46] Nonetheless, the 113th Congress started off with more headaches for the Speaker. The Speaker was reelected only after an attempted leadership coup was called off at the last minute and twelve Republicans voted against him.[47] Budget battles continued, and the federal government shut down for sixteen days in 2013. Congressional observers judged the 113th Congress harshly for its low productivity, and approval of Congress dipped to a record low of 9 percent during the 113th Congress.[48] Nonetheless, Republicans maintained the majority in the House, winning their largest majority since the 71st Congress.

Although Boehner was reelected Speaker in the 114th Congress, with twenty-five Republicans supporting another candidate, he resigned less than a year later. Boehner could not effectively lead a Conference divided over political strategy and institutional loyalty, and it seemed that he had had enough. Boehner's support had already eroded in the wake of past budget battles that had been resolved by compromises between Boehner, President Obama, and Democrats in Congress. In January 2015, around forty conservative Republicans disgruntled with Boehner's leadership, many of whom had previously identified as Tea Party Republicans, formed the Freedom Caucus. They worked to undermine Speaker Boehner on several key votes in 2015, arguing that Boehner was too conciliatory toward Democrats, even as Democrats opposed Boehner on many of these votes. They combined with Democrats to defeat a three-week continuing resolution to keep the Department of Homeland Security open, they tried to defeat a free trade bill, and they threatened to defeat a resolution of disapproval of the Iran nuclear agreement.

An intraparty battle in the fall of 2015 over Republicans' strategy to avert (or not) a government shutdown, this time in connection with Republican plans to defund Planned Parenthood, was exacerbated by calls from around twenty-five House Republicans to bring a no-confidence vote about the Speaker to the House floor.[49] To keep the government running after the September 30 deadline for Fiscal Year 2016 appropriations and to survive the no-confidence vote Boehner would have needed the votes of several Democrats, further weakening his fragile hold on the speakership.

Republicans ultimately got enough votes to pass a budget compromise that President Obama signed into law, but only after Boehner resigned so they could save face in supporting a compromise they had previously opposed to prevent a government shutdown.

Although many of those Republicans most critical of Boehner were also among the most conservative Republicans, the deepest disagreements within the conference were over strategy, not policy preferences. Republicans are unified on most policy issues, including in their support to eliminate funding for Planned Parenthood. Indeed, Boehner had brought a bill to defund Planned Parenthood to the House floor four days before he resigned, and it passed with the support of 239 Republicans, with opposition from only three Republicans. But, with a Senate filibuster blocking Senate action and threats of a presidential veto, the measure had no chance of becoming law on its own. The intraparty division centered on whether to force a government shutdown by linking the defunding measure to legislation to keep the government funded. In rejecting that strategy, and recognizing the limits and responsibilities of governing in the context of divided government, Boehner once again angered a vocal group of conservatives who were willing to incur damage to the party's reputation to press the issue.

As Speaker, Boehner had many institutional advantages, including agenda-setting power and several tools and prerogatives at his disposal to exert party discipline and reward members for their loyalty to the party, providing incentives for their cooperation. Yet Boehner's challenges and ultimate resignation demonstrate that even with highly centralized power in the hands of party leaders, balancing the dual imperatives of the speakership—responsibility for the institution and for one's party—is increasingly difficult in the context of divided government, polarized and competitive parties, and, perhaps most important, with a significant number of members who are less concerned about Congress' institutional legitimacy and place in the system of separated and shared powers than they are about particular policy goals. Boehner's job might have been easier with the support of more committee chairs with a greater stake in the legislative process. When he announced his resignation, Boehner highlighted the importance of protecting the institution: "The first job of any Speaker is to protect this institution that we all love . . . prolonged leadership turmoil would do irreparable damage to the institution."[50]

Paul Ryan did not immediately agree to be Speaker after Boehner announced his resignation, highlighting just how difficult the job of managing the majority party has become. After Ryan finally agreed, and most of the Freedom Caucus agreed to support him, he vowed to make institutional changes. After taking the oath of office as the 54th Speaker of the House, Ryan gave a speech on the House floor that made clear his agreement that party leaders had accrued too much power at the expense of committees and rank-and-file members: "We need to let every member contribute, not once they earn their stripes, but now. The committees should take the lead in drafting all major legislation: If you know the issue, you should write the bill. Let's open up the process. . . . In other words, we need to return to regular order."[51]

It was ironic that in a departure from previous eras, the call to return to regular order came in response to majority, not minority, party complaints (although minority party members were still vociferously complaining).

Six months into his speakership, Ryan has been praised for deferring more to committee chairs in the drafting of legislation and opening up the process by allowing more members to offer amendments.[52] He also has established a committee to reexamine GOP rules in the next year, including a change to Steering Committee rules to better reflect the geographic diversity of the Conference.[53] Ryan has also been criticized for falling short of his promise to return to regular order, as party leaders and their appointed task forces still make key decisions.[54] Ryan himself seems to recognize that the lack of institutional loyalty on the part of many GOP members, most visibly demonstrated by the disgruntled Republicans in the Freedom Caucus, causes bigger problems for House Republicans than does any divide over policy. In a speech at Heritage Action, he called upon Republicans to stop fighting over tactics: "And so what I want to say to you today is this: Don't take the bait. Don't fight over tactics."[55] As Ryan moves forward in the appropriations process, it seems likely that he will encounter challenges as he reconciles the competing institutional demands of the speakership and the demands of Conference members who place ideological and strategic goals ahead of their commitment to Congress's role in the constitutional system.

Conclusion

The Constitution divided power and created veto points in the legislative process to avoid tyranny and, in doing so, created a legislative obstacle course. In the contemporary era, competitive and polarized parties that view the president as the leader of his congressional party's team—what Mann and Ornstein refer to as "parliamentary style parties"—make governing within the constraints of the U.S. constitutional system even more difficult than anticipated.[56] As partisan polarization continued to increase following the reforms of the 1970s, and electoral competition between the two parties dramatically increased after the 1994 elections, party leaders gained strength over their own caucus and over the legislative process, but they were less able to effectively work across party lines, including with presidents of the other party. In the context of divided government, ideologically polarized parties increased legislative gridlock.[57]

Parties were not mentioned by name in the Constitution, and they were unpopular among the Framers.[58] Nonetheless, parties quickly emerged as a solution to the collective action problem inherent in getting a majority of individual members to support legislation and govern effectively. Parties also provide members with incentives to protect Congress's institutional standing and reputation relative to that of the president, but these incentives have broken down in the current era.

The committee system emerged as another important solution to legislating, and as a way to foster incentives for members to develop expertise and counterbalance the power of the executive branch. During the textbook era, committee leaders enjoyed gatekeeping power, as well as the ability to bring legislation to the floor, even over the objections of party leaders. The DSG bemoaned committee chairs' lack of responsiveness to the Democratic Caucus, and as liberal strength increased, the DSG prompted Democrats to reform the institution to give party leaders considerably more power at the expense of committee chairs' power. Republican innovations continued to strengthen party leaders' power.

Committee power has diminished considerably over the past four decades, with important implications. When crafting major legislation, party leaders have been increasingly likely to bypass the committee of jurisdiction altogether or make "postcommittee adjustments," changing the content of the bill. Data collected by Barbara Sinclair shows the extent to which party leaders ignore committees. According to Sinclair, when major bills reached the House floor in 1975–76, none had bypassed House committees of jurisdiction and only 15 percent were subject to postcommittee adjustment. A steady growth in bypassing committees and postcommittee adjustments occurs between the mid-1970s and the contemporary era. By 2009–10, Sinclair found, 34 percent of the House's major legislation bypassed the committee of jurisdiction and 39 percent of major House bills were subject to postcommittee adjustment.[59] Further, as power shifted from committee leaders to party leaders, committees did significantly less work. In 1979–80, House committees held 7,033 meetings. By 1999–2000, committees held only 3,347 meetings.[60] Committee chairs' declining power means that the agenda is often a function of partisan goals rather than the work of standing committees.

Despite the decline of committees, for the most part committee chairs and party leaders worked as a team during the postreform era. More recently, however, as Republican innovations continued to strengthen party leaders' power and diminish the overall role of committee chairs in the legislative process, resistance from intraparty factions have made it clear that majority party leaders would be stronger and more effective with the active support and engagement of their committee chairs. As Speaker Ryan considers rules changes, he would be wise to bolster the power of committees and committee chairs.

Intraparty divisions since House Republicans returned to the majority following the 2010 elections have limited party leaders' power, even in an era of strong party leaders and weak committee chairs. Intraparty factions within the Republican Conference, specifically the Tea Party Caucus in the 112th and 113th Congresses and the Freedom Caucus in the 114th Congress, and polarization between the parties have hindered Speakers' attempts to negotiate with the president and strike agreements over appropriations bills. As spelled out in Article 1, Section 7 of the Constitution, Congress has the power of the purse, which means it has the responsibility to pass appropriations bills to fund the federal government. In the contemporary era, Congress has struggled to fulfill this responsibility, particularly during times of divided government, leading to government shutdowns in 1995, 1996, and 2013. At the same time, sending "must pass" legislation to the president has, at times, been the only means for Congress to get anything accomplished. Reducing the use of omnibus legislation and ending the ban on congressional earmarks would engage more rank-and-file members in, and perhaps bolster support for, what has become a highly centralized process.

Unlike members of the DSG, Freedom Caucus members aren't seeking institutional reforms. Instead, they are willing to shut the government down if they can't achieve their policy goals. When twenty or thirty majority party members refuse to support bipartisan compromise and the Speaker is forced to rely on some minority party members, it erodes party leadership. At the same time, if Speaker Boehner had had stronger committee chairs supporting him, committee chairs with more power over the agenda and thus the lives of rank-and-file members, he might have been more successful.

As Speaker Ryan tries to forward a legislative agenda, or needs to forge a compromise with a Democratic president, he will be more likely to succeed with less centralization and more involvement from rank-and-file members. If more legislation worked its way through the committee process and committee members were assured that most of their work would be protected in the Rules Committee, committee chairs and majority party committee members would have influence over the process and investment in the outcome.[61] Even noncommittee members would be more invested if committee deference becomes important again, and resistance from intraparty factions may lessen.

The result of the current system, at least in the current 114th Congress, is nominally strong party leaders who are weakened by their own members, despite their many prerogatives, and weak committee chairs, leaving Congress with insufficient power and incentives to overcome institutional hurdles and fulfill its constitutional responsibilities.

Notes

1. *Federalist* No. 51, in *The Federalist Papers* (http://thomas.loc.gov/home/histdox/fed_51.html).

2. Senators' prerogative to engage in unlimited debate, or filibuster, is not written anywhere in the Constitution. Instead, the Framers anticipated that the Senate would operate under majority rule; see Sarah A. Binder and Steven S. Smith, *Politics or Principle? Filibustering in the United States Senate* (Brookings Institution Press, 1997).

3. Matthew N. Green, *The Speaker of the House: A Study of Leadership* (Yale University Press, 2010).

4. Randall Strahan, *Leading Representatives: The Agency of Leaders in the Politics of the U.S. House* (Johns Hopkins University Press, 2007).

5. Eric Schickler, *Disjointed Pluralism: Institutional Innovation and the Development of the U.S. Congress* (Princeton University Press, 2001).

6. Ibid.

7. Herbert B. Asher, "The Learning of Legislative Norms," *American Political Science Review* 67, no. 2 (1973), pp. 499–513; Lewis A. Froman Jr., *The Congressional Process: Strategies, Rules, and Procedures* (Boston, Mass.: Little, Brown,

1967); George Goodwin Jr., *The Little Legislatures* (University of Massachusetts Press, 1970).

8. Nelson W. Polsby, *How Congress Evolves: Social Bases of Institutional Change* (Oxford University Press, 2003).

9. David W. Brady and Charles Bullock III, "Is there a Conservative Coalition in the House?" *Journal of Politics* 42, no. 2 (1980), pp. 549–59; Richard Bolling, *House Out of Order* (New York: Dutton, 1965); Joseph Cooper and David W. Brady, "Institutional Context and Leadership Style," *American Political Science Review* 75, no. 2 (1981), pp. 411–25; Charles O. Jones, "Joseph G. Cannon and Howard W. Smith: An Essay on the Limits of Leadership in the House of Representatives," *Journal of Politics* 30 (1968), pp. 617–46; Polsby *How Congress Evolves*; Kathryn Pearson and Eric Schickler, "Discharge Petitions, Agenda Control, and the Congressional Committee System, 1929–1976," *Journal of Politics* 71, no. 4 (2009), pp. 1238–56; Kathryn Pearson and Eric Schickler, "The Transition to Democratic Leadership in a Polarized House," in *Congress Reconsidered*, 9th ed., edited by Lawrence C. Dodd and Bruce I. Oppenheimer (Washington, D.C.: CQ Press, 2009); Kenneth A. Shepsle, "The Changing Textbook Congress," in *Can the Government Govern?*, edited by John E. Chubb and Paul Peterson (Brookings Institution Press, 1989).

10. Eric Schickler and Kathryn Pearson, "Agenda Control, Majority Party Power, and the House Committee on Rules, 1937–65," *Legislative Studies Quarterly* 34, no. 4 (2009), pp. 455–91.

11. Pearson and Schickler, "Discharge Petitions."

12. David W. Rohde, *Parties and Leaders in the Postreform House* (Chicago University Press, 1991); Polsby, *How Congress Evolves*; Kathryn Pearson, *Party Discipline in the U.S. House of Representatives* (University of Michigan Press, 2015).

13. Bolling, *House out of Order*, p. 70.

14. Eric Schickler and Kathryn Pearson, "The House Leadership in an Era of Partisan Warfare," in *Congress Reconsidered*, 8th ed. (Washington D.C.: CQ Press, 2004).

15. Burton D. Sheppard, *Rethinking Congressional Reform* (Cambridge: Schenkman Books, Inc., 1985); Arthur G. Stevens Jr., Arthur H. Miller, and Thomas E. Mann, "Mobilization of Liberal Strength in the House, 1955–1970: The Democratic Study Group," *American Political Science Review* 68 (1974), pp. 667–81.

16. Rohde, *Parties and Leaders in the Postreform House*; Polsby, *How Congress Evolves*.

17. Ibid.

18. Rohde, *Parties and Leaders in the Postreform House*; Eric Schickler, Eric McGhee, and John Sides, "Remaking the House and Senate: Personal Power, Ideology, and the 1970s Reforms," *Legislative Studies Quarterly* 28 (2003), pp. 297–331.

19. Sara Brandes Crook and John R. Hibbing, "Congressional Reform and Party Discipline: The Effects of Changes in the Seniority System on Party Loy-

alty in the U.S. House of Representatives," *British Journal of Political Science,* 15, no. 20 (1985), pp. 207–26.

20. Rohde, *Parties and Leaders in the Postreform House*; Eric Schickler, *Disjointed Pluralism: Institutional Innovation and the Development of the U.S. Congress* (Princeton University Press, 2001).

21. Schickler, *Disjointed Pluralism.*

22. Roger H. Davidson, "The Emergence of the Postreform Congress," in *The Postreform Congress,* edited by Roger Davidson (New York: St. Martin's Press, 1992).

23. Rohde, *Parties and Leaders in the Postreform House.*

24. William Connelly and John J. Pitney Jr., *Congress' Permanent Minority? Republicans in the U.S. House* (Lanham, Md.: Rowman and Littlefield, 1994).

25. Connelly and Pitney, *Congress' Permanent Minority?*; Rohde, *Parties and Leaders in the Postreform House.*

26. Connelly and Pitney, *Congress' Permanent Minority?*

27. Pearson, *Party Discipline.*

28. Thomas E. Mann and Norman J. Ornstein, *The Broken Branch: How Congress Is Failing America and How to Get It Back on Track* (Oxford University Press, 2006); Schickler and Pearson, "The House Leadership in an Era of Partisan Warfare."

29. Pearson, *Party Discipline.*

30. Pearson and Schickler, "The Transition to Democratic Leadership in a Polarized House."

31. Barbara Sinclair, *Party Wars: Polarization and the Politics of National Policy Making* (University of Oklahoma Press, 2006); Juliet Eilperin, *Fight Club Politics: How Partisanship Is Poisoning the U.S. House of Representatives* (Lanham, Md.: Rowman and Littlefield Press, 2006); Mann and Ornstein, *The Broken Branch.*

32. Pearson, *Party Discipline.*

33. Edward Epstein, "Upset Is Not First Shock to the Seniority System," *CQ Weekly,* November 24, 2008, p. 3150.

34. Stanley Bach and Steven S. Smith, *Managing Uncertainty in the House of Representatives: Adaptation and Innovation in Special Rules* (Brookings Institution Press, 1988); Bruce I. Oppenheimer, "The Rules Committee: New Arm of the Leadership in a Decentralized House," in *Congress Reconsidered,* 1st ed., edited by Lawrence C. Dodd and Bruce I. Oppenheimer (New York: Praeger, 1977); Barbara Sinclair, *Legislators, Leaders, and Lawmaking: The U.S. House of Representatives in the Postreform Era* (Johns Hopkins University Press, 1995); Rohde, *Parties and Leaders in the Postreform House*; Schickler, *Disjointed Pluralism.*

35. Bach and Smith, *Managing Uncertainty*; Sinclair, *Party Wars.*

36. Rebecca Kimitch, "CQ Guide to the Committees: Democrats Opt to Spread the Power," *CQ Weekly,* April 16, 2007, pp. 1080–83.

37. Ronald M. Peters Jr. and Cindy Simon Rosenthal, *Speaker Nancy Pelosi and the New American Politics* (Oxford University Press, 2010).

38. Alan K. Ota, "Boehner Braces for Post-Election Title Fight," *CQ Weekly*, October 13, 2008, p. 2751.

39. Joseph J. Schatz, "The Trials Ahead for John Boehner," *CQ Weekly*, November 8, 2010, pp. 2520–23.

40. Ibid.

41. Jennifer Steinhauer, "Paul Ryan Brings Sharply Different Leadership Style to House," *New York Times*, December 7, 2015.

42. Anthony J. Chergosky, "Boiling Point: Tea Party Politics, Intra-Party Conflict, and the Republicans of the 112th Congress," Senior Thesis University of Minnesota-Twin Cities, 2013.

43. Ibid.

44. Ibid.

45. Ryan Kelly, "GOP Majority: Once More, Unto the Breach" *CQ Weekly*, January 7, 2013, p. 7.

46. Pearson, *Party Discipline*.

47. Jonathan Strong, "Speak Softly or Carry a Big Stick," *CQ Weekly*, January 14, 2013, pp. 62–64.

48. "Congress and the Public," *Gallup* (www.gallup.com/poll/1600/congress-public.aspx).

49. Jennifer Steinhauer, "John Boehner, House Speaker, Will Resign From Congress," *New York Times,* September 25, 2015.

50. "Statement by House Speaker John Boehner" (www.speaker.gov/press-release/statement-house-speaker-john-boehner).

51. "Speaker Ryan's Remarks to the House of Representatives," October 29, 2015 (www.speaker.gov/press-release/speaker-ryans-remarks-house-representatives).

52. Jennifer Steinhauer, "Paul Ryan Brings Sharply Different Leadership Style to House," *New York Times*, December 7, 2015; "Anatomy of a Vote: A Freewheeling Process Under Ryan," *CQ Weekly,* November 9, 2015.

53. "Congressional Affairs: If Not New Laws, Maybe New Rules," *CQ Weekly*, January 4, 2016.

54. Dana Milbank, "Paul Ryan Quickly Restores the House's Regular Disorder," *Washington Post,* November 18, 2015.

55. Paul Waldman, "Paul Ryan to the Tea Party: You Are the Problem," *Washington Post,* February 3, 2016.

56. Thomas E. Mann and Norman J. Ornstein, *It's Even Worse Than It Looks: How the American Constitutional System Collided with the New Politics of Extremism* (New York: Basic Books, 2012); Frances E. Lee, *Beyond Ideology: Politics, Principles, and Partisanship in the U.S. Senate* (University of Chicago Press, 2009).

57. Sarah A. Binder, "The Dynamics of Legislative Gridlock, 1947–96," *American Political Science Review* 93 (September 1999), pp. 519–33.

58. Although Madison conceded that political parties were inevitable, his concern about factions still resonates among political theorists and political observers today.

59. Barbara Sinclair, *Unorthodox Lawmaking* (Washington, D.C.: CQ Press, 2012), p. 147.

60. See Norman J. Ornstein, Thomas E. Mann, and Michael J. Malbin, *Vital Statistics on Congress, 2001–2002*. (Washington, DC: AEI Press, 2002), p. 146.

61. In today's polarized era, it is unrealistic to assume that minority party committee members are likely to be invested absent bipartisan compromise.

Ending the Omnibus

Restoring Regular Order in Congressional Appropriations

PETER C. HANSON

The annual appropriations process is in a state of collapse, and it is time to take some serious steps to restore it to health. A primary symptom of the collapse of appropriations is the decline of what is known as "regular order." Regular order is a time-tested system in which a dozen or so (the exact number has varied) appropriations bills are debated and adopted on an individual basis by the House and Senate. It is advantageous because it breaks the budget into bite-sized pieces and facilitates oversight.

Today, a depressingly familiar pattern has replaced regular order. Most appropriations bills pass the House of Representatives only to die in the Senate. In response, lawmakers bundle appropriations bills together into massive "omnibus" packages near the end of a session. These packages may be thousands of pages long, include over a trillion dollars in spending, and are adopted with little debate or scrutiny. In fact, limiting scrutiny is the goal. Leaders count on end-of-session pressures and the fear of a government shutdown to allow adoption of the package with minimal debate. In their view, it's the only way to push a budget through the gridlocked Senate floor.

The pattern is clear; both chambers have a hand in the creation of omnibus legislation, but the Senate is disproportionately responsible for the breakdown in appropriations.

The cost of its failure is high. Omnibus legislating prevents rank-and-file members from exercising genuine oversight over the budget. Unwise spending and policies are more likely to go uncontested. Funding is likely to be provided after the beginning of the fiscal year, forcing agencies to rely on temporary continuing resolutions that create waste and inefficiency. And, disruptive government shutdowns are larger and more likely.

It is time to restore regular order in appropriations. My research shows the following:

- Senators prefer regular order, but turn to omnibus packages because the Senate's individualistic rules permit appropriations bills to be delayed or used to force votes on politically painful amendments.
- Lowering the threshold for cloture on appropriations bills to a simple majority would let the majority party better manage debate on the Senate floor to keep the trains running smoothly.
- Other reforms, such as easing transparency requirements and restoring earmarking, might also ease the path through Congress for these critical bills.

This chapter summarizes a lengthier paper presented to the National Budgeting Roundtable in 2015.[1] It explains the research behind these findings and makes the case for reform.

Appropriations Transformed

Appropriations bills fund about a third of the budget, including all discretionary spending that must be authorized on an annual basis by Congress. The wide range of programs funded through discretionary spending gives it an importance beyond its share of the budget. If Congress fails to provide discretionary funds, FBI agents won't be paid, cancer research won't be funded, and passports won't be processed. The lives of those who depend on these programs will be disrupted. An effective appropriations process also provides a critical way for Congress to oversee federal agencies, manage the budget, and carry out policy.

Historically, Congress provided discretionary funds by adopting appropriations bills through a standard set of procedures known as "regular order."[2] Appropriations bills originated in the subcommittees of the House

Appropriations Committee. Each bill covered a particular area of jurisdiction, such as defense or agriculture. The bills were approved by the full Appropriations Committee, debated and adopted on the House floor, and then sent to the Senate. The Senate repeated these steps. Both chambers then negotiated a final version of each bill, passed it again, and sent it to the president.

Regular order was standard practice in the House and Senate until the late 1970s. There have been two waves of omnibus appropriating driven by a collapse of regular order in the Senate. Figure 9-1 illustrates this collapse using the proportion of spending bills receiving an individual vote in each chamber each year as its measure. It also illustrates the proportion of bills enacted as part of a package each year.[3] Between 1975 and 2012, a total of 88 percent of regular appropriations bills received a vote in the House of Representatives, but only 74 percent received a vote in the Senate.[4] Fully 61 percent of bills were enacted on an individual basis in regular order. The remaining bills were enacted as part of an omnibus package, or funding was provided through a yearlong continuing resolution. The trend has grown worse over time. Today, virtually all appropriations bills are passed in a package rather than in regular order.

The roots of the collapse run deep. Research suggests that broad changes in the congressional environment originating in the 1960s made it more difficult to pass spending bills on an individual basis in the Senate. Senators abandoned a culture of deference that characterized the chamber in the mid-twentieth century in favor of a culture of individual activism.[5] Where senators once would have deferred to the decisions of appropriators, they were now more likely to contest them. Sunshine laws opened senators to more public scrutiny than in the past.[6] Good government advocates welcomed this transparency, but it also had the effect of making compromise more difficult by raising the cost of straying from publicly held positions. Rising polarization caused by deep societal changes created an ideological rift between the two parties, increasing the likelihood of filibusters and intensifying partisan competition.[7] Deficit politics raised the stakes of budgetary decisions.[8]

These developments are problematic in the Senate because the chamber operates on a principle of accommodation.[9] The Senate's rules permit unlimited debate on virtually any matter unless sixty senators vote to end it. They also allow unlimited amending by members, including on matters not germane to the topic at hand. The net effect of these rules is that they prevent the majority party from controlling the legislative agenda in the Senate as is possible in the House. The majority generally cannot adopt (or

FIGURE 9-1. The Collapse of Regular Order in the Appropriations Committees, U.S. Congress, 1975–2012

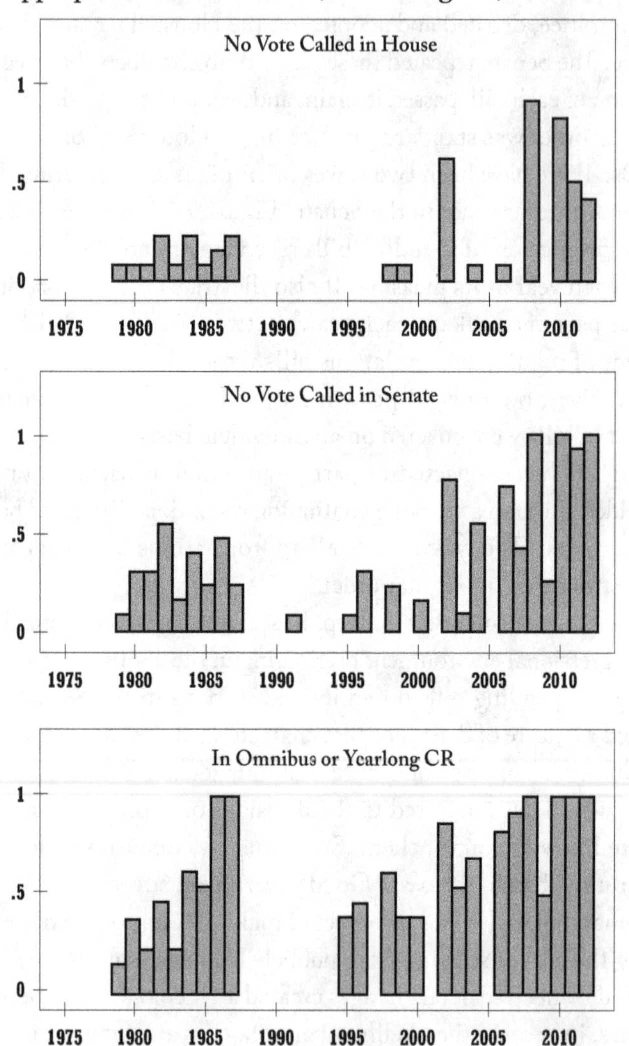

sometimes even debate) legislation without some buy-in from the minority, and the minority can usually ensure that its preferred policies receive a vote. In today's activist, polarized Senate, such agreement is hard to find and gridlock is the common result.[10]

Figure 9-2 illustrates why gridlock is more likely in today's Senate than in the past. Each marker represents a Democratic or Republican senator

FIGURE 9-2. Ideological Distance from 51st to 60th Voter, U.S. Senate, 95th and 112th Congresses

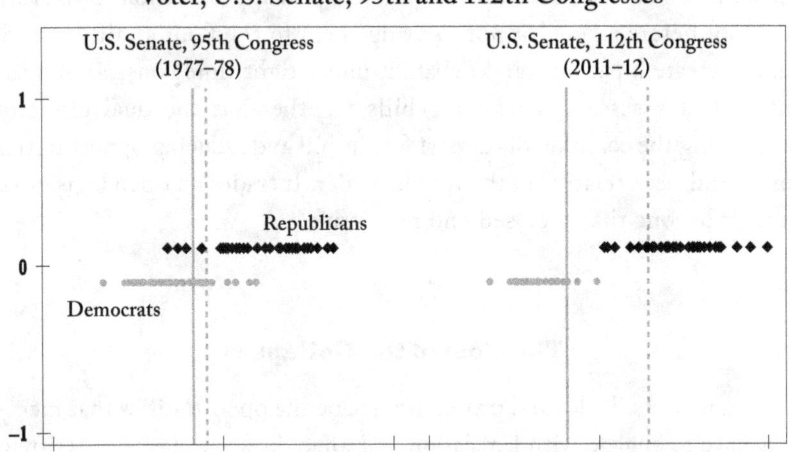

placed on his or her estimated position on the DW-Nominate ideological scale. On this scale, –1 represents the most liberal position and 1 represents the most conservative. To end a filibuster, a Democratic majority would have to secure sixty votes by building a coalition from the left to the right. In the 95th Congress (1977–78), the majority had to bridge only a small ideological distance to move from fifty-one votes (solid vertical line) to sixty (dotted vertical line). Agreements would have been relatively easy to reach. By the 112th Congress (2011–12), the gap between the fifty-first voter and the sixtieth had widened into a gulf. The policy concessions required today to build a sixty-vote coalition are much larger than in the past, and such agreements are harder to reach. More often than not, members cannot reach agreement and the result is gridlock.

These changes have made the task of adopting appropriations bills in the Senate particularly difficult. My research shows there are two main problems. First, the Senate pays for the sins of the House. The House passes most appropriations bills, but not all. By tradition, the Senate usually will not debate an appropriations bill if the House has not passed it first. Second, appropriations bills that do reach the Senate are caught in the quagmire of the Senate floor. Members target appropriations bills with swarms of amendments designed to cause the other party damage in the next election. They also filibuster spending bills and cause delays that ripple through the already crowded legislative calendar. The net effect of these tactics is to persuade the majority party to pull appropriations bills from the floor before a vote, or not to bring them to the floor at all. Instead, leaders create a package and debate it under tight time constraints near the end of a session. Packaging bills together has the dual effect of broadening the coalition of support for the bill and reducing opportunities for amendment relative to the regular order. It trades an open legislative process for one that is closed and restrictive.

The Cost of the Collapse

Process matters. Rules and procedures shape the opportunities that members have to engage with legislation and affect how legislation is written. Better process, better contents.

Political scientist Matt Green has argued that the advantage of regular order is that it allows members to challenge problematic provisions in open debate and strike or amend them. Unwise policies can be adjusted and wasteful spending can be removed. Abandoning regular order "risks enacting substandard legislation" because it eliminates this natural check in the legislative process.[11] Omnibus legislating moves lawmaking behind closed doors. Rank-and-file members are given few if any opportunities to change the final package. More errors, mistakes, and waste may creep into the final legislation as a result.

The dramatic decline of amending in the Senate illustrates why the collapse in regular order makes it harder to adjust spending bills. Figure 9-3 plots the total number of roll call votes on amendments to appropriations legislation (both regular and omnibus bills) in the House and Senate for each year from 1981 to 2012, weighted by the number of members in each chamber. The solid line is fitted to Senate amendments, the dotted to House amendments. The number of amendments per member in the House has crept steadily upward over time. Amendments from both parties are debated and voted on in the House. Minority amendments sometimes win. In the Senate, amending has collapsed. The number of votes per member on amendments is trending toward zero. The cause of this decline is simple: senators rarely debate individual appropriations bills on the floor anymore.

While more research is needed on the policy consequence of the collapse of regular order (see, for example, McCarty 2014),[12] the net result of the shift toward omnibus legislating is legislation that is likely worse

FIGURE 9-3. Weighted Roll Call Votes on Amendments, U.S. Congress, 1981–2012

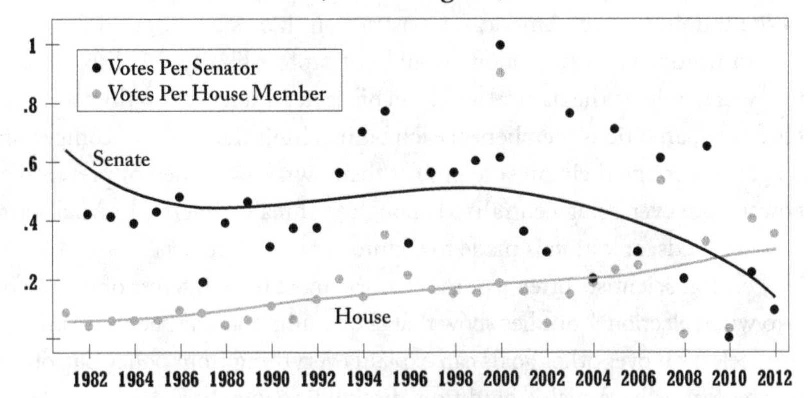

than what Congress would produce in effectively managed regular order. Budget hawks say omnibus packages are wasteful. Good government groups say unwise policies are buried in them. As Senator Susan Collins (R-Maine) observed: "Those bills are often thousands of pages in length. A lot of times some of the provisions have not had the opportunity to be thoroughly vetted. They really are not very transparent. They contribute to the public's concern about the way we do business here in Washington."[13]

There also is evidence that the late passage of appropriations bills contributes to poor management of federal agencies and wasteful spending. When Congress fails to adopt appropriations bills by the beginning of the fiscal year, it must adopt a temporary continuing resolution to provide stopgap funding to federal agencies. The Government Accountability Office reports that temporary continuing resolutions lead to inefficient spending and inhibit federal agencies' ability to carry out their appointed tasks.[14] It also increases the risk of a government shutdown and the serious disruptions to the lives of the American people. Standard and Poor's estimated that the 2013 shutdown cost the economy $24 billion.[15]

Appropriations Reform

Many of the root causes of the collapse in appropriations are with us for the foreseeable future. We can't turn back the clock on partisan polarization or persuade senators to restrain themselves from offering amendments. But, the appropriations process, obviously, can be improved.

Successful reforms must follow an important rule: they must advance the interests of members to be effective. This rule reflects an insight dating back to the framing of the American Constitution. James Madison understood that institutions and rules alone would not protect liberty. Madison's solution was to rely on the natural ambition of elected leaders to do this work. In his design, ambitious members of each branch limit the power of competing branches through their effort to protect their own power, thereby preventing power from ever being centralized enough to threaten liberty. In Madison's famous words, ambition is made to counteract ambition.

Political scientists often assume that the most basic interest of members is to win reelection.[16] Studies show that the assumption that members prioritize reelection over other goals can explain everything from policy outcomes to why parties have such a hard time disciplining members. It also explains why budget reforms usually fail; too often they are thinly disguised efforts to compel members to take steps that will cause them political harm. Members either water down reforms or circumvent them at the first opportunity.[17]

My research shows that well-managed regular order would advance member reelection interests. Debating appropriations bills gives members the chance to claim credit for accomplishments and take positions on matters important to their constituents, both activities that help them win reelection. Members prefer to follow regular order when they adopt appropriations bills, and they only abandon it when runaway amending and filibusters threaten to impose unacceptable political costs on them. Members have an incentive to return to regular order as long as those costs can be managed.

Restoring regular order will not be easy, especially because newer members may never have experienced a time when omnibus legislating was not routine. Here, I suggest a set of Senate reforms designed to smooth the path of appropriations bills through the floor and be compatible with the reelection interests of members.

Reform the Filibuster

Allow a simple majority of senators to end debate on all matters related to appropriations bills. Effective debate in regular order requires one of two things. Either members must exercise restraint during debate, as was common in the past, or leaders must manage debate to keep it under control. In today's Senate, senators no longer exercise restraint and leaders lack basic tools to manage debate. The majority party faces an unpalatable choice. It can bring bills to the floor in regular order and face runaway amending and filibusters, or it can bypass the floor, make an omnibus, and bring it up at the last minute, when debate will be expedited. Reforming the filibuster would give Senate leaders a third option: managed debate.

By filibuster reform, I mean changing the Senate's rules to allow a simple majority of senators to end debate on all matters related to appropriations bills. This step would simultaneously allow a majority to control amending as well as prevent dilatory tactics by a minority. Existing germaneness requirements would also have to be strengthened to prevent senators from being tempted to add non-appropriations legislation to spending bills as well.

Senators have already demonstrated that they believe filibuster reform is in their interest and that it can improve the Senate's productivity. In November 2013 Democrats exercised the so-called "nuclear option" to allow the Senate to proceed to a vote on certain presidential nominations by a simple majority vote. The number of federal judges confirmed by the Senate jumped dramatically as a result.[18] The Senate could be equally productive with appropriations bills.

Policy would be impacted as well. In a reformed Senate, legislation would be written to satisfy the preference of the member needed to provide a majority, just as the 60th senator whose vote is needed for cloture must be satisfied today. Members would debate spending, scrutinize the budget, and offer amendments. If they abused the process, the majority would have the option of ending debate and moving to a vote.

Critics of this idea have expressed several concerns. Some say the filibuster protects debate in the Senate and eliminating it would allow the majority to suppress debate on appropriations bills. The evidence suggests otherwise. As shown, senators now have a worse opportunity to debate spending bills than members of the House because Senate leaders are determined to avoid the floor. Meanwhile, House leaders have taken minimal steps to suppress debate on appropriations bills even as polarization has risen to historic levels. Bills come to the floor under modified open rules that allow any amendment to be debated as long as it is preprinted in the *Congressional Record*. When the members abuse this system, the majority cracks down with a structured rule.[19] There is no reason to think the Senate would do worse than the majoritarian House.

A second criticism is that the filibuster is a critical part of the nation's system of checks and balances that protects the public from bad legislation. This criticism also does not withstand scrutiny. First, the Framers' system of checks and balances only requires majorities in the House and Senate plus the president to agree on legislation. The filibuster is an additional hurdle that was created accidently when senators updated their rules and failed to include a motion to call previous question.[20] Second, senators would still be able to filibuster general legislation. Appropriations bills would be treated differently because of the requirement to pass them every year. General legislation could continue to simmer as long as it takes sixty senators to reach agreement.

Use Concurrent Consideration of Appropriations Bills

The House of Representatives also fails at times to pass appropriations bills. These failures are infrequent and idiosyncratic in their causes, but they are consequential because the Senate typically respects a tradition that it will not adopt (or often even debate) appropriations bills that have not first passed the House.

There is no reason senators should be denied the opportunity to debate an appropriations bill because of a failure in the House. It is a common misunderstanding that the Constitution requires appropriations bills to be initiated by the House of Representatives, like tax legislation. The Senate should debate appropriations bills concurrently with the House instead of waiting for the House to adopt them first. This step would ensure that at least one chamber debates a spending bill in regular order and that members have an opportunity to work their will on the legislation. It would also be in the interest of senators because it would give them expanded opportunities to take positions and claim credit for accomplishments.

Restore Limited Earmarking

Political science research shows that earmarking helps congressional leaders build a coalition of support for a bill.[21] The ban on earmarking in appropriations bills has had the unintended effect of making it harder to pass this vital legislation. Restoring limited earmarking could create an important tool for coalition-building, thus facilitating passage of appropriations bills.

The backlash against earmarking was rooted in the fact that the number of earmarks rose rapidly from the 1990s to the early 2000s. Appropriators complained they were overwhelmed with requests and budget hawks claimed earmarks were wasteful spending.

A limited restoration of earmarks could satisfy both concerns. Member requests could be capped to prevent appropriators from being flooded with requests. Members have historically understood earmarks to be in their reelection interest, and would likely do so again as long as the number of requests is effectively managed.

Reduce Transparency

Good government reformers have made a decades-long push to make the activities of members more transparent to the public so that members can be held accountable for their decisions. Some political scientists say these efforts have been too successful and that the deal-making needed for orderly government is now too difficult because members are criticized the moment they stray from an established public position.[22]

One option would be to return to an earlier system in which total vote tallies rather than the votes of individual members are reported for appropriations bills. Members might be more willing to cast tough votes, and there would be a reduced incentive for "gotcha" amendments aimed only at causing members political harm. The path of appropriations bills through the floor would likely be smoother.

Conclusion

Fixing appropriations requires a clear understanding of where the process is breaking down and why. My research shows that the Senate is the primary culprit. The House occasionally fails to pass spending bills, but the reasons for this are idiosyncratic and hard to fix. Meanwhile, the main breakdown is happening in the Senate. Leaders bypass the floor because they have no way to control amendments and filibusters. Instead, they turn to omnibus bills despite widespread agreement that these are a poor way to legislate. It's time to return to a more rational way of legislating.

Some of the reforms outlined in this chapter are likely to be controversial, particularly reforming the filibuster. As the parties have grown farther apart, the perceived stakes each party sees in stopping its opponent from enacting its agenda have grown higher. Defenders of the filibuster see it as the only thing protecting them from a policy catastrophe. The problem is that inaction also has a cost. When neither party can implement a coherent policy agenda, critical problems go unaddressed. Ultimately, critics must understand that it is not the responsibility of a Senate minority to protect the public from bad policy. Senate majorities should be allowed to govern in conjunction with the House and the executive branch. Voters can hold them accountable for their decisions in elections.

Restoring regular order in appropriations won't solve all our budget woes or slay the deficit dragon. But, as President Barack Obama said of foreign policy, sometimes policymakers must hit singles and doubles to advance national interests one step at a time.[23] The same is true of the budget. Taking the steps outlined here to restore regular order would improve the capacity of Congress to adopt appropriations bills in a timely way with appropriate scrutiny by lawmakers. Omnibus bills and last-minute budget deals would be smaller and more infrequent. After nearly two decades of careening from budget train wreck to budget train wreck, that would be a good start.

Notes

1. Peter C. Hanson, "Restoring the Regular Order in Congressional Appropriations," New Ideas for Federal Budgeting: A Series of Working Papers for the National Budgeting, Centers on the Public Service (George Mason University, 2005) (http://psc.gmu.edu/wp-content/uploads/New-Ideas-for-Federal-Budget-Working-Paper-No.-1.pdf).

2. Allen Schick, *The Federal Budget: Politics, Policy and Process*, 3rd ed. (Brookings Institution Press: 2007).

3. Peter C. Hanson, *Too Weak to Govern: Majority Party Power and Appropriations in the U.S. Senate* (Cambridge University Press, 2014); Peter C. Hanson, "Abandoning the Regular Order: Majority Party Influence on Appropriations in the United States Senate," *Political Research Quarterly* 67.

4. The vast majority of bills voted on by a chamber are approved.

5. Barbara Sinclair, "Senate Styles and Senate Decision Making, 1955–1980," *Journal of Politics* 48 (1986), pp. 877–908; Richard Fenno, "The Senate through the Looking Glass: The Debate over Television," *Legislative Studies Quarterly* (1989).

6. Donald R. Wolfensberger, *Congress and the People: Deliberative Democracy on Trial* (Washington, D.C.: Woodrow Wilson Center Press, 2000).

7. David Brady and Craig Volden, *Revolving Gridlock: Politics and Policy from Jimmy Carter to George W. Bush* (Boulder, Colo: Westview Press, 2006); Nolan McCarty, Keith Poole, and Howard Rosenthal, *Polarized America: The Dance of Ideology and Unequal Riches* (MIT Press: 2006).

8. Aaron Wildavsky and Naomi Caiden, *The New Politics of the Budgetary Process*, 5th ed. (New York: Pearson Longman, 2004).

9. Steve Smith, "Parties and Leadership in the Senate," in *The Legislative Branch*, edited by Paul J. Quirk and Sarah A. Binder (Oxford University Press, 2005).

10. Barbara Sinclair, "The "60-Vote Senate": Strategies, Process and Outcomes," in *U.S. Senate Exceptionalism*, edited by Bruce Oppenheimer (Ohio State University, 2002).

11. Matthew Green and Daniel Burns, "What Might Bring Regular Order Back to the House?" *PS: Political Science and Politics* 43 (2010), pp. 223–26.

12. Nolan McCarty, Keith T. Poole, and Howard Rosenthal, *Polarized America: The Dance of Ideology and Unequal Riches* (MIT Press, 2006).

13. *Congressional Record*, February 27, 2012, S1041.

14. Government Accountability Office, "Effects of Budget Uncertainty from Continuing Resolutions on Agency Operations" (http://www.gao.gov/products/GAO-13-464T).

15. Josh Hicks, "How Much Did the Shutdown Cost the Economy?" *Washington Post*, October 18, 2013 (www.washingtonpost.com/blogs/federal-eye/wp/2013/10/18/how-much-did-the-shutdown-cost-the-economy).

16. Richard Fenno, *Congressmen in Committees* (Boston, Mass.: Little, Brown and Company, 1973); David Mayhew, *Congress: The Electoral Connection* (Yale University Press, 1974).

17. David Primo, *Rules and Restraint: Government Spending and the Design of Institutions* (University of Chicago Press, 2007).

18. Christina L. Boyd, Michael S. Lynch, and Anthony J. Madonna, "Nuclear Fallout: Investigating the Effect of Senate Procedural Reform on Judicial Nominations," *The Forum* 13 (2016), pp. 623–41.

19. Peter C. Hanson, "Open Rules in a Close House: Agenda Control in House Appropriations from 1995–2012," Paper Presented at the Congress and History Conference, Vanderbilt University, 2015.

20. Sarah Binder and Steve Smith, *Politics or Principle: Filibustering in the United States Senate* (Brookings Institution Press, 1997).

21. Diana Evans, *Greasing the Wheels: Using Pork Barrel Projects to Build Majority Coalitions in Congress* (Cambridge, Cambridge University Press, 2004).

22. Sarah A. Binder and Frances E. Lee, "Making Deals in Congress," in *Political Negotiation: A Handbook,* edited by Jane Mansbridge and Cathie Jo Martin (Brookings Institution Press, 2016).

23. Barack Obama, Remarks by President Obama and President Benigno Aquino III of the Philippines in Joint Press Conference, Manila, April 28, 2014 (www.whitehouse.gov/the-press-office/2014/04/28/remarks-president-obama-and-president-benigno-aquino-iii-philippines-joi).

Political Realism

How Hacks, Machines, Big Money, and Back-Room Deals Can Strengthen American Democracy

JONATHAN RAUCH

In December 2014, progressives and Tea Partiers found common ground, not something that happens every day. Congressional leaders had attached to an omnibus spending bill a rider increasing by a factor of almost ten the amount that individuals could donate to the national parties for conventions and certain other purposes. Progressives denounced the measure as among "the most corrupting campaign finance provisions ever enacted," a gift to special interests and plutocrats.[1] Tea Partiers denounced the measure as "a sneaky power grab by establishment Republicans designed to undermine outside conservative groups," a gift to incumbents and party insiders.[2] For quite different reasons, it seems, these two antagonistic factions managed to agree that the flow of money to party professionals is a menace.

It was a small but telling instance of one of America's oddest but most consequential political phenomena: the continuous and systematic onslaught against political machines and insiders by progressivism, populism, and libertarianism, three very different political reform movements that, nonetheless, all regard transactional politics as, at best, a necessary evil and more often as corrupt and illegitimate. This attack, though well intentioned, has badly damaged the country's governability, a predictable result (and one accurately predicted more than fifty years ago). Fortunately, much of the damage can be undone by rediscovering political realism.

The politicos of our grandparents' generation did a pretty good job of governing the country despite living in a world of bosses and back rooms and unlimited donations, and many of them understood some home truths that today's political reformers have too often overlooked or suppressed. In particular they understood that transactional politics, the everyday give-and-take of dickering and compromise, is the essential work of governing and that government, and thus democracy, won't work if leaders can't make deals and make them stick. They would have looked with bafflement and dismay upon a world where even deals that command majority support within both political parties—something as basic as keeping the government or the Department of Homeland Security open—set off intraparty confrontations and governmental crises instead of being worked out among responsible adults. Not being fools or crooks, they understood that much of what politicians do to bring order from chaos, like buying support with post offices and bridges, looks unappealing in isolation and up close, but they saw that the alternatives were worse. In other words, they were realists.

Today, a growing number of scholars and practitioners are bringing new sophistication to our grandparents' realism. Though they use diverse approaches and vocabularies, they can be meaningfully regarded as an emerging school, one characterized by respect for grubby but indispensable transactional politics and by skepticism toward purism, amateurism, and idealistic political reforms. This essay builds on their work. In particular it argues that:

- Government cannot govern unless political machines or something like them exist and work, because machines are uniquely willing and able to negotiate compromises and make them stick.
- Progressive, populist, and libertarian reformers have joined forces to wage a decades-long war against machine politics by weakening political insiders' control of money, nominations, negotiations, and other essential tools of political leadership.
- Reformers' fixations on corruption and participation, although perhaps appropriate a long time ago, have become destabilizing and counterproductive, contributing to the rise of privatized pseudo-machines that make governing more difficult and politics less accountable.

- Although no one wants to or could bring back the likes of Tammany Hall, much can be done to restore a more sensible balance by removing impediments that reforms have placed in the way of transactional politics and machine-building.
- Political realism, while coming in many flavors, is emerging as a coherent school of analysis and offers new directions for a reform conversation that has run aground on outdated and unrealistic assumptions.

And where better to begin than with Tammany Hall?

The Realist Mindset

What I'm calling political realism has roots as deep as Aristotle, Thucydides, and Machiavelli. In more modern times, it found a colorful exponent in the person of George Washington Plunkitt (1842–1924), a Tammany Hall functionary who championed the virtues of patronage employment and "honest graft," by which he meant insider deals rewarding political loyalists, and which he distinguished from purely personal corruption. "The looter goes in for himself alone without considerin' his organization or his city," Plunkitt said. "The politician looks after his own interests, the organization's interests, and the city's interests all at the same time." Reformers who ignored the distinction and tried to stamp out honest graft, he believed, courted anarchy. "First, this great and glorious country was built up by political parties; second, parties can't hold together if their workers don't get the offices when they win; third, if the parties go to pieces, the government they built up must go to pieces, too; fourth, then there'll be h—to pay."[3]

Plunkitt's argument, though amusingly presented, found support in twentieth-century political science: for example, in the work of James Q. Wilson, whose 1962 book, *The Amateur Democrat,* deserves rediscovery. Political parties, professionals, and machines, Wilson observes, play a vital role in what he called "assembl[ing] power in the formal government." Their displacement by ideologically motivated amateurs, a process his book observed up close in three cities, would, Wilson foresaw, make governing harder. "The need to employ issues as incentives and to distinguish one's party from the opposition along policy lines will mean that political conflict will be intensified, social cleavages will be exaggerated, party leaders will tend to be men skilled in the rhetorical arts, and the party's ability to produce agreement by trading issue-free resources will be reduced."[4]

As the very different casts of mind of Plunkitt and Wilson imply, political realism is not a single theory or doctrine, but rather a set of attitudes and dispositions. Attitudinally, it shares many traits and premises with foreign policy realism. It sees governing as difficult and political peace and stability as treasures never to be taken for granted. It understands that power's complex hydraulics make interventions unpredictable and risky. (Banning some ugly political practice, for instance, won't necessarily make it go away.) It therefore values incrementalism and, especially, equilibrium—and, therefore, transactional politics. If most of the players in a political system are invested in dickering, the system is doing something right, not something wrong. Back-scratching and logrolling are signs of a healthy political system, not a corrupt one. Transactional politics is not always appropriate or effective, but a political system that is not reliably capable of it is a system in a state of critical failure.

Deal-making and power-balancing do not happen by themselves. They require, in foreign policy, structures and forums that are both legally constituted (for example, the United Nations Security Council and the World Trade Organization) and informal (such as diplomatic and personal channels, alliances, and understandings). In politics, likewise, deal-making and balancing require both constitutional structures like legislatures and informal ones like parties and political networks. Like Wilson and Plunkitt, realists try always to keep sight of the importance and health of informal channels, especially parties. If realists have one view in common, it is that parties play (or should play) a central role in governing but have been too often overlooked or marginalized by the reforms of recent decades.

A realist is likely to take a fairly indulgent view of the shenanigans politicians get up to, provided they get good results. To govern and keep the peace, politicians need to do things that don't look attractive when examined in isolation and placed under a moral microscope, and the good and great politicians are no exceptions. "No one used the power of patronage more ruthlessly than Abraham Lincoln," Wilson reminds us.[5] Asked quietly, a realist may acknowledge that, in any political system, the right amount of corruption is greater than zero, because a zero-tolerance approach criminalizes politics without actually ending corruption.

And always the realist, while acknowledging the importance and value of ideals and issues in politics, will insist on the ineluctability of trade-offs. Governing is hard, inherently and always hard, and good intentions and pure practices will not reliably bring it about. You need deals and deal-makers, too, and you need the kinds of informal channels and incentives for which the Constitution does not provide.

When it comes to specifics, political scholars with generally realist worldviews tend not to be doctrinaire. Some thinkers emphasize the importance of parties, others the dynamics of negotiations, still others the impracticality of campaign finance rules. Without denigrating any of those viewpoints, I want to make the case for a realist emphasis on machine politics. Here, to me, is a distinctive, important, and greatly underappreciated realist proposition: *For governments to govern, political machines or something like them need to exist, and they need to work.*

By "govern," I mean reliably and reasonably reach accommodations on the problems and conflicts that demand resolution from day to day.

By "political machines," I mean informal (as opposed to legally constituted) and mutually accountable hierarchies, networks, and relationships that allow politicians to organize their environment by reaching and honoring accommodations, rewarding and protecting supporters, punishing and marginalizing defectors, and exerting coordinated influence through multiple formal channels.

By "or something like them," I mean to indicate that the famed big-city party machines of yesteryear are merely one kind of machine and that other, less sharply defined political organizations or networks can do the work of machines: for example, the "regular order" system in Congress, with its hierarchy of committees and seniority rules. Until the 1990s, the U.S. House of Representatives had a pronounced machine-like aspect, with minority Republicans claiming a piece of the appropriations action in exchange for cooperation with majority Democrats (an arrangement gleefully demolished by Newt Gingrich). Even coalitions that are independent of formal political parties and structures, groupings like the Tea Party or the Koch brothers' network, can have some machine-like aspects.

Finally, by "need to exist and need to work," I mean that they need to establish incentive structures that enable political leaders to lead and that encourage political followers to follow, thereby assisting with what Wilson called the assembling of power in government.

What Machines Do Well

The downsides of machines are so well known that they need no elaboration here. If, indeed, there is a pejorative adjective, it has been applied to machine politics. Too often lost sight of are machines' considerable capabilities and, yes, virtues. It is important to see both sides of the ledger.

So how does the positive side look? Pretty impressive, actually. Machines can accomplish a variety of ends that otherwise are quite difficult to achieve. Most important is that they can compromise even when many of the people associated with them would rather not compromise. They can negotiate, package, and present elaborate bundles of compromises liberally salted with incentives that attract support. In America, the Constitution's system of distributed power forces politicians and factions to compromise in order to get much of anything done; but machines—party organizations, congressional hierarchies, even to some extent interest group congeries—are the kitchen where the deals are cooked up. Show me a political system without machine politics and I'll show you confusion, fragmentation, and a drift toward ungovernable extremism.

For many of the same reasons, machines tend to be a force for moderation. They must engage in transactional politics to survive, and that often requires them to put ideology aside, or at least to dial it back, in the interests of holding power. Recent research finds that states in which a larger share of political money flows through parties have less polarized legislatures because the parties, desiring to win, press legislators and candidates toward the center.[6]

Instinctively, machine culture is skeptical of or hostile to freelancers and insurgents, though it may pay them lip service. It is friendly to loyalists and repeat players, the people who have skin in the game and will most reliably respond to incentives, people sometimes known as hacks. Machine hierarchies are pretty adept at marginalizing grandstanders and solo entrepreneurs. In a machine-dominated Senate, there isn't much a figure like Ted Cruz can do except talk. He certainly can't shut down the government.

On the flip side of the coin, a core machine function is to protect loyal insiders who "take one for the team." After President Clinton personally pressured Representative Marjorie Margolies-Mezvinsky (D-Pa.) to cast the tie-breaking vote for his budget in 1993, his inability to protect her from defeat the following year registered as an epic fail. An insulated system is to some extent undemocratic and sacrifices some degree of responsiveness ("You can't fight City Hall"), yet it can also provide leaders with the critical margin of support and cover they need when difficult policy choices need to be made.

Politicians, like voters, are short-sighted, and machines help with that, too, because they are capable of strategizing and transacting across time. Machines are to politics as banking is to the economy: being long-term, repeat players, they can extend something like political credit. By acting as favor banks, they can induce politicians to sacrifice something today in exchange for a larger benefit in the next round. By trading on the present value of future political returns, they can conduct transactions across spans of time—something very hard, frequently impossible, for activists and freelancers to do.

Perhaps the most important thing machines are good at is empowering leadership by inducing followership. All the vision or foresight or statesmanship in the world on the part of political leaders comes to naught if followers will not follow. Loyalty is tenuous, interest is capricious, and ideology is divisive; though all can help inspire followership, they are no substitute for systematic inducements like money, power, prestige, protection, and the other stocks-in-trade of machine politics.

In the U.S. system, lacking as it does a parliamentary system's structural discipline, inducing followers to follow is all the more important. When asked by the late-night talk show host Jay Leno why he pursued a government shutdown strategy that was sure to fail, John Boehner, then the House Speaker, replied, "When I looked up, I saw my colleagues going this way. A leader without followers is simply a man taking a walk."[7] Without followers there can be no leaders, and without leaders there will be chaos. America today has generally capable, honest, hard-working political leaders (former Speaker Boehner among them). What the country faces is not a crisis of leadership but a crisis of followership. Richard Pildes of New York University Law School puts the case well: "The problem is not that individual leaders are now 'weak,'" but that "broader structural changes, including legal ones, have disarmed party leaders of the tools they previously had used to unify their members around deals that were thought to be in the best interest of the party as a whole."[8]

The Three-Front War on Hacks and Machines

The excesses of Tammany and its ilk needed reining in, to be sure. But what began as a necessary rebalancing became a relentless ideological attack from three different directions. Progressivism, populism, and libertarianism have many differences, and they also have many virtues. But however laudable their intentions, they have collaborated relentlessly and effectively to reduce the space for transactional politics.

The progressive tradition scorns transactional politics for deviating from meritocracy. Where the realist tends to believe that governing is inherently difficult, that politics is inherently transactional, and that success is best judged in terms of reaching social accommodation rather than achieving some abstract end, the progressive tradition tends to see government as perfectible and politics as a path toward a higher public good. Where realism tends to see the public interest in terms of negotiated settlements ("This is the best we could get this time around"), the progressive tradition tends to see it as an ideal benchmark against which real-world politics continually falls short—so that transactional politics, even if sometimes unavoidable, is a lamentable deviation from meritocratic decision-making. Where the realist sees interests as the very stuff of politics, the progressive sees them distracting or detracting from issues, the ideological currency that James Q. Wilson warned is so often nonnegotiable. Where realism sees money as an intrinsic and morally neutral part of politics, the progressive sees it as a contaminant. And where realism seeks to balance many competing political values (competence, stability, broad buy-in, integrity, and other variables all figure in the equation), the progressive tradition views integrity as paramount and self-interested activity as corrupt.

And the progressive tradition defines corruption very broadly, indeed. In a famous colloquy on the Senate floor in 1999, Senator John McCain declared that "we are all corrupted" by political contributions, but, under challenge by Senator Mitch McConnell ("Someone must be corrupt for there to be corruption"), he refused to name a single corrupt individual. The *system* is corrupt, he said, a good statement of the ideology that has made modern progressivism an inherently unstable and uncontainable doctrine. One academic propounds that "an act is corrupt when private interests trump public ones in the exercise of public power, and a person is corrupt when they use public power for their own ends, disregarding others," a definition that seems to erase altogether any boundary between self-interested transactional politics and corruption.[9] As progressives, ever disgusted with politics, search for new dragons to slay, one struggles to understand what sort of real-world political system is *not* corrupt. Here, then, is a classic case of overshoot. What began as a useful correction of Tammany-style excess has become a neurotic obsession.

The populist reform tradition scorns transactional politics for deviating from democracy.[10] The populist critique is closely aligned with the progressive one, but its emphasis is slightly different. While agreeing with progressivism that the leading problem in politics is corruption, the populist school equates legitimacy with direct participation by ordinary individuals and corruption with intermediation or influence on the part of organizations or interests, especially large or wealthy ones. For the populist reformer, the solution to almost any political problem involves more democracy, more participation, and more power for the little guy. Populism turns the progressive activist's instinctive suspicion of political insiders and careerists into an explicit ideology. By their very nature, political professionals are interlopers who speak for special interests and for the political class; amateurs are the true custodians of the public interest, and a goal of policy should be to empower them, everywhere and always.

The third member of the troika does not get along with the other two, except in one crucial respect: libertarians never saw a political machine they liked. They, too, scorn transactional politics, although not because it deviates from meritocracy or democracy but because it deviates from market outcomes. The libertarian critique of government goes back centuries to venerable sources, but its distinctive contemporary incarnation dates, perhaps, to the 1970s and Reaganism's critique of special-interest government. In 1975, a young congressional aide named David Stockman published a seminal article called "The Social Pork Barrel," in which he argued that formula-driven social welfare and entitlement programs were no less wasteful and corrupt than the Appropriations Committee logrolling and Tammany-style favoritism that they were supposed to clean up. Government, Stockman argued, had become a game of providing the "greatest goodies for the greatest number," paying off strong clients rather than strong claims and insidiously coopting even conservative opposition.[11] Today, Stockman's libertarian and libertarian-ish descendants despise political machines less because they are machines than because they are political. If market decisions are, with rare exceptions, more just (because less arbitrary) and more efficient (because less economically distorting) than political decisions, then transactional politics is inherently unjust and wasteful, and thus corrupt.[12]

As you might expect, when all three of the country's major political reform movements concentrate their fire on transactional politics continuously for decades, a lot of governing capacity will be lost. There is hardly an aspect of machine politics that reformers have not at least partially dismantled or disabled. To emphasize: many of the specific reforms and ideas of the past decades were reasonable and appropriate in the context of their time and place. My goal here is to consider their cumulative effect, which has been to replace relatively accountable machine politics with fragmented and unaccountable private actors.

The crown jewel in the populist political reform movement is the political primary system. Once upon a time, the party's nomination to appear on a general election ballot was largely, though not entirely, in the gift of party elders and professionals, who may have fought with each other but could normally make their eventual choices stick. Today, selection by amateurs—usually by voters in primaries but occasionally by partisan caucus-goers—is *de rigueur.* Without attempting to recapitulate the huge literature debating this change, I'll note that the switch to direct voter nomination has been probably the modern political world's most conspicuous example of unintended and perverse consequences. A crucial premise of populist reform, namely that most people want to participate more in politics, turns out to be wrong. And so, instead of opening decision-making to a broader, more diverse, and more representative spectrum than party hacks represented, primaries have skewed decision-making toward the notably narrow, ideologically extreme, and decidedly nonrepresentative sliver of voters who turn out in primary elections. "The universe of those who actually cast primary ballots is small and hyper-partisan, and rewards candidates who hew to ideological orthodoxy," write Jill Lawrence and Walter Shapiro in their recent evaluation of the 2014 cycle of House primaries.[13]

Primary contests also turn out to be unequaled pressure points for special interests. Especially in the Republican Party, insurgents like the Tea Party and interest groups like the Koch brothers' network have discovered that they can strike fear in the heart of Republican members of Congress by "primarying" them. The mere threat of a primary will influence political behavior.

If the loss of control over the nominating process was devastating for political professionals and machines, the reduced control over money has been almost as debilitating. To rank-and-file politicians, knowing that being a good team player will open money taps and that defecting will close them is an important and time-honored inducement to play well with others. To the individuals and groups that form politicians' bases and networks, giving money is an important and time-honored way to reward reciprocity and earn insider status. The first wave of progressivism, a century ago, took aim at dishonest graft, like bribery and extortion, and also at some forms of "honest graft," such as featherbedding and patronage, but it left ordinary political donations mostly alone. Disappointed by the results, a second wave, beginning in the 1970s, spread the net much more widely, establishing a web of legalistic rules and regulations that have made it much harder for candidates and parties to raise money, on the general theory that fundraising and dependence on big-dollar donors are inherently corrupting. The result was not to reduce the amount of money in politics or to reduce the influence of special interests but to drive money to unrestricted channels, such as party committees. When progressive legislation restricted those channels too, the result was to push money into so-called "independent" spending by Super PACS, nonprofit organizations, billionaires, and other actors who are less accountable, less pragmatic, and less transparent than Tammany ever was. According to the Brennan Center for Justice at New York University Law School, "outside spending [in Senate races] has exploded in the last three federal elections and is highly focused on competitive races. In 80 percent of competitive 2014 races, outside spenders outspent the candidates—sometimes by more than double." In 2014 so-called dark money, whose donors are not disclosed, accounted for almost half the outside spending.[14]

To be sure, many social and political changes, not just progressive laws and regulations, have contributed to the growth of the gray market for political money. Some of what is happening would have happened anyway. But to acknowledge as much does not get the progressive paradigm off the hook. Its *raison d'être* for four decades or more has been to sequester political professionals from political money, opening the way for amateurs to take over the job. Raymond J. La Raja, a political scientist at the University of Massachusetts, points out that money raised by party committees almost tripled in real dollars from 1988 to 2004. After the Bipartisan Campaign Reform Act of 2002 (the so-called McCain–Feingold Act) banned unrestricted donations to parties, party fundraising went into a mild decline and spending by outside groups rushed in to fill the gap, going from trivial in the 1990s to $1 billion or so by 2012. "The campaign finance system has strengthened the hand of partisan activists by limiting the flow of financial resources to the formal party organization and its technocratic staff," he writes. "The campaign finance rules constrain coherent, party-based organizing to such an extent that partisans have sidestepped the rules to create organizations such as Super PACs."[15]

To organize coalitions and deals, political machines and professionals need to talk to and organize their networks and supporters. But that imperative runs afoul of the weirdest and most perverse of modern progressive obsessions: the attempt to restrict "coordination" of campaign efforts between political parties and either their own candidates or their outside supporters. In the progressive worldview, limiting the money that private interests can give directly to candidates and parties does little good if the interests can pretend to spend independently while quietly letting candidates and parties direct the spending. For progressives, in other words, coordination is a way of circumventing the quarantine on political contributions. For a machine, of course, coordination is something else: the whole point of politics. If a machine can't organize, assist, and direct its politicians and supporters, it might as well not exist.

"The restrictions on party coordination force parties to spend 'independently' of candidates," writes La Raja. "This arrangement is not only a parody of what parties are about in most democracies, but encourages inefficient use of resources (hence ever more money is needed), legal gamesmanship, and diminished political accountability."[16] Predictably, trying to disconnect politicians and parties from each other and their supporters has created a gray market in coordination; driven resources, professional talent, and influence to unaccountable outside groups; hindered candidates' and parties' ability to control and transmit their message; and underwritten the growth of a burgeoning independent political infrastructure that is difficult (at best) for leaders to organize and influence.

If anti-coordination rules are an example of a bad idea that can't work, transparency requirements are an example of a good idea that can work but that entails trade-offs whose existence advocates are reluctant to acknowledge. If there is one thing that progressives, populists, and libertarians all agree on, it is that sunlight is the best disinfectant. Lying, cheating, and stealing are certainly more difficult when the world is watching. But so are dickering, floating trial balloons, being candid, and working out complex deals. Public attention, note Sarah Binder and Frances Lee, induces politicians to posture and adhere to partisan talking points. Closed-door negotiations, by contrast, give them more freedom to explore policy options and multidimensional, integrative solutions.[17] Above all, privacy lets negotiators work out complex packages *in toto* before individual pieces are shot down. No wonder that "candidate Obama vowed to televise negotiations over health reform," said *The Economist*, but "President Obama did no such thing." Instead he went behind closed doors with congressional leaders and industry groups to hammer out secret agreements.[18] In 2013, budget negotiations between the House and Senate budget committee chairs succeeded partly because, as a Democratic aide told Jill Lawrence, "their leaders empowered them to figure it out themselves, very, very privately."[19]

There isn't much hard evidence that transparency reliably improves real-world decision-making or makes the public happier, and some evidence points to ill effects. One recent study finds that, in developing countries, transparency makes the public more fatalistic about corruption rather than stimulating outrage and action; the same dynamic of cynicism and numbness may apply in the United States, especially when transparency is coupled with paralysis. The public sees more of the sausage-making while getting less sausage.[20] La Raja finds that disclosure rules seem to induce small political donors to halve their giving.[21]

The point is not that sunshine rules and disclosure laws are always bad or even to deny that up to a point they are a public good in and of themselves; it is only that they can be counterproductive and that reformers' dogmatic and often moralistic commitment to them needs a reality check. As Pildes writes, "If negotiations among leaders are a key to effective governance, particularly in polarized times, then we need a less moralistic, more realistic sense of the conditions under which negotiations effectively take place."[22] Sometimes, in other words, the only thing wrong with smoke-filled rooms is the smoke. Yet, note Binder and Lee, "private negotiations in Congress are increasingly difficult to secure."[23]

One important attribute of smoke-filled rooms was that, usually, you had a pretty good idea who was entitled to be in them—and the selection, to the dismay of idealists, was not always based on merit. To the contrary, political leaders delegated deal-making to functionaries who had earned a place at the table by dint of seniority, loyalty, or cunning, as well as expertise. Keeping freelancers and interlopers out of the room and maintaining control over the agenda inside the room are instrumental to making bargaining manageable and delivering on deals; giving loyalists and time-servers a place at the table rewards them and marginalizes outsiders.

In Congress, for many years, the seniority and committee systems served those incentivizing and boundary-setting functions well—arguably too well, because a senior committee chair could become an entrenched baron. When rank-and-file members from below and congressional leaders from above demanded and received more control over who got top committee slots, they were responding to a real problem. Over time, however, the downside of weakening committee hierarchies and the "regular order" process on Capitol Hill has come into clearer focus. The committees and subcommittees are the compromise factories of Congress. The chairs (and ranking members) are the factories' managers; mid-ranking and junior committee members are their sales force and their eyes and ears. The House Speaker and Senate Majority Leader, capable though they and their staffs may be, don't have the capacity to do a fraction of the work that committees can do, nor can they replace the committees' networks and expertise and finely tuned political antennae. Ad hoc arrangements like Senate "gangs" may have their occasional uses, but they are no substitute for "the negotiating advantages afforded by long-standing repeated interactions," as Binder and Lee put it.[24] When today's legislators call for a return to regular order—the routines of consensus-building led by delegated professionals—they are expressing an important insight about how the mechanism of transactional politics needs to work.

And then there are earmarks and pork. For years they were the hard currency of Capitol Hill's political economy. Sometimes abused, they could also be a powerful inducement to win a wavering vote or break an impasse. Lyndon Johnson famously won critical support for the 1964 Civil Rights Bill by "proposing, and personally securing, a NASA research facility at Purdue University," in the district of House Republican leader Charles Halleck of Indiana.[25] Pork remains alive but diminished in vigor, thanks to the relative shrinkage of the discretionary budget and the decline of the appropriations process. Earmarks were banned outright in 2010 under pressure from Tea Partiers, who saw them as emblematic of Washington corruption. Ironically, by the time they were barred, earmarks had been successfully reformed; they were, in fact, the least expensive and most transparent kind of pork, because they were narrowly targeted and routinely disclosed.[26] Their abolition stripped leaders on the Hill of one of the few tools still remaining to them for influencing behavior. Avoiding a government shutdown in 2013 would have "absolutely" been easier if House Speaker Boehner had been able to dispense earmarks, Trent Lott (R-Miss.), a former Republican Senate Majority Leader and House minority whip, told CNN: "Trying to be a leader where you have no sticks and very few carrots is dang near impossible. Members don't get anything from you and leaders don't give anything. They don't feel like you can reward them or punish them."[27]

The Rise of Shadow Machines

Little wonder, as reforms bear down on machines led by professional politicians, that shadowy rivals have sprung up, mimicking some of the functions of machines but unaccountable to voters through elections or to citizens through disclosure. Under the campaign finance rules, reports *Politico,* "state-party-run phone banks for federal candidates had to be staffed only by volunteers. They could make calls only for presidential elections—not congressional races. Mail, campaign literature, and get-out-the-vote operations around federal races were regulated by similarly strict rules, conditions and requirements regulating volunteer time, coordination with the national party and what kind of funds could be spent."[28] Funding, constrained by red tape and limits, has fallen for many state party organizations. Where is it going? To unconstrained private machines. The Koch network's $899 million commitment for 2016 "is challenging the primacy of the official parties," which, together, spent just over $700 million in 2012, according to the *Washington Post.*[29] In the 2014 North Carolina senate race, the Koch-funded Americans for Prosperity was "by far the most significant player" in get-out-the-vote activity on the Republican side, bringing "far more clout" than either the Senate candidate or the party.[30]

The shadow machines, although anything but amateurish, distinctly resemble Wilson's "amateur Democrats" in the important respect that their interest is often in issues and purity, not in the messy and compromising work of governing. "The aim, says Donald Bryson of [Americans for Prosperity], is to build a movement rather than to win elections. 'You may win or lose but at least you have been intellectually consistent—your principles haven't been defeated.'"[31] As they grow, the shadow machines weaken traditional ones, which find themselves ever less able to maintain order in their environment and in their own ranks. *Politico* quotes Thomas Mills, a North Carolina-based political consultant and observer who has worked on local, state, and presidential races: "There's nobody refereeing the fights. We're not seeing party bosses or strong chairs that can try to work out deals behind closed doors to keep it from breaking out into the public."[32] The shadow machines also weaken candidates' accountability to voters as well as to leaders. "Candidates raise as much as they can, but they can be smothered with expenditures from interest groups and Super PACs, which are not subject to the same fundraising limitations as candidates or parties," write former House members Tom Davis and Martin Frost and the journalist Richard E. Cohen.[33]

Little wonder, in turn, that more and more often, on any number of pressing issues—the budget, immigration, and even keeping the government open—congressional leaders have found themselves helpless to exert enough discipline to negotiate and deliver on deals even when getting a deal was in the interest of the party and when a majority of the caucus wanted one. Little wonder that lone-wolf politicians and outside groups and private machines have acquired veto power of a sort that would have shocked politicians of earlier generations.

Paralysis born of inability to forge consensus on a tough issue is frustrating and disappointing, but it accurately reflects political reality. Paralysis born of politicians' incapacity to organize a deal even when they want and need one is true systemic dysfunction, a distortion of political reality. To paraphrase something Daniel Patrick Moynihan said in a different context, a polity that demolishes its political machines and demonizes its political professionals asks for and gets chaos.

Rebalancing: Let Politicians Do What Comes Naturally

A frequent criticism of realism is that it is not realistic, because the world has changed and the age of political machines is over. In one respect, that objection is true but trivial; no realist imagines it is either possible or desirable to reincarnate the ward heelers, block captains, and party clubhouses of old. The realist claim is that we can learn from the past, not relive it; that generations of political knowledge and practice are still relevant today; and that today we can profitably seek modern processes that provide the functional equivalent of what our grandparents did that was valuable. In another respect, however, the objection that realism is unrealistic is nontrivial but the opposite of true. Organizing their political environment, transacting exchanges with each other and their supporters, favoring friends over foes, building and joining informal hierarchies, controlling access to power and perquisites: those behaviors are instinctive for political professionals. They can be encouraged simply by being allowed.

The realist mission is not to rig the system to favor political professionals and machines over amateurs and outsiders; rather, it is to move law, rules, and public opinion closer to neutrality in the contest between professionalism and amateurism, thereby giving the professionals more space to do what they need to do. The good news for realism is that today there is no shortage of strong minds at work on the question of how to strike a less lopsided balance. Realists are cropping up in the academy and elsewhere, examining various aspects of the problem, and making creative suggestions.

A logical place to begin is by reducing the artificial fundraising advantages that current law gives to political amateurs and outsiders. Today's tight restrictions on donations to candidates and parties have not reduced the amount of money in politics, nor have they demonstrably reduced corruption, improved policy outcomes, facilitated governance, or pleased the public. What they have done is channel money into "proto-parties disguised as independent groups run by party-affiliated political operatives," resulting in "a nightmare of fractionalized spending," as the Stanford University political scientist Bruce Cain puts it.[34] Because many or most donors would give directly to parties and candidates rather than shadow machines if they could, a logical remedy is to raise dramatically the contribution limits to candidates and parties, bringing more money back inside the system.

But where inside the system? There is a case for moving beyond neutrality by deliberately advantaging the parties in the fundraising game. In recent research, the political scientists Ray La Raja and Brian Schaffner, of the University of Massachusetts Amherst, compare states that have candidate-centered funding systems with those using party-centered systems. In states where parties do more of the fundraising and spending, the legislatures are less polarized and the parties' own behavior is more moderate. "Party organizations do, in fact, behave differently than other partisan groups by mediating ideological sources of money and funneling it to moderate candidates," they write.[35] That is not necessarily because parties are made up of moderates, but because they want to win. Moreover, party mediation "helps to insulate candidates from ideologically driven donors who might pull candidates in their direction, either by threatening to withhold funding or by financing other candidates who agree with them." Insiders, they find, direct electoral resources in ways that appeal to the median voter. "Moderation," they conclude, "is a byproduct of their pursuit of power."[36]

A good way to create space for transactional politics, then, might be simply to lift all restrictions, except disclosure requirements, on donations to political parties, an approach La Raja and Schaffner call building canals, not dams. With more resources of their own and relatively less flowing outside, parties would be in a stronger position to "assemble power in the formal government": in other words, to behave like machines. One could make a similar case for allowing top leaders in Congress (and perhaps committee chairs and ranking members) to raise much larger or even unlimited donations for their leadership PACs, helping leaders support and protect loyalists. Channeling contributions through parties and bosses would be reinforced by eliminating today's counterproductive restrictions on the coordinating of parties' campaign efforts with those of candidates and outside groups. Directing political traffic and organizing political coalitions are what machines exist to do.

They also act as gatekeepers to power, a function that today's system of primary elections has weakened, at high cost to leadership in government. Realists have proposed a number of ways to balance today's disproportionate influence of amateurs. As in the presidential nominating process, the primary vote in congressional contests could be supplemented with a designated role for officeholders and party grandees. Such super-delegates would be year-round professionals and elected officials, not amateur caucus-goers. Despite their influence, extremists might still get the nod in extreme districts, but allowing professionals to do more gatekeeping could give candidates and officeholders second thoughts about going rogue after the election. Another approach is to make getting on the primary ballot harder, filtering out candidates who have little party or institutional support. Yet another approach lets the party clearly indicate its preferred candidate on the primary ballot, telling voters unambiguously which candidate has earned official endorsement. "The point here," writes Nathaniel Persily, of Stanford Law School, "is to give the party organizations a thumb on the primary election scale so that potential nominees must factor in how much their apostasy means to them. In some circumstances, perhaps it will mean a lot. Candidates could still 'run against' the party. But when they do, it will be clear to voters that they are doing so."[37]

In Congress, realism prescribes seeking ways to strengthen the hand of congressional leaders and hierarchies. Here is a simple enough idea, far from revolutionary but probably incrementally helpful: bring back earmarks, well regulated, as they were before they were abolished. Jason Grumet, the president of the Bipartisan Policy Center, suggests that "bills passed out of committee by large enough majorities should be placed *auto-*

matically on a calendar that propels them to floor consideration without delay," a step that "would strengthen the committee chairs and increase the engagement of committee members who have grown weary of a process that has little chance of shaping outcomes."[38] A growing movement on Capitol Hill supports the reinvigoration of regular order and committee work. Taking steps to protect and expand private spaces for negotiations also would not go amiss.

Rethinking: Toward a New—or Is It Old?—Paradigm

Perhaps more important than making any particular change in law or policy or rules is to change the country's argumentative defaults. For too many years, anti-realists have enjoyed an oligopoly on the public conversation. Too many assumptions have gone unchallenged and have hardened into dogma.

It is often assumed that polarization is today's foremost problem for governance. Maybe not. As important, and perhaps more so, may be what Pildes calls fragmentation. "By fragmentation," he writes, "I mean the external diffusion of political power away from the political parties as a whole and the internal diffusion of power away from the party leadership to individual party members and officeholders."[39] The ideological gap between the two parties may, indeed, make negotiating more difficult and deals harder to strike (and may also present clearer choices to voters—not a bad thing), but the target for policy, the thing we could actually do something about, is "re-empowering party elites and leaders and giving them the tools to more effectively enforce party discipline in the service of effective governance in a highly polarized political era that is likely to remain so for years."[40] The question is not only how far apart the parties are but also whether their leaders have the capacity to meet in the middle when compromise is in their interest.

It is generally assumed that moderation comes from moderates, so the way to reduce polarization is to increase participation. Maybe not, on both counts. Moderation may come more from machines than from moderates, and direct participation naturally favors extremists and independent operators. If so, efforts that seek to foster moderation by encouraging voter independence and weakening party control—for instance, by establishing nonpartisan primaries, as California has done in hope of increasing the influence of moderate voters—may backfire.[41] To get moderation in governance, the better bet may be to empower leadership and parties that have incentives to compromise.

It is generally assumed that making districts more competitive in general elections would reduce obstructionism and extremism. Maybe not. From the point of view of governing, making general elections more competitive may be less important than making primary elections *less* competitive but more subject to leadership influence. Leaders who can protect their followers from retention contests—or who, conversely, can green-light a challenge to an obstreperous incumbent—will have a lot more leverage in seeking help on tough votes.

It is generally assumed that the system will be healthier if more individuals give small sums of money, thereby increasing participation and reducing the relative weight of special interests. Maybe not. Small donors tend to be polarized and polarizing. Pildes notes that individual contributions to campaigns "today are by far the largest source of direct money to campaigns (about 61 percent for Congress)" but that "as our campaign finance system has become more democratized, our politics has become more polarized."[42] Though a candidate funded by small donors may be less accountable to a high roller like Sheldon Adelson or Tom Steyer, she is also less accountable to a leader like Paul Ryan or John Boehner, which right now is the more pressing problem.

A similar analysis holds for public financing more generally. The question that needs to be asked more often is not whether financing is public or private, or whether donations are large or small, but whether flows of money are accountable to political and party insiders or outsiders. Super PACS and mega-donors like Adelson and Steyer are facts of life, and the sensible thing to do now is make the best of their big bucks by attaching them to machines or parties that offer some hope of mediating and directing their influence. Using the public purse to pay for all or part of campaigns might (or might not) reduce the influence of special interests and wealthy donors at the margins, but public subsidies to candidates also help politicians set up shop as independent entrepreneurs, reducing the power of parties and leaders to act as gatekeepers and traffic cops.

Deciding what the public has a right to know about the transactions that go on within government is difficult; there is no perfect sweet spot. At present, however, neither public discourse nor reform consensus is inclined to acknowledge that there is a cost to exposing the inner workings of politics to

24/7 public scrutiny. Recently, when it emerged that Hillary Clinton had used a private account for her e-mails when she was secretary of state, Democrats and Republicans debated whether she had broken the rules, but no one suggested that the secretary of state's e-mails are none of the public's business or that shielding them might be helpful when there are sensitive tasks to perform. Clinton herself felt obliged to announce, "I want the public to see my e-mail." Transparency advocates say they do not expect or want politicians and public officials to work in a fishbowl, but at what point will they draw a line against the encroachment of scrutiny? As Jason Grumet has said, the opposite of transparency in politics is not corruption, it is privacy. Even granting that there is no perfect balance to be struck, acknowledging the need for balance and the value of privacy would mark a welcome change.

It is time, too, to acknowledge that what Pildes calls the romanticization of democracy, the unquestioning pursuit of ever more participation, needs reexamining. The general assumption that politics will be more satisfying and government will work better if more people participate more directly is poorly supported and probably wrong. What is true of donors is also true more generally: where direct engagement with politics is concerned, the polarized and financially interested have an inherent advantage. Pildes argues for acknowledging a "tragic trade-off" between unmediated popular participation and government's effective functioning. There may be no perfect balance between the two, but just accepting that more democracy is not always the answer would mark a sea change in American political discourse.

And then there is that Tasmanian Devil of entrenched assumptions, the tail-chasing, tree-munching, all-consuming, ever expanding, and by now entirely counterproductive war on corruption. Perhaps the hardest of all default assumptions to reset is the idea that most of America's political and governmental ills are the result of some version of corruption and that the remedy involves some version of amateurism. Changing this default is a tall order in a country where politicians and the public are addicted to diatribes against politics, where inexperience in politics is regularly touted as proof of virtue, and where two generations of reformers are deeply invested in the war on corruption.

Still, mounting a frontal challenge to the premises that the war on corruption is based on now seems at least possible. Realists are beginning to step forward confidently into a debate that until recently stigmatized them as cynics or ignored them altogether. Their advocacy of political home truths is already suggesting new directions in a reform conversation that has reached a dead end.

Notes

This is a shortened version of *Political Realism: How Hacks, Machines, Big Money, and Back-Room Deals Can Strengthen American Democracy* (Brookings Institution Press, 2015). The unabridged version can be found at www.brookings.edu/research/reports2/2015/05/political-realism-rauch.

1. Lindsay Wise, "New Federal Budget Bill Lets Political Parties Cash In," *McClatchyDC*, December 16, 2014 (www.mcclatchydc.com/2014/12/16/250243/new-federal-budget-bill-lets-political.html).

2. Tarini Parti and Anna Palmer, "Tea Party Fumes over Campaign Finance Plan," *Politico*, December 11, 2014.

3. William L. Riordan, *Plunkitt of Tammany Hall*, Project Gutenberg digital edition, chapters 7 and 3 (www.gutenberg.org/ebooks/2810).

4. James Q. Wilson, *The Amateur Democrat: Club Politics in Three Cities* (University of Chicago Press, 1962; reprinted with a new preface in 1966), p. 358.

5. Wilson, *The Amateur Democrat*, p. 22.

6. The research, by Raymond La Raja and Brian Schaffner, is discussed later.

7. Emma Dumain, "Boehner Tells Leno Government Shutdown a 'Predictable Disaster,'" *Roll Call*, January 24, 2014 (http://blogs.rollcall.com/218/boehner-tells-leno-government-shutdown-a-predictable-disaster).

8. Richard Pildes, "Romanticizing Democracy, Political Fragmentation, and the Decline of American Government," *Yale Law Journal* 124 (2014), p. 833.

9. Zephyr Teachout, *Corruption in America: From Benjamin Franklin's Snuff Box to Citizens United* (Harvard, 2014), p. 9.

10. By "populist reform tradition" I mean to distinguish the modern political reform movement from populism in the broader sense of any politics that appeals to anti-elite sentiment.

11. David Stockman, "The Social Pork Barrel," *The Public Interest* (Spring 1975). Stockman went on to win election to Congress and head Reagan's Office of Management and Budget.

12. A good contemporary example of the libertarian critique of transactional politics as inherently corrupt is Jay Cost, *A Republic No More: Big Government and the Rise of Political Corruption* (New York: Encounter Books, 2015).

13. Jill Lawrence and Walter Shapiro, "Phoning It In and Failing to Show: The Story of the 2014 House Primaries," Brookings Institution, September 2014 (www.brookings.edu/~/media/research/files/reports/2014/09/30-candidates-voters-primaries-lawrence-shapiro/primaries_lawrence_shapiro.pdf).

14. Ian Vandewalker and Eric Petry, "Election Spending 2014: Outside Spending in Senate Races since Citizens United," Brennan Center for Justice, January 13, 2015 (www.brennancenter.org/publication/election-spending-2014-outside-spending-senate-races-citizens-united).

15. Raymond J. La Raja, "Why Super PACs: How the American Party System Outgrew the Campaign Finance System," *The Forum* 10, no. 4 (February 2013), pp. 93, 98.

16. Ibid., p. 103.

17. Sarah A. Binder and Frances E. Lee, "Making Deals in Congress," in *Political Negotiation: A Handbook,* edited by Jane Mansbridge and Cathie Jo Martin (Brookings Institution Press, 2016), pp. 91–117.

18. "Good, Bad, and Ugly," *The Economist*, January 17, 2015, p. 79.

19. Jill Lawrence, "Profiles in Negotiation: The Murray–Ryan Budget Deal," Brookings Institution, February 2015 (www.brookings.edu/research/papers/2015/02/profiles-negotiation-murray-ryan-lawrence).

20. Monika Bauhr and Marcia Grimes, "Indignation or Resignation: The Implications of Transparency for Societal Accountability," *Governance* 27, no. 2 (April 2014), pp. 291–320.

21. Raymond J. La Raja, "Political Participation and Civic Courage: The Negative Effect of Transparency on Making Small Campaign Contributions," *Political Behavior* 36, no. 4 (December 2014).

22. Pildes, "Romanticizing Democracy," p. 846.

23. Binder and Lee, "Making Deals in Congress," p. 64. The common rejoinder that members of Congress can still find places for private discussions misses the point, which is the difficulty of conducting organized negotiations out of public view. Until the 1970s, committees routinely met and did business behind closed doors, and they often reported only vote tallies rather than how individuals voted. The resulting dynamic was quite different from a hallway conversation.

24. Binder and Lee, "Making Deals in Congress," p. 66.

25. Michael O'Donnell, "What the Hell's the Presidency For?" *The Atlantic*, April 2014, p. 93.

26. Jonathan Rauch, "Earmarks Are a Model, Not a Menace," *National Journal*, March 14, 2009.

27. Dan Merica, "Longing for Pork: Could Earmarks Help Congress Get Things Done?," CNN, October 17, 2013 (www.cnn.com/2013/10/17/politics/earmarks-help-congress).

28. Byron Tau, "Last Call for State Parties?," *Politico*, February 16, 2014.

29. Matea Gold, "Koch-Backed Network Aims to Spend Nearly $1 Billion in Run-Up to 2016," *Washington Post*, January 26, 2015.

30. Ashley Parker and Jonathan Weisman, "For Midterms, Betting on Feet and Good Apps," *New York Times*, October 25, 2014.

31. *The Economist*, "How to Spend It," *The Economist*, October 25, 2014, p. 36.

32. Tau, "Last Call for State Parties?"

33. Tom Davis, Martin Frost, and Richard E. Cohen, *The Partisan Divide: Congress in Crisis* (Campbell, Calif.: Premiere, 2014), p. 164.

34. Bruce Cain, *Democracy More or Less: The Quandary of American Political Reform* (Cambridge University Press, 2015), pp. 167, 202.

35. Ray La Raja and Brian Schaffner, "Want to Reduce Polarization? Give Parties More Money," *Washington Post,* July 21, 2014 (www.washingtonpost.com/blogs/monkey-cage/wp/2014/07/21/want-to-reduce-polarization-give-parties-more-money).

36. Raymond J. La Raja and Brian Schaffner, *Campaign Finance and Political Polarization: When Purists Prevail* (University of Michigan Press, 2005), pp. 24, 11.

37. Nathaniel Persily, "Are Parties the Cause or Solution to Polarization?" Conference Paper, October 2013. Quoted by permission of the author.

38. Jason Grumet, *City of Rivals: Restoring the Glorious Mess of American Democracy* (Guilford, Conn.: Lyons Press, 2014), p. 132. Italics in original.

39. Pildes, "Romanticizing Democracy," p. 809.

40. Richard Pildes "Fragmentation, Not Polarization: Reduce Participation and Empower Leadership," Conference Paper, October 2013. Quoted by permission of the author.

41. I've supported the California experiment, and I still do, at the state level. Reforms like nonpartisan primaries and redistricting commissions deserve to be tried. But so do reforms like strengthening parties, which have received less attention.

42. Pildes, "Romanticizing Democracy," p. 826.

A Return to Madisonian Republicanism

Strengthening the Nation's Most Representative Institution

WILLIAM F. CONNELLY JR.
AND JOHN J. PITNEY JR.

Critics contend that our politics today is dysfunctional because it is contentious, polarized, and partisan. Frances Lee, however, notes that "intense partisan conflict has been the norm for U.S. congressional politics."[1] The 1950s baseline popular with critics of partisan polarization today may give us an inaccurate impression of what is normal. The days of tranquil politics, due in part to Democratic congressional supermajorities, may not be the appropriate standard for judging our politics today.

Wilson and the Broken Congress

Nevertheless, critics continue to bemoan contentious partisanship as if it were new. Ironically, the conventional critique has been with us at least since the 1885 publication of Woodrow Wilson's *Congressional Government* with its criticism of our constitutional system. Knowingly or unknowingly, contemporary critics start from his benchmark of simple majoritarianism. Wilsonian political scientists and political reformers often idealize the British parliamentary system in which voters choose a majority party, and presto, it enacts its program, largely liberated from the separation of powers. (Real parliamentary systems are more complex than the Wilsonian model would suggest.) As Daniel Stid writes, Wilson's influence on twentieth-century political science is most evident in the 1950 APSA report *Toward a More Responsible Two Party System*. Thus, the conventional critique draws inspiration from Wilson, as do many commonplace criticisms of our constitutional system. In 1885, Wilson went straight for the constitutional jugular by highlighting the central structural principle of the Constitution, the separation of powers, as its "radical defect."[2]

James Madison saw the separation of powers as the Constitution's central virtue. In *Federalist* No. 49, Madison argued in favor of "veneration" for the Constitution. In his conclusion to *Congressional Government*, by contrast, Wilson insisted "the Constitution is not honored by blind worship," calling instead for "fearless criticism of that system."[3] By Wilson's benchmark, Congress has always been broken.

Wilson's antagonism toward the Constitution stemmed from a frustration with the unleashing of self-interest and factionalism. Wilson was leery of institutional checks and he disparaged Congress as "a disintegrate mass of jarring elements."[4] He scorned the complexity of Madison's separation of powers for hampering genuine accountability of politicians to the people: "How is the schoolmaster, the nation, to know which boy needs the whipping?"[5] In *Congressional Government*, Wilson made explicit his "mission" to "set reform a-going."[6] Did Wilson's advocacy compromise his political science? Wilson saw himself as a statesman and acknowledged that he was studying American politics to change it. His progressive inclination informed his dislike for "the too tight ligaments of a written fundamental law" such as the U.S. Constitution, along with his desire to explore the "living reality" of the nation's underlying constitution rather than any mere "literary theory."[7]

"The British system is perfected party government," Wilson declared, and parliamentary party government promotes accountability.[8] He elaborated, "*Power and strict accountability for its use* are the essential constituents of good government."[9] After all, "*somebody must be trusted*" and that somebody must be held to the "highest responsibility."[10] Responsible party government permits the concentration of authority, thereby fostering efficient policymaking. Parliamentary government prevents the paralysis that, in his view, troubles our separation of powers system. Wilson would join today's neo-Wilsonian reformers in lamenting divided government and our purported gridlock.[11]

Many political scientists, journalists, and others have been happy to engage in criticism of Madison's Constitution ever since, starting with

Wilson's contemporary Herbert Croly in *The Promise of American Life*. Later, James MacGregor Burns's "deadlock of democracy," and James Sundquist's "stalemate" both echoed Woodrow Wilson's belief that "you cannot compound a successful government out of antagonisms."[12] Later still, journalists such as Ron Brownstein in *Second Civil War* reprised many of Wilson's concerns, as did economist Lester Thurow in *The Zero-Sum Society*.

Similarly, congressional reformers of both parties often have taken their cue from Wilson. Daniel Stid describes the Democratic reform movement that strengthened House party leadership. A Republican version began in June of 1980, when Jack Kemp proposed Governing Team Day. Newt Gingrich led the project with a press release stating: "Governing Team Day Is a Step Toward a De Facto Parliamentary System." The Woodrow Wilson of *Congressional Government* and Newt Gingrich both admired the parliamentary ideal and were inclined to see Congress as central to our constitutional system with presidents serving largely as administrators. Both criticized the separation of powers, reducing it to checks and balances. Both disliked standing committee hegemony and both sought to elevate the role of legislative parties. They disliked "committee government," preferring "party government," in part, to promote "grand partisanship" in place of the "petty" politics of competing and compromising interests.[13] They preferred party government, with its confrontation of ideas, to pluralism, with its compromise among interests. Both professorial politicians proposed the use of devices like Gingrich's 1994 Contract with America.[14] Finally, both Wilson and Gingrich had limited regard for constitutional forms, perhaps especially the separation of powers.

Wilson saw the separation of powers in mechanistic terms. In *Constitutional Government* he concluded that the Framers built the Constitution upon an unconscious copy of Newtonian theory: "The trouble with the theory is that government is not a machine, but a living thing. It falls, not under the theory of the universe, but under the theory of organic life. It is accountable to Darwin, not to Newton."[15]

To the contrary, Martin Diamond argued that the Constitution's "functional parceling out of political power" promotes "not only free but effective government."[16] Our separation of powers system arguably fosters ambition counteracting ambition as well as ambition vying with ambition. Madison wanted stability and energy; limited, yet effective government. Wilson's own practical effort to create "responsible government under the Constitution" succumbed to "the countervailing and constitutionally entrenched logic of the Founders' separation of powers," according to Daniel Stid.[17] Ever since, he says, neo-Wilsonian reformers have often found themselves "confounded by the alternative logic of the separation of powers."[18] Accordingly, their reforms have had unintended consequences. In 1994 House Republicans drew on Democratic 1970s precedents by strengthening party leadership, driving Congress toward "party government" and farther from regular order. Both parties in Congress sought to strengthen the parties as teams.[19] One ready measure of these congressional party-building reforms can be seen in Frances Lee's *Beyond Ideology* charts showing growth in funds and staff for Senate party leaders relative to committee offices and members' personal offices.[20]

Before delving deeper into Wilson's bitter fruit, we should turn to James Madison's perspective.

The View from Montpelier

Why look to Madison for guidance on appraising Congress? He died in 1836 and could not have imagined C-SPAN and many other features of legislative life in the twenty-first century. During the 1950s, scholars faulted his work as simplistic and unscientific. Deploring a "pessimistic view of human nature," Louis Hartz said that Madison's view of experience "seems to be exhausted by the human propensity to fight."[21] Robert Dahl wrote of his premises: "These axioms are Hobbesian in character and run something like this: Men are instruments of their desires. They pursue these desires to saturation if given the opportunity. One such desire is the desire for power over individuals. . . ."[22]

Madison turns out to be a more sophisticated thinker than his critics understood. Although *The Federalist* warns about human nature, the critics erred by suggesting that Madison's analysis stops there. "As there is a degree of depravity in mankind which requires a certain degree of circumspection and distrust, so there are other qualities in human nature which justify a certain portion of esteem and confidence," says *Federalist* No. 55. "Republican government presupposes the existence of these qualities in a higher degree than any other form." Madison saw people in all their complexity: individualistic and social, selfish and benevolent.[23] The task for government was both to curb their bad qualities and nurture their good ones.

Dahl claimed that Madison overstated the importance of institutional checks on power while ignoring internal checks: "the conscience (super-ego), attitudes, and basic predispositions."[24] Even aside from the now-obsolete Freudian language ("super-ego"), this observation overlooks Madison's clear assertion that a "dependence on the people is, no doubt, the primary control on the government" and that the institutional checks are "auxiliary precautions."[25] The people control the government by choosing lawmakers who "possess the most attractive merit and the most diffusive and established characters."[26]

"Delay and deliberate confusion," wrote Hartz, were the real goals of the constitutional structure.[27] Hartz failed to grasp that Madison did not support delay for its own sake, and he did not aim for confusion. "Energy in government is essential to that security against external and internal danger, and to that prompt and salutary execution of the laws which enter into the very definition of good government," Madison wrote in *Federalist* No. 37.[28] Far from sowing confusion, he believed, the constitutional structure would encourage deliberation, a topic mostly absent from the work of Hartz, Dahl, and other critics.

Madison saw that there are two kinds of public voice. On the one hand, there are passions and snap judgments. On the other hand, there is a more deliberative opinion, which takes longer to form and rests on deeper review of arguments and information.[29] Madison wanted the latter voice to prevail, as "it is the reason, alone, of the public, that ought to control and regulate the government. The passions ought to be controlled and regulated by the government."[30] Madison anticipated modern social psychology far better than did his twentieth-century critics. His distinction between passion and reason corresponds roughly to what Nobel laureate Daniel Kahneman calls "fast and slow thinking"; that is, the contrast between intuitive judgments and "a slower, more deliberate and effortful form of thinking."[31] Speaking as a lawmaker in 1796, Madison said that "this House, in its Legislative capacity, must exercise its reason; it must deliberate; for deliberation is implied in legislation."[32] In *Federalist* No. 42, he explained that such deliberation was hard to achieve because "the mild voice of reason, pleading the cause of an enlarged and permanent interest, is but too often drowned, before public bodies as well as individuals, by the clamors of an impatient avidity for immediate and immoderate gain."[33] The constitutional system, he wrote, would "refine and enlarge the public views, by passing them through the medium of a chosen body of citizens . . . [so that]

the public voice, pronounced by the representatives of the people, will be more consonant to the public good than if pronounced by the people themselves, convened for the purpose."[34]

Because enlightened statesmen would not always be at the helm, the Framers added guardrails on the path to deliberation. Terms of office would be long enough for lawmakers to learn the issues. The chambers would be big enough to encompass diverse views but small enough "to avoid the confusion and intemperance of a multitude."[35] Bicameralism would ensure that bills would undergo scrutiny by two distinct bodies.

Dahl complained that "no modern Madison has shown that restraints on the effectiveness of majorities imposed by the facts of a pluralistic society operate only to curtail 'bad' majorities and not 'good' majorities."[36] Again, however, the Framers' idea was not just to curb majorities but to encourage deliberation. Alexander Hamilton acknowledged that the process might thwart "good" majorities from time to time, but said that the outcome was worth it. "The injury which may possibly be done by defeating a few good laws, will be amply compensated by the advantage of preventing a number of bad ones."[37]

"In republican government, the legislative authority necessarily predominates," wrote Madison.[38] But the Framers knew that circumstances could shift the balance. Hamilton noted one example: "It is of the nature of war to increase the executive at the expense of the legislative authority."[39] Congress would, thus, have to watch out for presidential efforts to encroach on its power. "Ambition must be made to counteract ambition," Madison wrote in *Federalist* No. 51. "The interest of the man must be connected with the constitutional rights of the place."[40]

Today's critics of Congress argue it moves too slowly and passes too few bills. But from a Madisonian perspective, the real question is not speed or quantity of legislation but the quality of deliberation. Similarly, the issue of representation is not whether Congress reflects the polls but whether it heeds deliberative opinion. And oversight is not just about preventing tyranny but keeping the executive within its proper bounds so it can do what it does best.

To think constitutionally is to keep these ideas in mind no matter which party controls which branch. In 1990, Representative Mickey Edwards (R-Okla.) offered some far-sighted advice. Although his party had held the White House for nearly a decade and had not controlled the House since 1954, he defended congressional prerogatives. "I am frustrated by continued liberal domination of the Congress. . . . But there was a reason why wits of earlier ages cautioned us not to toss out the babies when we dump the bath water. Let us reform the Congress, but let us hold it dear as the guardian of our liberties against the centralization of power."[41]

Representation

Some critics have said that Congress is unrepresentative because its demographic characteristics do not mirror those of the general population.[42] Others have complained that its decisions fail to reflect public opinion on key issues. The Framers, however, would scorn both perspectives.

In *Federalist* No. 35, Hamilton spurned the idea "that all classes of citizens should have some of their own number in the representative body," saying that "this will never happen under any arrangement that leaves the votes of the people free."[43] Historically, much of the demographic mismatch between Congress and the public has been a symptom of discrimination and unequal opportunity. And it is surely good that the reduction of such barriers has opened the Capitol doors for more women, African Americans, and Hispanics. But in other respects, as Hamilton said, it is unrealistic to think that free elections will produce a statistically representative sample of the public.

Adherents of the "instructed delegate" school would hold that the key to representation lies in adherence to popular sentiment. One problem is that there is often no public opinion to guide them. Most voters, most of the time, are unaware of the bills before Congress and their legislators' positions on those bills. In such cases, lawmakers can only try to anticipate what voters would think if they did learn about the bills.[44]

On those issues where polling data do reveal public sentiments, Congress has arguably been responsive to a fault. Consider the federal budget. Despite a few recent years of falling deficits, the retirement of the baby boom generation will soon send them upward again. Congress's failure to address the looming debt balloon has its roots in public opinion because voters favor spending cuts in the abstract while opposing them in the particular. When Pew surveyed respondents about nineteen major programs, majorities wanted either to maintain or increase spending for eighteen of them.[45] According to a more recent Gallup poll, 63 percent are dissatisfied with the amount Americans pay in taxes. Most of this group, 46 percent of the public, want Americans to pay less in taxes. Only 4 percent would prefer they pay more.[46] The late survey expert Andrew

Kohut wrote in 2012: "In my years of polling, there has never been an issue such as the deficit on which there has been such a consensus among the public about its importance—and such a lack of agreement about acceptable solutions."[47] In other words, Congress cannot decide because the public cannot decide.

Another argument on unrepresentativeness involves polarization; the congressional parties are purportedly much more ideologically divided than the general public. Some of those who make this argument place most of the blame on the GOP.[48] There are flaws in this argument, both in general and in its more partisan form.

Survey data show ideological sorting in the public, with Democrats becoming more consistently liberal and Republicans becoming more consistently conservative. A 2014 Pew survey found that 92 percent of Republicans are to the right of the median Democrat, compared with 64 percent twenty years before. And 94 percent of Democrats are to the left of the median Republican, up from 70 percent in 1994.[49] Meanwhile, congressional constituencies have become more consistently partisan. Major cities and majority–minority areas have become more uniformly Democratic, resulting in heavily liberal districts where Democrats win by huge majorities. Elsewhere, districts tilt Republican, and thus conservative, though by smaller margins.[50] Senate electorates have also polarized. Of thirty-six senate races in 2014, only three—Colorado, Iowa, and Maine—went to a candidate of the party that lost the 2012 presidential race in that state.[51] The Senate in the 114th Congress included just sixteen members from states that favored the opposite party in the 2012 presidential race. "Rather than indicating that there is a 'disconnect' between politicians and voters," writes Alan Abramowitz, "polarization in Congress actually indicates that Democratic and Republican members are accurately reflecting the views of the voters who elected them."[52]

As for the notion that Republicans are uniquely responsible for the partisan division on Capitol Hill, a glance at *Congressional Quarterly*'s party unity scores supplies correction. Between 2007 and 2014, a period in which each party had a House majority for four years, the average House Republican voted with his or her party 88.9 percent of the time. That number seems high, but the figure for the average House Democrat was even higher: 89.5 percent. Similarly, the average party unity score for Senate Republicans was 84.3 percent, compared with 90.9 percent for Senate Democrats.[53]

From a Madisonian perspective, it is largely beside the point whether the congressional parties accurately replicate public opinion, much less which party is more partisan. Although the Federalists insisted that lawmakers would broadly share the people's "sentiments" and "interests," they did not expect Congress to serve as an ongoing poll. They wanted representatives, Madison wrote, who were notable for their "wisdom," "patriotism," and "love of justice."[54]

Does the current political environment encourage the selection of such people? Back in the days of strong party organizations, local party leaders often chose high-quality candidates for Congress. It is not that the bosses were idealistic; rather, they understood that such candidates had a better chance of winning. The success of their recruiting efforts hinged on their ability to offer fallback jobs or future nominations in case of electoral defeat. Jamie L. Carson and Jason M. Roberts say that this system ended with a Progressive initiative: "Our analysis of the direct primary reveals that a reform that was designed to provide a more open electoral system had the unintended consequence of gradually reducing the emergence of high quality candidates in House races."[55]

It is difficult to quantify the wisdom and patriotism of candidates who emerge from the current system of nominations and elections. It is likely, however, that it tends to favor those who have mastered what Madison called "the vicious arts by which elections are too often carried,"[56] particularly fundraising. Because of the low ceilings on hard-money contributions to House races, candidates and incumbents have to spend a great deal of time dialing for dollars. A PowerPoint presentation to incoming freshmen by the Democratic Congressional Campaign Committee laid out a model ten-hour day, including four hours for "call time" and another hour for "strategic outreach," including fundraisers and press work.[57] Advancement does not necessarily go to those most gifted at deliberation, but to those who are most shameless about raising money.

Deliberation

Deliberation involves reasoning on the merits of public policy.[58] Madison said that a legislator would need:

> A certain degree of knowledge of the subjects on which he is to legislate. . . . Some portion of this knowledge may, no doubt, be acquired in a man's closet; but some of it also can only be derived from the public sources of information; and all of it will be acquired

> to best effect by a practical attention to the subject during the period of actual service in the legislature.[59]

Congressional reforms between the 1960s and 1980s had mixed results for deliberation. Congress strengthened its ability to gather and analyze information by, among other things, creating the Congressional Budget Office. Allowing live television coverage of the House and Senate allowed citizens to witness the workings of their government, which has been good for deliberation in the public sphere. According to one study, the cameras also caused House and Senate sessions to get longer.[60] But has more talk really meant more thought? In their study of congressional deliberation, Gary Mucciaroni and Paul J. Quirk conclude: "Anyone listening to debate in Congress will be treated to a stream of half-truths, exaggeration, selective use of facts, and, in a few instances, outright falsehoods."[61]

While sunshine may well be the best of disinfectants, as Justice Brandeis said, disinfectants can have toxic side effects. In open meetings, lawmakers posture for the cameras and avoid positions that might anger interest groups. A former staff director of the Senate Armed Services Committee told Colleen J. Shogan that he was proud that his committee had resisted open markups. "Why should we do it in the open? It would wreck the seriousness of the purpose. Staff needs to give candid views to senators, and you can't do that in open session. Governing in the sunshine shouldn't be applied to everything."[62]

Alongside the transparency reforms of the late twentieth century came practices that concentrated procedural power in congressional party leaders. In the 1970s, the impetus came from House liberals. In the late 1980s and early 1990s, House Republicans followed suit. Leadership staffs grew in size and budget at the expense of committee staffs.[63] In both chambers, "unorthodox lawmaking" bypassed regular order and committee consideration, shifting key decisions on policy and process to the closed-door offices of the leaders.

The old committee system could be cumbersome, but it did allow members to develop deep expertise in their issues and usually ensured serious scrutiny of major bills. Things are different under the new leader-based system, writes James Wallner. "Reasoned deliberation has nearly disappeared in the modern Senate as decision-making has gradually migrated from committee hearings and the Senate floor to informal and ad hoc meetings of interested members typically held under the auspices of the party leadership and out of public view. The death of public deliberation has ultimately undermined our representative democracy."[64]

The deals resulting from these ad hoc meetings have often deprived rank-and-file members of the ability to read the bills, much less deliberate about legislative language. Twenty years ago, Representative David Dreier regretted the GOP rush to pass the Contract with America within the first 100 days of the 1995 session. "We're going against the Founding Fathers. They wanted us to be deliberative."[65] The 2009 stimulus bill and the 2010 Affordable Care Act both ranked among the least-read pieces of English prose since *Finnegan's Wake*. James Curry writes: "When decisions are made and bills are drafted behind closed doors by party leaders and committee chairs and presented to the rest of the chamber just hours before the vote, the participation of most lawmakers is minimal. . . . This may be efficient, but it is not representation, nor is it deliberation."[66]

Though some members have dismissed such concerns, the Affordable Care Act illustrated the importance of reading the bills. Murky language involving subsidies led to costly litigation that put the whole law in jeopardy. Even while voting to uphold the act, Chief Justice Roberts observed that it "does not reflect the type of care and deliberation that one might expect of such significant legislation."[67]

In today's complex society, it takes staff support to acquire the kind of knowledge that Madison said was indispensable to legislative deliberation. On this score, Congress has weakened itself. In 1995, lawmakers scrapped the Office of Technology Assessment, which had provided analysis of scientific and technical issues since 1972. The Government Accountability Office (GAO) and the Congressional Research Service (CRS) employ 20 percent fewer staffers than they did in 1979.[68] And CRS now has to divert much of its diminished capacity toward answering constituent questions instead of casting light on legislative issues.[69] Similarly, cuts in federal data agencies such as the Bureau of Labor Statistics have made it harder to get a clear picture of unemployment and other key issues.[70]

These cutbacks are purportedly about saving money for the taxpayers, but they are a false economy. For the sake of trimming a microscopic share of federal spending, Congress has greatly reduced its ability to understand the economy, oversee the budget, and legislate responsibly.

Legislation

When it comes to Congress's legislative function, the progressive impulse points to a simple diagnosis and cure. Gridlock is the problem. Productivity is the solution. But is productivity for its own sake the proper standard?

Neo-Wilsonians use a spurious "box score" method to rate Congress: the more enactments, the better. Kevin R. Kosar argues we cannot judge Congress by tallying legislation. Counting is a "crude, biased, and meaningless metric" given the lack of consensus among Congress watchers on any quantitative measure.[71] Kosar adds that focusing on legislative productivity alone ignores Congress's other functions, including representation, deliberation, and oversight.

The Madisonian perspective turns the gridlock presumption upside down: passing lots of long, complex bills is a problem "if the laws be so voluminous that they cannot be read, or so incoherent that they cannot be understood."[72] Thomas Jefferson concurred: "The instability of our laws is really an immense evil."[73] Hamilton, too, noted "the mischiefs of that inconstancy and mutability in the laws, which form the greatest blemish in the character and genius of our governments."[74] Madison concluded that "the facility and excess of lawmaking seem to be the diseases to which our governments are most liable."[75]

Why the emphasis today on productivity for its own sake? The answer seems to be Woodrow Wilson and the progressive passion for efficient government. David Mayhew's historical studies even cast doubt on the progressive premise and gridlock presumption.[76] Congress, he argues, has been fairly consistently productive over the long run.

Sometimes, gridlock may be good. Former Congressman Tom Davis (R-Va.) defended the obstruction of Congressional Republicans in the 113th Congress: "I think a lot of Republicans feel they were put there to stop the Obama agenda. . . . You can look at it as the least productive Congress, but a lot of them see that as their job."[77] Walter Oleszek says: "Partisan stalemates can prevent mistakes that could occur if bills were passed without adequate deliberation and amendment opportunities for each party. In short, legislative deadlock may be the best option absent consensus in Congress and the country over how to address consequential issues and problems."[78] Lee Rawls, a longtime senate staffer, acknowledges increased partisanship, but he doubts whether partisanship is truly undermining our ability to tackle essential policy challenges. During policy debates in which he participated, Rawls saw "hard bargaining" rather than "gridlock."[79] Examples during the 114th Congress include: important accomplishments on surface transportation; reform of the No Child Left Behind education law; extension of the Children's Health Insurance program; the permanent "doc fix"; renewal of trade promotion authority; new restrictions on national security surveillance; and, of course, the big budget agreement precluding a shutdown in 2016.

Legislative productivity waxes and wanes, sometimes tracking presidential cycles. The first two years of President Obama's first term saw passage of the economic stimulus, Affordable Care Act, and Dodd–Frank financial regulatory reform. Then came the 112th Congress with its paucity of productivity, leaving neo-Wilsonians lamenting gridlock. How quickly they forget! Similarly, President George W. Bush was more successful legislatively in his first term than his second term, with budget and tax legislation, together with legislative productivity on the heels of 9/11 with the Patriot Act and creation of the Department of Homeland Security. Such cycles are common.

Again, Madison's constitutional system invites both stability and energy; both legislative productivity and gridlock have their place.

Oversight

Congress is powerful because it is independent of the executive branch and institutionally designed to best exercise its distinct functions, including oversight. This watchdog function involves legislative, budgetary, and investigative oversight, including Congress's power of the purse and impeachment power. The committee system, far from being an impediment to congressional action, made Congress more independent and more effective during the twentieth century. As Michael Malbin notes, "[t]he committee system originally grew out of Congress's desire to assert its independence of the executive."[80] Because it was independent, Congress needed committees; in turn, Congress became more independent because of its committees.

Committees can empower Congress by providing a division of labor and by ensuring that Congress is not completely dependent on the president or bureaucracy for expertise. Committees enable Congress to compete effectively with the executive. For example, when Congress wanted to regain budgetary power from the executive with the 1974 Budget

Impoundment and Control Act, it created the House and Senate Budget Committees. Wilson did not like committee government but did celebrate Congress's oversight or informing function, insisting that "[t]he informing function of Congress should be preferred even to its legislative function," largely for the purpose of educating the public. Congress should keep "all national concerns suffused in a broad daylight of discussion" to promote "the enlightenment of the people."[81]

But did the neo-Wilsonian "openness" strengthen congressional oversight?[82] The old closed committees ensured serious legislative scrutiny, while the new, more open, party-dominated Congress may actually be promoting more grandstanding than serious information gathering, and emphasizing the political rather than policy purposes of oversight.

Committee government or party government? According to Oleszek, this is the "eternal debate" in the "evolving Congress."[83] Congress has long had two sets of leaders, party and committee, which sometimes compete and sometimes cooperate with one another. Congress has sometimes been balanced and sometimes torn by the centripetal force of party leadership and the centrifugal force of committee leadership. Which is Congress? Both. Congress has both party leaders and committee leaders who thrive on Congress's independence from the executive and who help maintain that independence, simultaneously limiting and empowering Congress and the president. This never-ending tension within Congress, between party leaders and committee leaders competing and cooperating with one another, defines Congress. Lawrence Evans notes: "As the majority party becomes more unified internally about the major issues of the day and the gulf between the policy preferences of the majority and minority party members widens, party leaders become more central to the legislative process and the autonomy of committees tends to decline. Conversely, lower levels of partisan polarization are associated with stronger committees."[84]

Have neo-Wilsonian reforms made Congress more or less effective at fulfilling its oversight function? It depends.

Reforms since the 1970s have had a mixed effect. On the one hand, limited transparency under committee government may have allowed representatives to avoid certain issues, eroding public confidence. On the other hand, greater transparency today exposes the sausage-making to public scrutiny, ironically contributing to public distrust. The old committee oversight was subject to capture by organized interests and government agencies. Party control over committees today conceivably keeps committees from the clutches of the special interests, but that same party control may undercut committee independence. In fact greater exposure of committee deliberations may have increased the role of lobbyists; after all, who today fills Gucci Gulch outside the Ways and Means Committee hearing room? Furthermore, Don Wolfensberger sees the decline of conference committees as "one more sign of the decline of the committee system and its attributes of deliberation and expertise."[85] Sloppy legislation may be one result. Another may be the failure to head off fiascoes such at the scandal at the VA hospitals. Partisanship can be a spur to oversight, however, even if polarization is a consequence. One scholar has found that "data tend to show that the Congress has increased its oversight activity over history, particularly over the past three decades."[86]

So is Congress more or less effective at congressional oversight thanks to reforms? Ironically, the answer may be "yes, both." Congress may be promoting two different kinds of oversight depending on whether it perceives itself as part of the government or part of the opposition. Committee "comity clubs" may engage in serious administrative scrutiny and study of policy proposals, thereby educating members, while partisan oversight clashes may enlighten public deliberations, providing voters a choice not an echo in the next election.

Yet Wilson's ideas also contributed to the growth of government, creating a burgeoning administrative state that may be too complex for effective oversight. Madison noted in *Federalist* No. 58 that the "power of the purse may, in fact, be regarded as the most complete and effectual weapon with which any constitution can arm the immediate representatives of the people, for obtaining a redress of every grievance, and for carrying into effect every just and salutary measure."[87] Today, however, we sometimes see "lockbox government," a risky development providing a "guaranteed funding stream" to programs offering, in effect, an end run around the appropriations process.

The Framers ended legislative supremacy, creating instead two independent political branches: Congress and the president. Each is designed to best exercise its functions and each is powerful within its sphere. Congress may be prone to openness, while the president is inclined toward secrecy. Congress has the authority to demand information from the president, but the president has the prerogative, executive privilege, to withhold information. Inevitably, this institutional tension must, in practice, be resolved by a political struggle between the political branches.[88]

A New (Old) Paradigm?

We have argued against using the conventional Wilsonian standards for appraising Congress. We believe that Madisonianism provides a more sophisticated perspective. From this viewpoint Congress is not broken, but its members do not always represent what is best in the American public. It does not deliberate as thoughtfully, legislate as carefully, or oversee the executive branch as thoroughly as it should.

Some have blamed partisan polarization but this polarization is a reflection of public sentiment on both sides. On the right, the Tea Party movement emerged out of widespread dissatisfaction with perceived government overreach. On the left, many Democrats embraced the 2016 presidential candidacy of an avowed socialist. Congress is divided because we, the people, are divided.

By Madisonian standards, there is nothing inherently wrong with strong opinions and strong words. Madison himself was familiar with tough politics, and he fired his share of rhetorical bombshells. Spirited debate on fundamental issues can be good for public deliberation, but it is also possible to see ways in which polarization has been problematic. As the previous section explained, committee "oversight" has often involved sound bites instead of meticulous analysis. On the floor, procedural warfare has limited opportunities for debate and amendment. Contrary to the assertions of hyperpartisan pundits, Republicans and Democrats are both responsible. Don Wolfensberger reminds us that restrictive rules in the House have increased under both parties. And on the Senate side, Democratic Majority Leader Harry Reid (D-Nev.) blocked minority-party amendments by "filling the tree," and despite a professed commitment to regular order, GOP Majority Leader Mitch McConnell (R-Ky.) started to do the same thing.[89] Similarly, filibuster flip-flopping has approached comical proportions, with each party defending or damning the tactic depending on whether it holds the majority.[90]

Despite congressional rules limiting personal attacks on the floor lawmakers often work very close to the line, and occasionally cross it. On the Internet and television shout shows they are even less restrained. Breaches of civility are unhelpful, for as the Annenberg Public Policy Center puts it: "Central to the ability to deliberate is the presumption of mutual respect."[91] Over time, opinions change, passions cool, and politicians adapt. But for the time being we have to accept the reality of polarization and ponder ways in which Congress can nevertheless address its own problems. We have to "think institutionally," recognizing the unintended consequences of past reforms. If we cannot turn Congress into a platonic model of wise lawmaking, we can at least stop making things worse.

The remedy is not to reject the constitutional design but to restore it. We can improve Congress by returning to a constitutional Congress, complete with proposed reforms premised on an appreciation for constitutional context. We have aimed in this collection of essays to promote a Madisonian roadmap for reform to return Congress to its proper place in our constitutional system.

We can revitalize Congress by remembering the Constitution and returning to Madison's realism and republicanism. We must relearn the value of Madison's realism about human nature and Madison's republicanism in government. We need to return to an appreciation for Madison's Constitution as the enduring context for contemporary politics and as the predicate for congressional reform. Any successful reform, free of unintended consequences, must be consonant with Madison's Constitution and grounded on a proper understanding of Madison's constitutional structure.

We need Madisonian republican reforms, not Wilsonian democratic reforms. Instead of the more "open and democratic" reforms championed by generations of Wilsonians, we need more republican and deliberative reforms that recognize that the purpose of government is the protection of liberty. The cure to the ills of democracy is not more democracy, but a more balanced Madisonian republicanism. We must recognize that unintended consequences of reform result from an inadequate understanding that the separation of powers promotes limited and effective government, not just "checks and balances."

A Constitutional Roadmap for Reform: Revitalizing Congress

What is to be done? There is a good deal of literature, including the essays in this volume, suggesting remedies.

A good place to begin is with Jonathan Rauch's "political realism." We cannot take the politics out of politics. Or as Rauch says, "governing is difficult and politics is transactional." Thus we need "political machines" that reempower party leaders, on the Hill and in party headquarters, with the necessary carrots and sticks to lead. Congressional party and committee leaders need leverage and opportunities to deliberate behind closed doors.

Rauch wants a return to the smoke-filled rooms, perhaps without the smoking.

Rauch wants to "rescue compromise," a republican virtue.[92] Arguably compromise does not need rescuing in our system, since it is inevitable. The Constitution forces compromise between and within our two parties, two branches, and two chambers. The Constitution requires compromise because neither party, neither branch, neither chamber governs by itself. Our system confronts all with a strategic dilemma or constitutional conundrum: whether to be part of the government or part of the opposition. Both parties, both branches, and both chambers are at all times both government and opposition. In this way, Madison promotes both stability and energy.

Yet there can be little compromise where there is no consensus. Our "perfect tie" politics today, in which our two parties may be more closely divided than sharply divided, often hampers compromise. Perhaps we will need to resort in time to a resolution via electoral politics, that is, a "choice not an echo" election. Our constitutional system invites compromise and confrontation, resolution of our differences in either the governing or campaigning phases of our policymaking and politics. This is Madison's republican balance. The unintended consequences flow from misjudging our constitutional system by the light of the British parliamentary standard. Like Madison, we need to think institutionally, beginning with an understanding of the complexity of our system. Examples of the unintended consequences of reform abound.

- *Campaign finance reform* has contributed to a deliberation deficit because lawmakers have to spend inordinate time "dialing for dollars." Ray La Raja cites another consequence: "The campaign finance system has strengthened the hand of partisan activists by limiting the flow of financial resources to the formal party organization and its technocratic staff," who may be more interested in winning than being right.[93]

- *Congressional primaries,* according to Rauch, are an egregious case of unintended consequences. Low turnout, activist-dominated nominations may have contributed to red versus blue polarization, though some political scientists doubt that the effect has been particularly pronounced.[94]

- *Redistricting reforms* seem to have largely failed to ease red versus blue polarization, according to Nathaniel Persily.[95]

- *Sunshine reforms* may have undermined deliberation, curbed legislative productivity, and weakened congressional leadership, all without truly augmenting accountability thanks to what David Frum calls a "transparency trap."[96]

  The earmark ban was meant to limit special interests; instead, it has limited leadership leverage. Robert Draper, in *Do Not Ask What Good We Do*, quotes Speaker Boehner saying wistfully: "It's not like the good old days. . . . Without earmarks to offer, it's hard to herd the cats."[97]

Perhaps we need to restock legislative leaders' larders. Bruce Cain thinks we need to give "representatives more room to negotiate, deliberate, and compromise."[98] Cain raises a cautionary concern: "The question is whether the effects of partisanship can be toned down without violating constitutional constraints."[99] Madison was the Father of the Constitution and the Bill of Rights. Compromising First Amendment freedoms in the name of good government reforms has proven to be one of the most challenging consequences of Wilsonian reforms. It may be a "cure worse than the disease" from Madison's perspective.

Do we really need to dial down partisanship? Some suggest we strengthen establishment elites over populist insurgents such as the Tea Party in the GOP or the Sanders wing of the Democratic Party. Yet a successful party needs both elements, in balance. As a wise old House staffer once told us: "If the establishment dominates the party, it becomes paralyzed and disintegrates; if the revolutionaries dominate, the party becomes wild and explodes."[100]

From a realist Madisonian republican perspective our congressional parties need both the establishment and the insurgents, and both need each other. Madison made certain congressional parties needed both their "government" and "opposition" wings; a party cannot soar without both wings. We can afford to strengthen political parties since we can trust Madison to have parties institutionally under control at all times. Madison is rather adept at managing factionalism.

Here are ways we can strengthen the republican character of Congress:

- *Campaign Finance.* We could raise the contribution caps for congressional party leadership PACs and also allow the Speaker and Senate Majority Leader to choose the chairs of the National Republican Campaign Committee (NRCC) and National Republican Senatorial Committee (NRSC). Michael Malbin has suggested allowing parties to help candidates by making unlimited coordinated expenditures using donor contributions less than $1,000.[101]

- *Transparency.* While shutting down cameras in the chamber might trigger a revolt by congressional scholars, perhaps settling for fewer cameras in committee markups and elsewhere still might be a working compromise. As Christopher DeMuth notes, there are reasons for optimism about reform possibilities: "Most arguments for particular congressional reforms—restoring regular order and annual budgets, empowering the committee chairs, eliminating roadblocks to legislative resolution—are determinedly bi-partisan."[102]

- *Procedure and Regular Order.* On taking the Speaker's gavel in the fall of 2015, Paul Ryan pledged a return to "regular order." Early signs were encouraging, but additional steps deserve consideration. DeMuth suggests ending "entitlement autopilot," along with budgeting by continuing resolution. "Return to the procedures of the Budget Act of 1974 and place all of the executive agencies on regular annual appropriations—and follow through by building a merit-based hierarchy with strong committees and committee chairmen." Perhaps we can restore policy authority to authorizing and appropriating committee chairs because bipartisanship is not yet dead in congressional "comity clubs," at least in the Senate, according to Ross Baker.[103] Reviving earmarks might help resuscitate the power of committee chairs, especially in the Appropriations Committees. Eliminating term limits on committee chairs might help as well.

  Senate filibuster reforms since the Progressive Era, designed to make the upper body more majoritarian, have had the unintended consequence of increasing abuse of the filibuster. Robert Dove and Richard Arenberg cite a particularly ironic example of majoritarian filibuster reform: "The authors of the 1974 Budget Act, by providing expedited procedures that prohibit filibusters on budget resolutions and reconciliation bills, and guarantee an up-or-down vote, thought they were building a budget process that would foster bipartisan cooperation. It had the opposite result." Might Harry Reid's "nuclear option" prove similarly counterproductive?

- *Strengthened Committees.* Executive "poaching" on legislative prerogative may provide the necessary incentive for strengthening committees since, historically, committees originated, in part, to assert congressional independence from presidents.[104] Might Congress take this cue to reinvest in committee resources, including rebuilding the CRS and the Congressional Budget Office? Wolfensberger details the shift in congressional staff resources in recent decades augmenting "politics at the expense of policy."[105] Party leadership and campaign and constituency service staff have expanded while committee staff have declined.

We cannot blame Congress for everything, even if it does usefully serve as our national lightning rod. There are causes of contentiousness beyond anyone's control. Media fragmentation thanks to the Internet, together with hyperpluralism or "demosclerosis" stemming from the explosion in the number of organized interest groups, have compounded the bellicosity of American politics. Moreover, while American politics has always been rambunctious, the coarsening of our culture has contributed to the willingness of Joe Wilson or Jim Wright to accuse sitting presidents of lying. The growth of government may be the key reason for the confrontational character of our politics. Oleszek notes that today we have "two parties with sharply different and distinct world views on a host of issues, many tied to the role and reach of the national government."[106] The growth of government, along with the rise of nondivisible agenda items, such as abortion and gay rights, even has contemporary commentators, liberals and conservatives, calling for a return to federalism. Some have gone so far as to raise doubts about the Progressive era's Seventeenth Amendment promoting direct election of senators.

Such a reforming of the reforms may no longer be practicable at this late date, of course, though it does bring the debate between James Madison and Woodrow Wilson front and center. Both Madison and Wilson were men of theory and men of practice who contributed to and participated in the contentious politics of their own eras. The country survived those confrontational times thanks, in large part, to the constitutional concrete of Madison's Constitution. Is our purported dysfunction really any worse today? Are we hyperpartisan today or are we hypersensitive to partisanship, having been taught by generations of good government reformers that factions are evil? Are we sharply divided, or closely divided, as Fiorina insists? Ultimately, elections, more than institutional reforms, may provide the necessary resolution of our differences. After all, today's political parties provide a "choice not an echo" just as the 1950s APSA reformers wanted.

Notes

1. Frances E. Lee, *Beyond Ideology* (University of Chicago Press, 2009), pp. 19–20.

2. Woodrow Wilson, *Congressional Government* (New Brunswick, N.J.: Transaction Press, 2002), p. 284.

3. Ibid., p. 333.

4. Ibid., p. 210.

5. Ibid., p. 282.

6. Daniel Stid, *The President as Statesman: Woodrow Wilson and the Constitution* (University Press of Kansas, 1998), p. 11.

7. Wilson, *Congressional Government*, pp. 311, 10.

8. Ibid., p. 117.

9. Ibid., p. 284. Italics in the original.

10. Ibid., pp. 283–84. Italics in the original.

11. See, for example, Lloyd Cutler's "To Form a Government," *Foreign Affairs* 59 (Fall 1980) or "A Bicentennial Analysis of the American Political Structure" (Washington, D.C.: Committee on the Constitutional System, 1987). See, also, David Mayhew's discussion of whether "divided government" has resulted in paralysis in his book *Divided We Govern; Party Control, Lawmaking, and Investigation, 1946–2002* (Yale University Press, 2005).

12. Wilson, *Constitutional Government*, p. 60.

13. See Wilson, *Congressional Government*, p. 85; Newt Gingrich, "Gingrich Address: New House Speaker Envisions Cooperation, Cuts, Hard Work," *CQ Weekly*, November 12, 1994, p. 3296.

14. Daniel Stid, "A Wilsonian Perspective on the Newtonian Revolution," paper presented at the annual meeting of the American Political Science Association, Chicago (September, 1995), p. 6. See also, Wilson, *Congressional Government*, p. 98.

15. Wilson, *Constitutional Government*, p. 56.

16. Martin Diamond, "The Separation of Powers and the Mixed Regime," in *As Far as Republican Principles Will Admit*, edited by William A. Schambra (Washington, D.C.: AEI Press, 1992), pp. 61, 67.

17. Stid, *The President as Statesman*, p. 2.

18. Ibid., p. 170.

19. Lee, *Beyond Ideology*, p. 23.

20. Ibid., pp. 15–16.

21. Louis Hartz, *The Liberal Tradition in America* (New York: Harcourt, Brace, and World, 1955), pp. 79, 83.

22. Robert A. Dahl, *A Preface to Democratic Theory* (University of Chicago Press, 1956), p. 8.

23. Joseph F. Kobylka and Bradley Kent Carter, "Madison, 'The Federalist,' and the Constitutional Order: Human Nature and Institutional Structure," *Polity* 20 (Winter 1987), pp. 190–208 (www.jstor.org/stable/3234779).

24. Dahl, *A Preface*, p. 18.

25. *Federalist* No. 51, Avalon Project at Yale Law School (http://avalon.law.yale.edu/18th_century/fed51.asp).

26. *Federalist* No. 10, Avalon Project at Yale Law School (http://avalon.law.yale.edu/18th_century/fed10.asp).

27. Hartz, *Liberal Tradition*, p. 85.

28. *Federalist* No. 37, Avalon Project at Yale Law School (http://avalon.law.yale.edu/18th_century/fed37.asp).

29. Joseph M. Bessette, *The Mild Voice of Reason: Deliberative Democracy and American National Government* (University of Chicago Press, 1994), p. 35.

30. *Federalist* No. 49, Avalon Project at Yale Law School (http://avalon.law.yale.edu/18th_century/fed49.asp); See, also, Daniel W. Howe, "The Political Psychology of *The Federalist*," *William and Mary Quarterly* 44 (July 1987), pp. 485–509 (www.jstor.org/stable/1939767).

31. Daniel Kahneman, *Thinking, Fast and Slow* (New York: Farrar, Straus, and Giroux, 2011), p. 13.

32. James Madison, Speech on House Floor, March 10, 1796 (http://press-pubs.uchicago.edu/founders/documents/v1ch10s21.html).

33. *Federalist* No. 42, Avalon Project at Yale Law School (http://avalon.law.yale.edu/18th_century/fed42.asp).

34. *Federalist* No. 10, Avalon Project at Yale Law School (http://avalon.law.yale.edu/18th_century/fed10.asp).

35. *Federalist* No. 55, Avalon Project at Yale Law School (http://avalon.law.yale.edu/18th_century/fed55.asp).

36. Dahl, *A Preface*, p. 29.

37. *Federalist* No. 73, Avalon Project at Yale Law School (http://avalon.law.yale.edu/18th_century/fed73.asp).

38. *Federalist* No. 51, Avalon Project at Yale Law School (http://avalon.law.yale.edu/18th_century/fed51.asp).

39. *Federalist* No. 8, Avalon Project at Yale Law School (http://avalon.law.yale.edu/18th_century/fed08.asp).

40. *Federalist* No. 51, Avalon Project at Yale Law School (http://avalon.law.yale.edu/18th_century/fed51.asp).

41. Mickey Edwards, "A Conservative Defense of Congress," *The Public Interest* 100 (Summer 1990), pp. 81–88 (www.nationalaffairs.com/public_interest/detail/a-conservative-defense-of-congress).

42. Hanna Fenichel Pitkin, *The Concept of Representation* (University of California Press, 1967), chapter 4.

43. *Federalist* No. 35, Avalon Project at Yale Law School (http://avalon.law.yale.edu/18th_century/fed35.asp).

44. R. Douglas Arnold, *The Logic of Congressional Action* (Yale University Press, 1990), pp. 8–13.

45. Jocelyn Kiley, "As Sequester Deadline Looms, Little Support for Cutting Most Programs," Pew Research Center, February 22, 2013 (www.people-press.org/2013/02/22/as-sequester-deadline-looms-little-support-for-cutting-most-programs).

46. Lydia Saad, "Americans' Satisfaction with Federal Taxes on Low Side," *Gallup*, January 22, 2015 (www.gallup.com/poll/181241/americans-satisfaction-federal-taxes-low-side.aspx).

47. Andrew Kohut, "Debt and Deficit: A Public Opinion Dilemma," Pew Research Center, June 12, 2012 (www.people-press.org/2012/06/14/debt-and-deficit-a-public-opinion-dilemma).

48. Jacob S. Hacker and Paul Pierson, *Off Center: The Republican Revolution and the Erosion of American Democracy* (Yale University Press, 2004); Thomas E. Mann and Norman J. Ornstein, *It's Even Worse Than It Looks* (New York: Basic Books, 2012).

49. Michael Dimock and others, "Political Polarization in the American Public," Pew Research Center, June 12, 2014 (www.people-press.org/2014/06/12/political-polarization-in-the-american-public).

50. Jowei Chen and Jonathan Rodden, "Unintentional Gerrymandering: Political Geography and Electoral Bias in Legislatures," *Quarterly Journal of Political Science* 8, no. 3, pp. 239–69 (www-personal.umich.edu/~jowei/florida.pdf).

51. Nathan Nicholson, "U.S. Senate Results Show Continued Rise in Predictive Power of Partisanship," FairVote blog, December 3, 2014 (www.fairvoteblog.com/2014/12/us-senate-results-show-continued-rise.html).

52. Alan Abramowitz, "U.S. Senate Elections in a Polarized Era, in *The U.S. Senate: From Deliberation to Dysfunction*, edited by Burdett A. Loomis (Washington, D.C.: CQ Press, 2012), p. 31.

53. Authors' calculations from data in Eliza Newlin Carney, "Standing Together Against Any Action," *CQ Weekly*, March 16, 2015, pp. 37–45 (http://library.cqpress.com/cqweekly/file.php?path=/files/wr20150316-2014_Party_Unity.pdf).

54. *Federalist* No. 10, Avalon Project at Yale Law School (http://avalon.law.yale.edu/18th_century/fed10.asp).

55. Jamie L. Carson and Jason M. Roberts, *Ambition, Competition, and Electoral Reform* (University of Michigan Press, 2013), p. 114.

56. *Federalist* No. 10, Avalon Project at Yale Law School (http://avalon.law.yale.edu/18th_century/fed10.asp).

57. Ryan Grim and Sabrina Siddiqui, "Call Time for Congress Shows How Fundraising Dominates Bleak Work Life," January 9, 2013 (www.huffingtonpost.com/2013/01/08/call-time-congressional-fundraising_n_2427291.html).

58. Bessette, *Mild Voice of Reason*, p. 46.

59. *Federalist* No. 53, Avalon Project at Yale Law School (http://avalon.law.yale.edu/18th_century/fed53.asp).

60. Franklin G. Mixon Jr., David L. Hobson, and Kamal P. Upadhyaya, "Gavel-to-Gavel Congressional Television Coverage as Political Advertising: The Impact of C-Span on Legislative Sessions," *Economic Inquiry* 39 (July 2001), pp. 351–64 (http://onlinelibrary.wiley.com/doi/10.1093/ei/39.3.351/epdf).

61. Gary Mucciaroni and Paul J. Quirk, *Deliberative Choices: Debating Public Policy in Congress* (University of Chicago Press, 2006), pp. 200–01.

62. Colleen J. Shogan, "Defense Authorization: The Senate's Last Best Hope," in *Party and Procedure in the United States Congress*, edited by Jacob R. Straus (Lanham, Md.: Rowman and Littlefield, 2012), p. 209.

63. Matthew Glassman, "Congressional Leadership: A Resource Perspective," in *Party and Procedure in the United States Congress*, edited by Jacob R. Straus (Lanham, Md.: Rowman and Littlefield, 2012), pp. 26–27; Lee, *Beyond Ideology*, pp. 15–16.

64. James Wallner, "The Death of Deliberation: Party and Procedure in the Modern United States Senate," in *Party and Procedure in the United States Congress*, edited by Jacob R. Straus (Lanham, Md.: Rowman and Littlefield, 2012), p. 168.

65. Elizabeth Drew, *Showdown: The Struggle Between the Gingrich Congress and the Clinton White House* (New York: Simon and Schuster, 1996), p. 99.

66. James M. Curry, *Legislating in the Dark: Information and Power in the House of Representatives* (University of Chicago Press, 2015), p. 204.

67. *King et al. v. Burwell, Secretary of Health and Human Services, et al.* (www.supremecourt.gov/opinions/14pdf/14-114_qol1.pdf).

68. Lee Drutman and Steven Teles, "Why Congress Relies on Lobbyists Instead of Thinking for Itself," *The Atlantic*, March 10, 2015 (www.theatlantic.com/politics/archive/2015/03/when-congress-cant-think-for-itself-it-turns-to-lobbyists/387295).

69. Kevin R. Kosar, "Why I Quit the Congressional Research Service," *Washington Monthly*, January/February 2015 (www.washingtonmonthly.com/magazine/januaryfebruary_2015/features/why_i_quit_the_congressional_r053467.php).

70. Michael R. Strain, "Congress Is Trying to Make It Harder to Know How the Economy Is Doing," *Washington Post*, August 14, 2015 (www.washingtonpost.com/posteverything/wp/2015/08/14/congress-is-trying-to-make-it-harder-to-know-how-the-economy-is-doing).

71. Kevin R. Kosar, "Five Reasons Why You Can't Judge a Congress by Counting Laws," *The Hill*, January 14, 2015 (http://thehill.com/blogs/congress-blog/politics/229396-five-reasons-why-you-cant-judge-a-congress-by-counting-laws).

72. *Federalist* No. 62, Avalon Project at Yale Law School (http://avalon.law.yale.edu/18th_century/fed62.asp).

73. See Alexis de Tocqueville, *Democracy in America*, edited by J. P. Mayer (New York: Harper Perrenial, 1969), p. 203.

74. *Federalist* No. 73, Avalon Project at Yale Law School (http://avalon.law.yale.edu/18th_century/fed73.asp).

75. *Federalist* No. 62, Avalon Project at Yale Law School (http://avalon.law.yale.edu/18th_century/fed62.asp).

76. David R. Mayhew, *Divided We Govern: Party Control, Lawmaking, and Investigation, 1946–2002* (Yale University Press, 2005).

77. See Alex Seitz-Wald, "Stop Complaining That Congress Doesn't Work Enough," *National Journal*, December 12, 2013 (www.nationaljournal.com/magazine/stop-complaining-that-congress-doesn-t-work-enough-20131212).

78. Walter J. Oleszek, "The Evolving Congress: Overview and Analysis of the Modern Era," in *The Evolving Congress* (Washington, D.C.: CRS, 2014), p. 46 (www.gpo.gov/fdsys/pkg/CPRT-113SPRT89394/pdf/CPRT-113SPRT89394.pdf).

79. Lee Rawls, *In Praise of Deadlock: How Partisan Struggle Makes Better Laws* (Johns Hopkins University Press, 2009), pp. 95–98.

80. Michael Malbin, "Framing a Congress to Channel Ambition," *This Constitution* 5 (Winter 1984), p. 12.

81. Wilson, *Congressional Government*, pp. 195, 196, 198.

82. Donald R. Wolfensberger, "The Dawning of the Sunshine Seventies," *Congress and The People: Deliberative Democracy on Trial* (Washington, D.C.: Woodrow Wilson Press, 2000), chapter 7, pp. 86–102.

83. Oleszek, "The Evolving Congress," pp. 14–15, 29, 35, 58.

84. C. Lawrence Evans, "Congressional Committees," in *The Oxford Handbook of the American Congress*, edited by Eric Schickler and Frances E. Lee (Oxford University Press, 2011), p. 398.

85. Don Wolfensberger, "Have House–Senate Conferences Gone the Way of the Dodo?" Woodrow Wilson Center for International Scholars, April 28, 2008 (www.wilsoncenter.org/publication/have-house-senate-conferences-gone-the-way-the-dodo).

86. See Walter J. Oleszek, *Congressional Procedures and the Policy Process*, 9th ed. (Washington, D.C.: CQ Press, 2014), p. 409.

87. *Federalist* No. 58, Avalon Project at Yale Law School (http://avalon.law.yale.edu/18th_century/fed58.asp).

88. Gary J. Schmitt, "Executive Privilege: Presidential Power to Withhold Information from Congress," in *The Presidency in the Constitutional Order*, edited by Joseph M. Bessette and Jeffrey Tulis (LSU Press, 1981), pp. 178–80, 183.

89. Sarah Mimms, "How Democrats Play the Obstruction Game," *National Journal*, April 6, 2014 (www.nationaljournal.com/congress/2014/04/07/how-democrats-play-obstruction-game); Manu Raju, "McConnell Employs Reid's Hardball Tactic," *Politico*, July 30, 2015 (www.politico.com/story/2015/07/mitch-mcconnell-harry-reid-hardball-tactic-120801).

90. See a now-amusing video at "Switching Sides on the Filibuster," Bessette-Pitney Text blog, November 25, 2012 (www.bessettepitney.net/2012/11/switching-sides-on-filibuster.html).

91. Annenberg Public Policy Center, "Civility in Congress (1935–2011) as Reflected in the Taking Down Process," September 28, 2011 (http://cdn.annenbergpublicpolicycenter.org/wp-content/uploads/Civility_9-27-2011_Final1.pdf).

92. Jonathan Rauch, "Rescuing Compromise," *National Affairs* (Fall 2013), p. 9 (www.nationalaffairs.com/publications/detail/rescuing-compromise).

93. Raymond J. La Raja, "Why Super PACs: How the American Party System Outgrew the Campaign Finance System," *The Forum* 10, no. 4 (February 2013), p. 93.

94. Nathaniel Persily, "Stronger Parties as a Solution to Polarization," in *Solutions to Political Polarization in America*, edited by Nathaniel Persily (Cambridge University Press, 2015), p. 125.

95. Ibid.

96. David Frum, "The Transparency Trap," *The Atlantic,* September 2014 (www.theatlantic.com/magazine/archive/2014/09/the-transparency-trap/375074).

97. Robert Draper, *Do Not Ask What Good We Do* (New York: Free Press, 2012), p. 272.

98. Bruce Cain, "Two Approaches to Lessening the Effects of Partisanship," in *Solutions to Political Polarization in America*, edited by Nathaniel Persily (Cambridge University Press, 2015), p. 159.

99. Ibid.

100. See Bill Gavin in William F. Connelly Jr., *James Madison Rules America: The Constitutional Origins of Congressional Partisanship* (Lanham, Md.: Rowman and Littlefield, 2010), p. 184.

101. Michael J. Malbin, "CFI's Malbin Calls for a 'Third Approach' to Party Coordination," Campaign Finance Institute press release, December 8, 2014.

102. Christopher DeMuth Sr., "Congress Incongruous," Library of Law and Liberty, September 2015 (www.libertylawsite.org/liberty-forum/congress-incongruous).

103. Ross K. Baker, *Is Bipartisanship Dead? A Report from the Senate* (Boulder, Colo.: Paradigm Publishers, 2015), pp. 15–16, 37.

104. On executive and judicial "poaching" on legislative prerogative, see Christopher Demuth Sr., "Congress Incongruous," *Library of Law and Liberty*, September 2015 (www.libertylawsite.org/liberty-forum/congress-incongruous).

105. Don Wolfensberger, "The New Congressional Staff: Politics at the Expense of Policy," March 21, 2014 (www.brookings.edu/blogs/fixgov/posts/2014/03/21-congressional-staff-politics-over-policy-wolfensberger).

106. Oleszek, "The Evolving Congress," p. 29.

About the Contributors

REBECCA BURGESS is program manager for the American Enterprise Institute's Program on American Citizenship in Washington, D.C.

ANDREW E. BUSCH is Crown Professor of Government and George R. Roberts Fellow at Claremont McKenna College. Additionally, he serves as director of the Rose Institute of State and Local Government at Claremont McKenna College. He is the author of *After Hope and Change: The 2012 Elections and American Politics.*

WILLIAM F. CONNELLY JR. is the John K. Boardman Politics Professor at Washington and Lee University. He is also founder and director of Washington and Lee University's Washington Term Program. He is the author of *James Madison Rules America: The Constitutional Origins of Congressional Partisanship.*

PETER C. HANSON is an assistant professor of political science at Grinnell College and a former senior aide to Senator Tom Daschle (D-S.Dak.). He is the author of *Too Weak to Govern: Majority Party Power and Appropriations in the U.S. Senate.*

MELANIE M. MARLOWE is a visiting scholar at the Georgetown University Law Center. She is also a visiting fellow at the Hudson Institute. She is coeditor of *The Obama Presidency in the Constitutional Order.*

DANIEL J. PALAZZOLO is department chair and professor of political science at the University of Richmond. He is also codirector, with Dr. Gary McDowell, of the John Marshall International Center for Statesmanship. He is the author of *The Speaker and the Budget.*

KATHRYN PEARSON is an associate professor of political science at the University of Minnesota, specializing in American politics, and a former legislative assistant for two members of Congress. She is the author of *Party Discipline in the House of Representatives.*

JOHN J. PITNEY JR. is the Roy P. Crocker Professor of American Politics at Claremont McKenna College. He previously served on the staff of Senator Alfonso D'Amato (R-N.Y.) and the House Republican Policy Committee. He is coauthor of the textbook *American Government and Politics: Deliberation, Democracy, and Citizenship.*

JONATHAN RAUCH is a senior fellow at the Brookings Institution and contributing editor to *National Journal* and *The Atlantic.* He is the author of *Government's End: Why Washington Stopped Working.*

GARY J. SCHMITT is the director of the American Enterprise Institute's Program on American Citizenship. He has served as the Democratic staff director of the Senate Select Committee on Intelligence, as executive director of the President's Foreign Intelligence Advisory Board, and is contributing editor of *The Imperial Presidency and the Constitution.*

DANIEL STID is director of the Madison Initiative at the William and Flora Hewlett Foundation. He served on the staff of the House Majority Leader. He is the author of *The President as Statesman: Woodrow Wilson and the Constitution.*

DONALD R. WOLFENSBERGER is a resident scholar at the Bipartisan Policy Center and a congressional fellow at the Woodrow Wilson International Center for Scholars. He previously served as chief-of-staff of the House Rules Committee.

Index

CPSIA information can be obtained
at www.ICGtesting.com
Printed in the USA
JSHW020109131221
21211JS00001B/3